Contents

Acknowledgements   vii

Notes on Contributors   ix

List of Illustrations   xiii

Foreword by David Martin   xv

1   Introduction: *Sartor Resartus* Restored: Dress
Studies in Carlylean Perspective   1
William J.F. Keenan

2   A Comparative Exploration of Dress and the
Presentation of Self as Implicit Religion   51
Eileen Barker

3   An 'Informalizing Spurt' in Clothing Regimes:
Court Ballet in the Civilizing Process   69
Norman R. Gabriel

4   Land of Hip and Glory: Fashioning the 'Classic'
National Body   85
Alison Goodrum

5   Multiple Meanings of the *Hijab* in Contemporary
France   105
Malcolm D. Brown

6   *Gestus* Manifests *Habitus*: Dress and the
Mormon   123
Douglas J. Davies

7   Vampires and Goths: Fandom, Gender and
Cult Dress   141
Milly Williamson

Contents

8   The Fall and Rise of Erotic Lingerie   159
     Dana Wilson-Kovacs

9   Dress Freedom: The Personal and the Political   179
     William J.F. Keenan

Name Index   197

Subject Index   203

DRESS, BODY, CULTURE

Dressed to Impress
Looking the Part

Edited by

William J.F. Keenan

Foreword by

David Martin

Oxford • New York

First published in 2001 by
Berg
Editorial offices:
150 Cowley Road, Oxford, OX4 1JJ, UK
838 Broadway, Third Floor, New York, NY 10003-4812, USA

Berg is an imprint of Oxford International Publishers Ltd.

Library of Congress Cataloging-in-Publication Data
A catalogue record for this book is available from the Library of Congress.

British Library Cataloguing-in-Publication Data
A catalogue record for this book is available from the British Library.

ISBN   1 85973 455 3 (Cloth)
       1 85973 460 X (Paper)

Typeset by JS Typesetting, Wellingborough, Northants.
Printed in the United Kingdom by Biddles Ltd, Guildford and King's Lynn.

Acknowledgements

Arguably, this volume has its remotest foundations in the accident that the school-boy crocodile of my early adolescent years snaked its weary weekend walk, under the watchful eye of religious Brothers, past the Scottish Lowland village of Ecclefechan, then etched on our impressionable memories as 'the birthplace of Thomas Carlyle, the grand historian of the French Revolution'. Four decades or so on, Carlyle – now reconfigured as 'the grand philosopher of dress' – came unexpectedly to life again through the pages of *Sartor Resartus* as I searched for intellectual foundations on which to erect a professional sociologist's interest in dressways. At the Annual Conference in 1998 of the British Sociological Association held at the University of Edinburgh – Carlyle's own *Alma Mater* – where the theme of that year was 'Making Sense of the Body: Theory, Research and Practice', I was able to meet and share ideas on dress with the seven other authors included in this collection. I wish to record here my deep appreciation of the generous response of this 'magnificent seven' in allowing me the opportunity to exercise – exorcise is too final a word here – my Carlylean ghost via the present extended Introduction to their work. I am indebted to Berg's Kathryn Earle who encouraged me initially to draw the collection together and Regents' Professor Joanne B. Eicher who supported the project from the first stitch – and to whom its title is due. For his inspiration and friendship, I am especially indebted to Emeritus Professor David Martin who graciously wrote the Foreword. The love and support of my wife and children are beyond measure. They exist for me as, in Carlyle's words, 'divine apparitions'. I like to be haunted by them.

Notes on Contributors

Eileen Barker, OBE, FRA, is Professor of Sociology with Special Reference to the Study of Religion at the London School of Economics. Her main research interests are 'cults', 'sects' and new religious movements and the social reactions to which they give rise, and changes in the religious situation in post-communist countries. Over 170 publications in eighteen languages, include the award-winning The Making of a Moonie: Brainwashing or Choice? and New Religious Movements: A Practical Introduction. In 1988, supported by the British Government and mainstream Churches, she founded INFORM, a charity based at the LSE that provides information about new religions which is as accurate, objective and up-to-date as possible. She is a familiar commentator on religious matters on both radio and television, and the only non-American elected President of the Society for the Scientific Study of Religion.

Malcolm D. Brown is a lecturer in the Department of Sociology at the University of Exeter, where he teaches the sociology of Migration and Racism. He has undertaken research (at the University of Glasgow) on the construction of Muslim identities in the United Kingdom and France, and has published work on Orientalism, Islamophobia and racism. He is currently doing research on racism in rural societies.

Douglas J. Davies is now Professor in the Study of Religion in the Department of Theology at Durham University, England. Before that he was Professor of Religious Studies at the University of Nottingham where he taught for many years. His academic background lies in both social anthropology and theology. His research interests and publications have focussed on Mormonism, death and funerary rites, especially cremation, Anglicanism and the history and theory of the study of religion. His major publications include The Mormon Culture of Salvation (2000), Death, Ritual and Belief (1997), and Meaning and Salvation in Religious Studies (1987). He also holds an honorary doctorate from The University of Uppsala. He is currently President of the British Sociology Association Sociology of Religion Study Group.

Norman R. Gabriel is a Lecturer in Early Childhood Studies at Suffolk College in Ipswich, Norfolk, England. He is involved in testing and applying the theoretical framework of Norbert Elias to different substantive areas of sociology.

He gained his doctorate from the University of Sussex in 1998, developing a non-relativistic sociology of scientific knowledge to assess the contribution of a set of statistical indicators for evaluating scientific research. He is currently working on the application of a suitable theoretical framework to understand the ways in which different cultural factors influence the early learning processes of young children.

Alison Goodrum is a postgraduate research student with the Geography and Environmental Management Research Unit (GEMRU) at Cheltenham and Gloucester College of Higher Education, Gloucestershire, England. She is currently involved in completing her PhD, looking at British fashion and the effects of globalization on the fashion industry from a critical cultural geography perspective.

William J.F. Keenan is Head of Sociology in the Department of Social Sciences, The Nottingham Trent University, England where he teaches cross-faculty in the Schools of Art and Design and Economics and Social Sciences. He has published extensively on higher education, knowledge technologies, mortality, animal rights, speech codes, monasticism and religious life, and sacred dress in modern and postmodern contexts. His most recent publications on the latter subject appear in Body & Society, Fashion Theory and the Berg volume Undressing Religion edited by Linda Arthur (2000). From studies in archives in England, Italy, France, Ireland and his native Scotland he has been preparing a historical socio-theology of religious dress codes since the French Revolution. He has served as a national subject assessor for sociology and is on the Scientific Ethics Committee of his university.

David Martin is Emeritus Professor in Sociology at the London School of Economics and Political Science where he taught for many years and served as Convenor of the Department of Sociology. His many publications include Pacifism: A Sociological Study, The Religious and the Secular, The Breaking of the Image, A General Theory of Secularization, Does Christianity Cause War?, Tongues of Fire: Pentecostalism in Latin America, Reflections on Sociology and Theology, and (with P. Heelas and P. Morris) Religion, Modernity and Postmodernity. He has held numerous prestigious Visiting Professorships in England and the United States of America and directed field research throughout Europe and Latin America. In 2000 he was awarded an honorary doctorate in theology by the University of Helsinki in the same year as receiving a Festschrift from the British Sociological Association Sociology of Religion Study Group of which he is Founder and Past President. His unique 'voice' on the shaping forces and deeper subterranean cultural currents of modern society is acknowledged internationally as among the most perceptive of the age.

Milly Williamson is Senior Lecturer in Mass Communications and Cultural Studies at the University of North London, England. Her publications include 'Vampires and the Gendered Body' in Reframing Bodies (edited by Nick Watson). Her main research interests include gender, fandom, subcultures, media audiences, and horror and vampire fiction.

Dana Wilson-Kovacs is a doctoral student in sociology at the University of Exeter, Devon, England. She has a background in philosophy and her main interests are in material culture, consumption and the sociology of gender, with particular reference to pornography. Her PhD research into intimacy and sexual consumption continues her earlier work on the construction of identities and encounters in British top-shelf magazines.

List of Illustrations

1.1   *Thomas Carlyle*, by John Linnell, 1844
      The Scottish National Portrait Gallery, Edinburgh
      Courtesy of the Picture Library, National Galleries of
      Scotland   2

1.2   *Thomas Carlyle*, by Walter Graves, c1879
      Scottish National Portrait Gallery, Edinburgh
      Courtesy of the Picture Library, National Galleries of
      Scotland   3

1.3   *Thomas Carlyle 1879*, by Helen Allingham 1848-1926
      Scottish National Portrait Gallery, Edinburgh
      Courtesy of the Picture Library, National Galleries of
      Scotland   41

4.1   *The Cutting Edge*
      Exhibition Catalogue, 'The Cutting Edge: Fifty Years of British
      Fashion 1947–1997', Victorian and Albert Museum, London,
      March-July 1997, London
      Courtesy of the V&A Picture Library   93

4.2   *Burberry Man*
      Burberry Autumn and Winter Catalogue 1996
      Courtesy of Burberrys of London   98

4.3   *Burberry Woman*
      Burberry Autumn and Winter Catalogue 1996
      Courtesy of Burberrys of London   99

9.1   Detail from *The Gunpowder Plot, 1605* by Unknown Artist
      c1605
      Courtesy of The National Portrait Gallery, London   185

The editor wishes to acknowledge his appreciation of the permissions granted by the holding authorities to publish the above illustrations.

Foreword

One indicator of the importance of a cultural item is the range of meanings and overtones you can pack into its core vocabulary. Think only of the implications built into the title of this book about the way we show off our prescribed or chosen role in the social scene by what we 'put on'. Dress mediates how we see ourselves and how others see us, and if we want to pass muster we had better make the right choice. My second son was threatened in Boston, Massachusetts, with the comment: 'You are wearing the wrong kind of jacket at the wrong time in the wrong place.' In a very different kind of context in the gospels the man dragged off the street to make up the wedding party found himself condemned for not being already togged up in his 'glad rags'. The message in both cases is that we should be ware[1] and be ready. We mustn't be caught 'improperly dressed' as military lingo has it. Living is a way of being on parade and demotion or excommunication or detention can mean stripping or being kitted out in the uniform of disgrace.

A fluid vocabulary able to shift the social scenery around with that kind of speed is truly an index of importance and richness of implication. And yet dress has not been all that central to sociological reflection until the arrival of postmodernity and the associated advent of cultural studies. The classic point of reference is Carlyle's *Sartor Resartus* and Carlyle is one of the great unread masters of Victorian literature. His writing is complex and very much needs the kind of illuminating reappraisal here provided by William Keenan.

Berg's pathbreaking *Dress, Body, Culture* series under the general editorship of the doyenne of comparative dress studies, Regents' Professor Joanne B. Eicher, helps greatly to disclose the breadth and depth of the intellectual foundations in this sector of enquiry. Each of the articles in the current book adds further insight to a work of analysis that inhabits an expanding universe subject to probe but which is not exhaustible. This is the 'soft wear' of sociology but as hermeneutically taxing as anything in the so-called 'hard' sectors of the subject: not a matter of arithmetical figures as in demography but of the figures we cut in the world. We are all of us part of what Shakespeare called 'the glass of fashion and the mould of form', advertising ourselves in our covering.

David Martin, Emeritus Professor of Sociology
London School of Economics and Political Science, London University

[1] *Editor's Note:* **ware**: careful, aware, observant (Old Scots and Old English usages). See also *The New Oxford Dictionary of English* (1998, Oxford University Press), page 2081 for additional sartorial resonances.

Introduction: 'Sartor Resartus' Restored: Dress Studies in Carlylean Perspective

William J.F. Keenan

Clothes, as despicable as we think them, are so unspeakably significant.

T. Carlyle *Sartor Resartus* (1869 ed.: 70)

Introduction: Founding Dress Studies

Who, today, outside of antiquarian literary circles, reads *Sartor Resartus*? Sadly, few appear to recognize, in his day as well as our own, the full significance and potential of this curious book by the eminent Victorian, Thomas Carlyle (1795–1881) (Fig.1.1), for shaping the intellectual field, as we moderns would say, of dress studies. A major purpose of this Introduction to a collection of contemporary academic essays on different facets of the inexhaustible world of dress is to make the general case for Thomas Carlyle's partly fictionalized, partly autobiographical, entirely original work as a seminal text for would-be contributors to the expanding field of dress studies. Through *Sartor Resartus*, it is claimed, Carlyle prepared deep and strong foundations for the study of clothes as a creative, challenging and credible realm of cultural enquiry.

Rather than introduce each of the essays to follow in turn as a self-conscious example of the new 'Carlylean' dress studies in action, the intention here is to let each contribution speak for itself in terms of its theoretical rationale and methodological underpinnings. After all, we hardly expect modern physicists to cite Newton in every scientific paper or Darwin to make a statutory appearance in contemporary academic biology reports or Adam Smith to monopolise contemporary economic theory. While none of the essays presented here explicitly

Figure 1.1 Thomas Carlyle, by John Linnell, 1844. Scottish National Portrait
Gallery, Edinburgh.

makes reference to Carlyle and his seminal text, the fact remains that *Sartor
Resartus* inaugurated the field of dress studies by giving the subject of clothes
its first sustained systematic scrutiny. As with other great intellectual founder
figures – few, if any, of whom purposefully set out to found an academic
subject area – Carlyle is owed credit by those who later build upon the original
foundations. This Introduction is, perhaps, the first extended tribute to the
forgotten Victorian Master in his role as Founder of dress studies (Fig.1.2).

Figure 1.2 Thomas Carlyle, by Walter Graves, c.1879. Scottish National Portrait Gallery, Edinburgh.

Consciously or unconsciously, it is on Carlyle's intellectual foundations that modern students of dress inescapably build, whatever new departures in theoretical approach and empirical subject matter have been taken since his work was originally published.

The main aim here, then, is to take the opportunity afforded by this Introduction to claim Carlyle as the putative founder of the recently and rapidly developing academic discipline of dress studies. In taking clothes seriously as a fitting and rewarding subject matter for their original research and scholarship, the spirit, if not the letter, of Carlyle's masterpiece, is interwoven throughout this collection of articles on a remarkable range of dressways. *Dressed to Impress: Looking the Part* is designed as an expression in 'late modern' form of the field of dress studies *Sartor Resartus* served to found, largely unintentionally, no doubt, at the launch of modernity.

Exploring Dressways

Though a patch over-embroidered, perhaps, the adage 'dress makes the (wo)man' contains a thread of sociological truth which this collection of state-of-the-art studies of 'dressways' across an impressive array of social life makes clear. How society 'covers' and leaves its impress upon our individual and corporate identities through dress signs and symbols is the warp and woof of *Dressed to Impress: Looking the Part*. Clothes are society's way of showing where we belong in the order of things, our role and position in the social pageantry. Until relatively recently, clothing has remained on the margins of the sociological project, albeit such luminaries as Herbert Spencer, Emile Durkheim and – primus inter pares amongst those with the keenest eye on the *'Orbis Vestitus'* – Thomas Carlyle, brought human dressways within the horizon of serious cultural reflection. He taught us to see how it was that 'a more or less incompetent Digestive-apparatus' (p. 65)[1] could become 'the Godlike rendered visible' (p. 216) by 'the covering Art' (p. 281) and 'how a Man is by the Tailor new-created . . .'(p. 280).

Whether as an expression of a postmodern cultural turn or simply an aspect of the coming of age of sociology, academic attention to dress and society has become a fitting part of the necessary agenda of contemporary social and cultural studies. *Dressed to Impress* attests to the attractiveness, salience and vigour of dress as a category and realm of cultural analysis. If Carlyle's *Sartor Resartus* can with ample justification be construed as the vade mecum of what in this reappraisal of the classic text is referred to as 'the new dress studies', the essays gathered up here provide splendid samplers of the layered and limitless wardrobe of human dressways across a wide diversity of historical and social circumstances. What sociological riches lie in prospect within 'the World in Clothes'!

A fresh 'Carlylean' light cast over the subject of dress, currently exhibiting a powerful renaissance, helps greatly to disclose the true depths and expansiveness of the intellectual foundations of this area of enquiry. Each of the chapters here contributes impressively to the permanently unfinished work of (un)covering the socially significant symbols – of which dress, arguably, is the most resonant – in which we 'live, move and have our being' within society. We learn from the volume as a whole how, in Carlyle's 'Swiftian' language (p. 55), 'a forked straddling animal with bandy legs' can be converted under diverse clothing regimes into, inter alia, a 'divine apparition', to give an indication of the immense span of the field. The sociological days have arrived when students of the 'hard' powers of economics, politics and technology have to learn to share the mantle of true science and scholarship with Carlyle's heirs – too long on the outskirts of academic life – for whom the 'soft' powers of dress and adornment mark an indelible impress upon the human condition that commands our attention and analysis as observers of all human life.

With regard to taking the measure of the dressways of humanity, Carlyle, it will be argued, was a man ahead of his time – and by some distance. *Sartor Resartus*, I shall claim, is a fitting foundational text for studies relevant to the 'society of the sign' (Baudrillard 1987). It is, in certain respects, not to put too fine a point on it, 'postmodern' *avant la lettre*, and highly apposite to the topical, exciting and challenging intellectual enterprise of academic studies of human clothing. A handful of contemporary texts (Wilson 1985: 154; Rubinstein 1995: 21, 39–40; Barnard 1996: 47–8, 53) make passing reference to Carlyle's evolutionary 'adornment hypothesis' – that the origins of clothes are to be found in the body decorations of 'wild people' – and his recognition that dress has a 'rhetorical' or 'emblematic' dimension beyond mere functionality. However, the case for Carlyle as the designer-in-chief of an important and enduring 'new look' at an old subject – dress – has never quite been put with the rigour and vigour it deserves. Too often, Carlyle the student of dress has been occluded underneath layers of scholastic interest in Carlyle the literary figure, Carlyle the philosophical historian, Carlyle the Victorian moralist. Important as these acknowledgements are of a many-sided major intellect, there is the danger that Carlyle, the Founder of dress studies, author of the perennially challenging guide to the heights and depths of reflections on dress, *Sartor Resartus*, becomes hidden from cultural and intellectual history. This chapter is an attempt to rescue a giant from the risk of oblivion, an effort to catch glimpses of a unique and powerful 'eye' on an incoming postmodern tide.

Every field of study, especially those emerging into partial intellectual autonomy from the chrysalis of obscurity and neglect within which they may have been long submerged, needs its heroic figures, its pathfinders and exemplars. Without them, it is hardly likely that older conservative paradigms of academic praxis will ever get busted or new areas of enquiry and innovative approaches enter the marketplace of ideas (Kuhn 1970). Carlyle, no stranger to the understanding of the hero in history (Bentley 1940) (see his *On Heroes, Hero-Worship, and the Heroic in History*, 1841), deserves full consideration in this principal historic role within the field of dress studies for his work in identifying the substance and value of human clothing as an independent realm of critical exploration and a subject matter worthy of the most creative intellectual efforts. *Sartor Resartus* not only opened up a limitless seam of behaviours and beliefs about dress for substantive study, it also and, perhaps, more importantly, set in train the unfinished and, probably, endless task of theorising the topic in ways that contribute significantly to our knowledge and understanding of the human being as a *dressed* subject. In *Sartor Resartus*, Carlyle proceeds to show that this blindingly transparent observation about the human social animal – counter intuitive to the human sciences, it would appear, from a review of the social sciences canon and curricula until relatively recently indeed – is not, by any means, the least significant social and cultural fact about us.

The purpose of this present Introduction to a collection of state-of-the-art essays on diverse aspects of dress and society, then, is to pay belated homage to Carlyle as Founder of what has become something of the quintessential discipline of 'the economy of signs and spaces' (Lash and Urry 1994), the multi-disciplinary study of dress and culture. Among the key interwoven 'environmental' factors in the contemporary evolution of dress studies as a self-confident subject area can be included the following: the 'cultural turn' (Chaney 1994) of late modernity and its associated valorization of the symbolic; the shift from 'production' to 'consumption' as a locus for understanding contemporary economic life (Featherstone 1990; Falk 1994); the generalized interest in and enthusiasm for, notably among social and cultural minority groups (and especially among women, young people, gays and lesbians, and ethnic communities), questions of identity, representation and lifestyles (Hall (ed.) 1997; Muggleton 2000); the proliferation of studies on the 'body' and subjects in close relation (Turner 1996; Shilling 1993); and the renewed attention to 'material culture' (Miller 1987; Gottdiener 1995) and 'visual culture' (Evans and Hall (eds) 1999) in the cultural and social sciences. While intimations of a dress studies efflorescence can be discerned earlier, particularly in the steady stream of contributions of the pathfinding social anthropologists, historians and social psychologists noted below, it was not until the 1960s and the associated 'expressive revolution' (Martin 1981), that the study of dress began to attract the attention of a wider academic community and 'grow' as a substantial intellectual field.

A Living Tradition

Detailed exploration of this conducive historical context for the resurgence of the field of dress studies as the territory of an independent 'academic tribe'

(Becher 1989) would carry us far beyond the remit of the present Introduction. What needs to be said here, however, is that the social, cultural and intellectual changes of the last few decades have helped to generate a supportive ambience for a critical mass of investigations of human dressways to begin to forge its way into academic and public visibility. Pivotal to this whole process of the blooming of dress studies have been the commanding works spanning, in many cases, modern and postmodern scholarly generations, of prominent dress scholars such as Joanne Eicher, Valerie Steele, Ruth Barnes, Mary Ellen Roach, Justine Cordwell, Elizabeth Hurlock, Aileen Ribeiro, Elizabeth Wilson, Anne Hollander, Alison Lurie, Griselda Pollock, Helen Callaway, Beatrice Medicine, Thorstein Veblen, Herbert Blumer, Ernest Crawley, Gregory Stone, René König, Ronald Schwarz, Solomon Poll, Roland Barthes, Ted Polhemus, Daniel Roche, Fred Davis, James Laver, Nathan Joseph, James Hall, John Wright, and Philippe Perrot. These writers kept the flame of dress studies flickering when it was not always fashionable or even quite academically respectable to do so, given prevailing 'masculinist' academic prejudices against 'women's subjects' of which dress and the body appeared the most extreme.[2] The 'campaigning' role of the 'heroic' generation in the definition and elaboration of the subject area of dress studies cannot be underestimated. If dress studies is to develop into a fully-fledged and autonomous academic subject it will be largely due to the contributions of this far-sighted cohort whose animating presence persists in the work on all aspects of supplementing and modifying the body of their growing retinue of latter-day descendants (such as, for example, C. Evans, C. Breward, P. Calefato, D. Ko, E.Tseëlon, R. P. Rubinstein, N. Pellegrin, L.B. Arthur, H. Clark, J. Entwistle, C. Tulloch, S. Kaiser, M. Barnard, J. Ash, N. White, B. Burman, L. Taylor, C. Cox, M. Garber, G. Lipovetsky, J. Schneider, I. Griffiths, G.D. McCracken, A. McRobbie, J. Craik, E. Rouse, V. Wilson, F. El Guindi, T. Abler, A. McLintock, S. Cole, A. Gay, E. Green, M. Banim, H.B. Foster, M. Garber, C.B. Kidwell, L. Welters, B. McVeigh, L.D. Sciama, A. Lynch, J. Perani, N. Wolff, B. Gordon, K. Soper, A. Brydon, S. Niessen, M.T. Haynes, S. Zdatny, and others).[3]

Today, the knowledge 'institutions', 'structures' and 'processes' are largely in situ for dress studies to assume its own identity and place as an 'organized knowledge' (Machlup 1962; Sklair 1973) field. Inter alia these include: a multiplicity of sub-fields of scholarship and areas of research specialization; a galaxy of dedicated metropolitan and provincial museums; a vibrant range of permanent and occasional exhibitions covering every conceivable aspect of dress from the costumes of native tribal communities and ancient civilizations, to ecclesiastical vesture and erotic fantasy wear, to occupational liveries, street styles and the ball gowns of Princess Diana; regional, national and international scholarly networks and conference circuits; high-quality academic journals and expanding publishers' lists serving as outlets for the empirical and theoretical work of professional scholars and researchers. On this formidable institutional base and expanding knowledge map, the prospects are reasonably good, while the 'quality' case is overwhelming (if one can be a little parti pris here in relation to those with whom one identifies one's knowledge interests), for the subject of dress studies to attain heightened academic visibility and prominence within the academy, develop its own reward system, prestige hierarchies and 'normative order' (Merton 1968), and assume full status as an independent subject. Dress studies may never assume – and may never aspire to – the mantle of 'big science' (de Solla Price 1969), but it has every intellectual justification and all the necessary knowledge supports to become an identifiable disciplinary field sui generis. In dress studies, where the cut and quality of the intellectual cloth, as it were, is of paramount importance and value, size per se – sheer volume of intellectual 'product', 'grant capture', 'project scale', 'social impact' and so forth – matters little, particularly at this stage of maturation into academic autonomy and intellectual independence.

In making confident, powerful strides into the future, it behoves those who stand on giants' shoulders to honour ancestral intellectual debts. A central purpose of this Introduction to a body of work which makes its own modest contribution to the development of dress studies, is to pause for reflection on one of the keystones of our common intellectual project and disciplinary culture, lest, in the absorbing business of enlarging, making more robust and edifying the building, we cover over and forget its unique part in giving shape – and, in Carlyle's case – substance and style to the whole edifice. As we move further and further into the 'network' or 'virtual' age and build the 'distanced interaction' systems of the 'knowledge society' around us, we need to recall to mind and take fuller stock and measure of those simpler, quotidian, taken-for-granted 'techniques of the body' (Mauss 1973) through which we have lived out and expressed our humanity down the ages. Clothes – Carlyle had the perspicacity and audacity to remind us at the very outset of the creation of the 'technical environment' (Friedmann 1947) – were of both a fundamental and an ultimate order of cultural and social significance. They transform 'a forked radish with a head fantastically carved' (p. 60), to use a favourite term of Carlyle for the 'Adamite', the raw, bare-boned human being, into a potent carrier of infinite cultural meanings. Depending on context, 'a snip of the scissors' (pp. 34–5) serves to transport mortal flesh 'to endless depths' (p. 49) of baseness and depravity, or render that self-same 'Garment of Flesh (or of Sense), contextured in the Loom of Heaven . . . skywoven, and worthy of a God' (p. 64).

Introducing this collection of key articles on dress as central to the impressions individual and collective bodies make on the world around them is to engage immediately with an essentially 'Carlylean' theme. The way dress figures in how we make our mark on those around us, how our clothing discloses much about our role in the drama of history, where our garments locate us in the social pageantry, the messages – economic, cultural, moral, philosophical, theological and spiritual given out by this most personal and intimate medium of social communication, for example, are all matters to which Carlyle applied his formidable learning and intelligence.

For contemporary students of the burgeoning, pre-eminently late modern or postmodern field of dress studies, Carlyle's enigmatically entitled master-piece, *Sartor Resartus* – 'The Tailor Retailored' or, sometimes, 'The Patcher Repatched' (Wilson 1924: 223) – constitutes a key foundation text. It merits attention by everyone drawn to the exploration of dress as a field of academic enquiry. Its author, Thomas Carlyle, widely honoured as an eminent Victorian essayist, figures only in passing as something of a curio within human sciences commentary in general. Regrettably, too, his pathbreaking entrée into the serious-minded enquiry upon dress as a fundamental aspect of the human social and cultural condition has somehow become bypassed in the modern academic development of the subject. However, in his highly interdisciplinary work ranging across anthropology, theology, history of civilizations, philosophy and ethics, Carlyle addresses in a powerful, perceptive and prescient fashion what he called, in Swiftian flourishes, 'the adventitious wrappings' of the 'omnivorous biped that wears Breeches'(p. 64). His literary style and investi-gative modus operandi may not be to conventional contemporary taste, it is true. However, the searching and soaring philosophical 'voice' and deep penetrating sociological 'gaze' on clothes found between the dusty covers of *Sartor Resartus* badly need to be rescued from the modern wash.

In this chapter I have drawn exclusively on the Chapman and Hall 1869 edition of *Sartor Resartus*. More recent editions (for example, Carlyle 1987 and 2000) are available albeit their primary focus is on the literary historical aspects of the work rather than, as here, on its theoretical and substantive interest in dress itself. There is, in any case, something intellectually and spiritually nourishing for 'anamnestic communities' (Yerushalmi 1982), even academic or epistemic 'communities of memory' (Connerton 1989), such as that implicitly becoming fashioned by the international 'invisible college' (Crane 1972) of dress scholars, to 'return to the *fons*' to commemorate a shared lineage (Schwartz 1982) and renew 'their story' (Fentress and Wickham 1992). This periodic 'ritual of remembrance' that occurs within mature, self-conscious disciplinary traditions is not undertaken merely for the purpose of preserving a fixed deposit of knowledge frozen in perpetuity. On the contrary, it is designed to contribute to the reconstruction of a sense of a dynamical, self-critical tradition (King 1971) – a 'progressive' tradition of knowledge (Lakatos and Musgrave (eds.) 1970) – aware of its own roots and heritage as a valuable reservoir of insight, but able to build upon this resource in ways responsive to new directions in thought and cultural and social life.

In this regard, honouring Carlyle as the 'Founder' of the intellectual domain of dress studies registers a monumental reference point in an unfolding tradition of knowledge growth from which contemporary scholars in this expanding field can take their bearings and the subject area as a whole gauge its development. For scientific communities, as much as for religious, ethnic and national communities, the 'communion between the living and the dead' (Warner 1975) through the channel of 'foundation' texts is highly significant if the bond between past and present within a living tradition is to be cultivated. *Sartor Resartus* is positioned here as the locus classicus of dress studies. It stands as the first *mapa mundi* of this field and charted the broad lineaments of the ideational cosmos of clothes. Foundation texts provide key linkages in the communal chain of being as well as access points to its fundamental and core principles (Eliade 1959). As 'objective knowledge' (Popper 1974) they can always be accessed with profit by those who would take stock of the 'long tradition' and locate potential means of revitalization within it (Eliade 1954). They become reference points to hand for the ongoing evolution of a critical hermeneutical response and the basis upon which the 'paradigm wars' of mature knowledge traditions – religious, scientific, literary and cultural – can perforce occur. Carlyle's point-of-view represents a necessary and perennially stimulating orientation to the matter of clothes. Had it not been propounded in *Sartor Resartus*, it would be necessary to invent it if for no other reason than to provide for as rich and extensive a vocabulary on and conspectus of the 'idea of dress' that we can possibly conceive and imagine. Carlyle's is an essential 'voice' on the whole subject of dress and one that merits an airing in any generation of dress scholarship.

Without the critical debate generated by engagement with the diverse layers that make up 'invented traditions' (Hobsbawm and Ranger (eds) 1983), then such a 'restorative' exercise as undertaken here becomes simply one of 'ancestor worship'. However, as put by MacIntyre (1982: 206) in terms that have relevance to the role of *Sartor Resartus* in the 'awakening' of dress studies as a self-aware, 'autocritical' knowledge field: 'a living tradition is an historically extended, socially embodied argument, and an argument precisely in part about the goods which constitute that tradition'. Going back to the 'Carlylean' roots is a way of seeing ourselves in the mirror of our own past, a means of identifying with our own household gods and wrestling with family ghosts, a way of putting in relief what it is we – our tribe – want to preserve and exorcize. Dress studies, arguably, is poised ready for full-bodied development as a knowledge field in its own right. The conditions for its coming out of the closet into the full light of academic day have never been better. A crucial part of such a 'coming of age' stage in the internal history of a mature academic subject area is the capacity to live confidently and critically with its own intellectual history. Owning the plenitude of the tradition, incorporating the methods and perspectives we identify closely with as well as those we have become distanced from emotionally and intellectually or even disavow is integral to this disciplinary crystallization process. Carlyle's nineteenth-century literary and discursive approach may well fit into this latter category for a number, perhaps the majority, of modern thinkers put off by his lengthy arcane asides and esoteric excurses. The important point, nonetheless, is that the intellectual substance of his work be recognized as a vital milestone in the cartography of dress studies albeit, it is presently considered, there are grounds for continuing to return to it as a reliable signpost for further voyages of exploration in an ever-expanding world of dress signs and symbols.

Acknowledgement of Carlyle's honourable place in the ancestry of dress studies is long overdue as is clear recognition of the value of his 'sacred text', *Sartor Resartus*, as an inspirational 'manifesto' still with 'something to say' to present-day generations of dress scholars. In identifying a place for a 'Carlylean' perspective within an epistemologically pluralistic and theoretically diversified field of dress studies, one wants, of course, to avoid that 'closed society' mentality that bedevils, as Becker and Barnes (1961: 10) have it: 'communities in which a sort of emotional halo encircles the ways of the fathers and thereby prevents profanation by change'. The Carlylean cap, as it were, fits only for appropriate occasions, the intellectual purposes for which it was designed. It should become neither a straitjacket nor a fetish, but an item – more a staple essential than an optional extra, it could be argued – in the wardrobe of ideas of the intellectually well-dressed student of dress. For present purposes of capturing something of the 'spirit' of the 'Founder', Carlyle's own idiosyncratic style, so to speak, I preferred the earlier 1869 edition (from which all quotations here are drawn) close to the original, even period, style of the classic as it first appeared in its germinal forms in the 1830s. As put by Carlyle (p. 233) in his disquisition on 'the Ghosts of Old Clothes': 'What still dignity dwells in a suit of Cast Clothes! . . . The Hat still carries the physiognomy of its Head.'

In his opening paragraph to *Sartor Resartus*, Carlyle sets out his store as follows:

It might strike the reflective mind with some surprise that hitherto little or nothing of a fundamental character, whether in the way of Philosophy or History, has been written on the subject of Clothes.

Modern writers on the subject of dress may today take issue with such a claim and are likely to eschew the sexist language that bespatters the text in which Carlyle imparts his reflections on 'the vestural Tissue . . . which Man's Soul wears as its outmost wrappings and overall' (p. 2). Yet, rarely, if ever, in our academic dealings with the multiple worlds of clothing, do we depart for long from the seminal themes and fundamental tropes addressed by Thomas Carlyle over a century and a half ago. While sketched out originally between 1830 and 1831, *Sartor Resartus* was first published in essay form in *Fraser's Magazine* between November 1833 and August 1834. Carlyle's unique philosophical treatise on the 'Dressed World' of his imaginary character, the learned Professor Diogenes ('Gneschen') Teufelsdröckh, remains unsurpassed as a map of the key themes and basic problematics of 'the world of dress'. Far from being an ephemeral subject fit only for a few throw-away remarks to embroider works of more serious intellectual import, Carlyle makes clear (ibid: 261), if with a light (even spoofish) touch, that 'this Science of Clothes is a high one, and may with infinitely deeper study on thy part yield richer fruit: that it takes rank beside Codification, and Political Economy, and the Theory of the British Constitution'.

If outmoded in his allegorical style of literary expression, 'the Sage of Chelsea', as this *émigré* from the remote Dumfriesshire weaver village of Ecclefechan to the sophisticated salon world of metropolitan London in mid-nineteenth century became known, can with justification be called the 'Vasari' or even the 'Darwin' of dress studies, so decisive was his contribution to that particular domain of knowledge on which he pressed his magisterial stamp, namely, human dress in all its grime and glory. Where the fore-mentioned luminaries have always held the advantage, of course, is that there has rarely been any doubt, either within the academy or in the public mind, as to the obvious intellectual merits and substance of the problematics with which the founders of art history (Vasari) and evolutionary science (Darwin) engaged. Carlyle's *problemstellung* or programme, to comprehend the nature and significance of human clothing, can easily appear, by contrast, somewhat puny and facile by comparison, a stigma which, unhappily, dress studies still carries in some more antediluvian and, perhaps, more snobbish and macho, circles today. One of the major aims of this present extended introductory essay is to suggest that what we can call 'the Carlylean paradigm' outlined below provides, for contemporary students of dress, a still highly serviceable compass and route map by means of which we can obtain not only unique guidelines through the complex worlds of dress, fashion and adornment, but also one distinctive philosophical point of departure and illuminating theoretical *point d'horizon*.

A Carlylean Paradigm

Carlyle broke with scholastic convention in so far as he perceived dress as a fully significant component of human culture and society, a power in its own right and not simply an accidental effect and incidental by-product of more salient historical forces and social conditions. 'Society, which the more I think of it, astonishes me the more', he opines in *Sartor Resartus* (p. 59), 'is founded upon Cloth'. His interest in the social efficacy of clothes has come of age in our own 'postmodern' (Lyotard 1984) 'new times' as increasing numbers of students and scholars turn their attention to this rich and universal seam of cultural life for clues as to how human beings shape and mould the world around them and impress their stamp upon their contemporaries and peers, be that, as he puts it in *Sartor Resartus* (pp. 64–5), 'in the highest imperial Sceptre and Charlemagne-Mantle, as well as in the poorest Ox-goad and Gypsy-Blanket'. Yet, the man who did most to bring dress within the purview of critical consciousness and the work which gave clothing its rightful place of prominence within the drama of social life has become well-nigh merely an obscure footnote reference in contemporary scholarship and research devoted to dress in all its manifold manifestations and meanings. A major objective of this Introduction to a collection of contemporary social and cultural studies of diverse aspects of dress is to establish Carlyle's original perspectives on this inexhaustible and still largely undercultivated field as still, in important respects, foundational, fresh and fecund in relation to the scholarly purposes of serious students of the subject today.

Carlyle's substantive range and intellectual vision when brought to bear upon clothes in *Sartor Resartus*, I wish to contend, illuminates a path forward for dress studies that is both 'scientific' and 'artistic'. Carlyle's distinctive modes of theorization and interpretation have all the marks of his intellectual generation and of his own somewhat idiosyncratic literary bent. As a clothes research programme, Carlyle's credo in *Sartor Resartus* (p. 65 and p. 70): 'The beginning of all Wisdom is to look fixedly on Clothes . . . till they become *transparent*' and 'the essence of all Science lies in the Philosophy of Clothes' is somewhat over-zealous for us today. Yet, the example of one who broaches the neglected subject of dress with a concern to observe and describe it carefully and reflect upon it with wisdom and *élan* still serves to encourage those who would follow the Master into this still largely uncharted and unchartered territory of the study of dress. In the language of Max Weber, the great German thinker on the complexities of the sociology of culture (a figure with whom, one suspects, Professor Teufelsdröckh – Carlyle's literary alter ego in *Sartor Resartus* – might have found partial sympathy), a 'Carlylean' approach to dress can be 'adequate at both the levels of causation and meanings' (Weber 1949). *Sartor Resartus* teaches us the value of finding our own path through the sheer density of human dressways and discovering our own 'voice' in the matter of narrating and interpreting what we see and experience. The work stands as a 'classic' in the field and an inspirational document not because it should be slavishly imitated by modern writers, but largely because it is an original work of quality providing an enduring conspectus of a universal subject which we moderns or late moderns do well to take into account in the further development of clothing studies.

Without reading too much into the phrase, we are all 'Carlyleans' now. Few books written about late modern culture and society fail to recognize, even if for the most part *en passant*, that in the postmodern economy of the sign, dress matters and matters considerably in the (re-)presentation of individual and corporate body-selves. *Sartor Resartus* anticipates our postmodern preoccupation with signs and signage – and body symbols especially – by some century and three quarters, almost the full span, indeed, of modernity itself. As a champion of political and intellectual liberty, Carlyle would have been among the last to have his academic followers in the field of clothing studies imitate him to the letter. In any case, his unique work on dress is, truly, far too idiosyncratic for that possibility. It is that 'Carlylean' freedom to explore and evaluate the manifold ways in which the emblematic nature of dress is woven into the warp and woof of human society – not necessarily anything more – that we find fully expressed in the articles in this present collection that allows us to construe the author of *Sartor Resartus* as the Founder of what we can call the new dress studies of the present day.

Inevitably, of course, the study of clothes has widened its empirical coverage and adjusted its ideological lenses since Carlyle's own day. It would be anachronistic to expect the contents of Carlyle's wardrobe trunk to exactly match our own. We find nothing in the archetypical Victorian, neo-Calvinist, provincial Carlyle, for instance, of bodies being 'genderized' (Kidwell and Steele (eds) 1989; Barnes and Eicher (eds) 1993; McDowell 1997; Griggs 1998; Tseëlon 1995), 'sexualized' (Ash and Wilson (eds) 1992; Garber 1992; Hollander 1993), 'eroticized' (Steele 1985; Keenan 1999b), 'fetishized' (Steele 1996; Steele (ed.) 1999), 'brutalized' (Arnold 2000), 'surgicalized' (Johnson and Lennon (eds) 1999), 'primitivized' (Vale and Juno (eds) 1989), 'racialized' (Eicher (ed.) 1995), 'colonized' (Abler 1999), 'ideologized' (Wilson 1985; McVeigh 2000), 'patronized' (Perani and Wolff 1999), 'mythologized' (Haynes 1998), 'rationalized' (Keenan 2000), 'fashionalized' (Hebdige 1979; Polhemus 1994; Warwick and Cavallaro (eds) 1998; Entwistle 2000), and 'profanized' (Keenan 1999a) through dress.

History and 'knowledge interests' have moved on apace since the Victorian age and a number of the contributions in this present volume exemplify aspects of the shift of direction taken by late modern dress studies, not least in terms of the greater transparency and explicitness about 'dress/body talk', the heightened academic criticism regarding the fine details of 'clothed world's apart', and the general public scrutiny of the naked power relations embedded in dress. At a time, however, when piano-legs were covered-up and 'Upstairs and Downstairs' inhabited largely hermetically sealed dressed 'Galsworthian' worlds of disdain, deference and dependency, propriety and patronage could dictate exacting in-built limits, often self-imposed, on the tongue and pen on such sensitive subjects close to the raw edges of Victorian sensibility.

But, en passant, it is worth noting that Carlyle's own particular 'nineteenth-century' preoccupations with the broadcloth of social class and religion refracted through the lenses of clothing as a marker of socio-economic status and as a medium of religious identity and belonging have persisted since as something akin to a continuous tradition within modern dress studies. Dress as 'cultural capital' (Bourdieu 1984; Bell 1992; Perrot 1994; Roche 1994; Rubinstein 1995; Gronow 1997) and as a vehicle for the 'sacralization' of individual and corporate bodies (Poll 1962; Yoder 1969; Mayo 1984; El Guindi 1998; Arthur (ed.) 1999; Arthur (ed.) 2000) remain firmly today as key foci of the new dress studies linking the 'Founder' with his present-day academic epigoni. Examples of this common 'Carlylean' interest in the implication of clothing in the ways of God and Mammon are also found in the present volume.

If by 'paradigm' is meant a set of specific assumptions and general concepts pertaining to some substantive areas or aspects of the world, the two key components of a 'Carlylean paradigm' for dress studies are as follows: (1) dress matters and is significant within human experience, cultures and societies in the everyday and ceremonial lives of individuals and groups; and (2) clothes reflect and symbolise traditions, values, ideologies and emotional states and can be understood by both scientific and artistic means. This, of course, offers a copious remit for the social, cultural and psychological sciences conceived in humanistic terms (Berger 1963; Nisbet 1976). The entire point of the 'Carlylean paradigm', and its main benefit as a *tours d'horizon*, is that it provides a broad enough context of interest and significance to allow scope for the individual subjects and disciplines – aesthetics, anthropology, archeology, psychology, sociology, philosophy, theology, religious studies, history, literary studies, geography, economics, art and design studies, fashion studies and so forth – to examine the dressways of the world according to their own particular modalities and methodologies, the details of which need not detain us here. The looming background presence of the Carlylean paradigm also scotches the old canard that the study of dress is constitutionally a 'women's subject' (Rouse 1989), a myth that persisted despite the 'classical' contributions of Darwin, Spencer, Tylor, Morgan, Durkheim, Westermack, Simmel, Sapir, Bogatyrev, Kroeber, Veblen, Flügel, Crawley, Blumer, König, Stone, Barthes and other male 'voices' on the subject (Simmel 1904/1957; Crawley 1912/1931; Stone 1962; Barthes 1967, 1983; Blumer 1968; König 1973a, 1973b; and contributors to Eicher and Roach-Higgins 1993 and Roach-Higgins, Eicher and Johnson (eds)1995). Clothing, perish the thought, has frequently traditionally been perceived as at best a minor feminine pastime on a par with crochet, jam making and the leisurely perusal of women's fashion, beauty and home-making magazines, a diversionary amateur activity on the distaff fringes of scholarship proper. Restoring the Carlylean foundations serves to debunk this myth.

Carlyle's own theoretical perspective on clothing is rooted in his 'post-Christian' socio-political denunciation of the falseness of material wealth (Roe 1969; Levin 1998) coupled with an idealist 'Romantic' spirituality full of humanitarian hope and optimism (Jessop 1997; Vanden Bossche 1991) which he refers to in *Sartor Resartus* as 'The Everlasting Yea'. Dress, for him, was a site where human beings can either succumb to the yoke of social conformity and the tyranny of cultural uniformity or, in however small a degree, in their clothing variations, express and assert individual and group differences. The view taken here in this Introduction is that this distinctive 'Carlylean' cast of mind – to be found, inter alia, in Wesley, Edwards, Arnold, Pater, Ruskin, Dickens, Melville, Hawthorne (cf. Arac 1979; Dale 1977) and, arguably, Nietzsche (Bentley 1940) – merits a place in its own right as a 'way of seeing' the cultural orders and social worlds around us. It resonates well with the contemporary resurgence of interest in 'agency' against the crudely deterministic focus on 'structure' of many strands of modern social theory (Archer 1988; Giddens 1984).

Carlyle avoids and, in fact, inveighs against the excessive and reductionist materialism of the social radicalism and liberalism of his times (Levin 1998). In *Sartor Resartus* he rings the changes on the 'sacramentalist' theme that there is more to matter than mere matter, that matter matters in a metapyhsical or spiritual, even theological sense (Milbank, Ward and Pickstock 1999). 'Art Thou not the "Living Garment" of God?', he proclaims (ibid: 108). It is the 'metaphysicality' of 'mere dress' which captivates Carlyle. He sums up his 'Natural Supernaturalism' (p. 261) thus (p. 260): 'that all symbols are properly Clothes; that all forms whereby spirit manifests itself to sense, whether outwardly or in the imagination, are Clothes'.

Dress was the 'sacred' medium on which he chose to enlarge upon and embroider his essentially romantic ideas, largely Germanic in inspiration through the influence of Goethe and Jean Paul Richter especially (Ashton 1994), about Creation, Culture and Humanity. Brantley (1993) points out that Carlyle's world view harks back to the epistemology of John Locke and the 'empirical-evangelical' vision that apprehends God-in-nature and valorizes reverence for our common spiritual foundations above all things. In *Sartor Resartus* (p. 258) Carlyle writes:

> Long and adventurous has the journey been from those outmost, palpable Woollen Hulls of Man . . . inwards to the Garments of his very Soul's Soul . . . Can many readers discern, as through a glass darkly, in huge wavering outlines, some primeval rudiments of Man's Being, what is changeable from what is unchangeable?

A Humanistic Perspective

Dress has ever played a part in commentary on morals, manners and mores from biblical injunctions against vanity, through literary satire – Chaucer, Erasmus, Swift – on human foibles and frailties, to innumerable books on etiquette, decorum and good taste ranging from early modern manuals on 'civilized' (cf. Elias 1978) conduct to 'dress for success' guides in our own day. Across this immense literature, clothes are perceived as presentational devices – 'secondary causes' – for underlying tastes and values, mere surfaces on which cultural and moral preferences and powers can be impressed. In dressing this way or that way we mirror our selves and societies. Whether in robes of splendour or ragged-trousered charitable hand-me-downs, be it to look as similar to or as different from those around us as clothes can possibly make us, we reveal something fundamental and telling about our humanity, that is to say, our connectedness and communicability with fellow members of 'the dressed race'. To put the point in the neo-Cartesian epigrammatic style of the hero of *Sartor Resartus*, Herr Professor Diogenes Teufelsdröckh (Carlyle's own stylized voice, his 'omniscient narrator'): 'I dress therefore human am I.' In the chapters that follow, we find exemplification and enlargement of this humanistic vision tailored to the vicissitudes of the actual clothing arrangements and circumstances of a considerable range of specific communities and cultures.

For Carlyle, dress could never be just something insignificant, incidental and irrelevant to Life. It was a solid, hard reality located full-square in the midst of human interaction and as such fully deserving of our most meticulous apprehension and utmost respect. As he puts it in *Sartor Resartus* (p. 34): 'Body and the Cloth are the site and the materials whereon and whereby . . . a Person is to be built.' In the panoply of theorizations available to us to try to make sense of the infinite complexity of our dealings with the stuff of creation in general, and dress – the embodied sign of the full spectrum of material and social difference – in particular, Carlyle's *Sartor Resartus* provides a highly different 'neo-Platonist' angle of vision from the more materialist social scientific orthodoxies of structural functionalism, Marxism, phenomenology and classical social theory (Turner 1999; Ritzer 2000).

Moreover, as we 'late moderns' struggle to come to terms with and make sense of the dense layerings of symbols and the power of signs that surround us in contemporary society, Carlyle's perspective on such matters as dress – where, in effect, the 'hard' power of political economy hits the 'soft' power of raw human flesh – may be found not only insightful and instructive, but also 'prophetic' (Kelman 1924; Symons 1952). This may be so as much in the 'postmodern' style of Carlylean address – ironic, playful, metaphysical, humorous and pluralistic – as in the substantive focus on the social, cultural and human significance of clothing itself. In all the immense draughts of almost-Proustian introspection, the multiple extended metaphors and the brilliance of the ironic wit, there remains in *Sartor Resartus* a peasant's acuity of description of the real. For all his jaunts to the fashionable parts of Glasgow, Edinburgh, London, Birmingham and Paris, Carlyle remained throughout his life a Lowland peasant (Oliphant 1892: 115). His nomadic life as upwardly mobile social aspirant and cosmopolitan writer made for a deracinated, marginal relationship with the world around him, an anticipatory 'postmodern condition' conducive, perhaps, to the cultivation of an uneasy 'sociological imagination' (Mills 1959).

As the pioneer philosopher-theoretician of dress, a reappraisal of Carlyle's significance for the now burgeoning field of dress studies is long overdue. Better known for his historical studies (cf. Tarr 1989) such as *The French Revolution* (1837), *Chartism* (1839) and *Heroes and Hero-Worship* (1841), Carlyle, a Victorian Scottish émigré to England, produced, first in Edinburgh in serial magazine form (1833–4) and then in book form in North America in 1836 and London in 1838, what remains the most eloquent and sustained conspectus of, in the 'Humean' language of his times, the 'moral philosophy' of clothing to date. His 'vitalist' perspective on dress is original and unsurpassed in this particular respect. Carlyle sees beyond the purely or merely material life of clothes and penetrates something of their deeper spiritual meaning in the cultural lives of their wearers. As a richly layered text, *Sartor Resartus* offers multiple 'takes' on its subject. Through the literary device of his fictional narrator, Herr Professor Diogenes Teufelsdröckh, Carlyle undertakes to reveal the full measure of clothes as elemental markers of the human spirit and character. He is impressed by what we wear and, at the same time, not taken in by them. He perceives the part our clothes assign us to in the grand design but refuses to believe that that is all there is to us.

In the variety and variability of our dressed lives there is much scope for all manner of human vulnerability and frailty to surface. As regards our beliefs and states of feeling about ourselves and the world, guise and disguise interweave as in a gigantic 'masked' ball (Tseëlon 1992 and 1995). What we wear is and is not who we really are. Clothes speak, as it were, in a semi-transparent language that is partly literal and prosaic and partly mysterious and poetic (Lurie 1992; Barnard 1996). Carlyle cottoned on to this in a very strong way. Dress tells us only so much and thereafter keeps us guessing. Dress conceals and reveals at one and the same moment. Clothes are a flimsy disguise for our naked ambitions and inhibitions. At the same moment, they offer assurance and reassurance that we are one of a kind, recognizably members of this clan or that sub-tribe, this team or that nation, this or that type, generation, gender, sorority, sexual preference community, style group or ideological fraternity. His chapters in *Sartor Resartus* on 'The Dandiacal Body' (pp. 263–77) and 'Church Clothes' (pp. 207–10), contrasting occasions to dress to impress, be it noted, the former designed to catch the faddish eye of one's fellows, the latter aimed more at the all-seeing eye of the Creator, give full vent to the panoptic Carlylean gaze on the full spectrum of dress in all its social and spiritual entanglements. Taking the diverse dressways of 'Drudges', 'Dandies', 'Saints', 'Sects' and 'all manner of Utilitarians, Radicals, refractory Potwallopers, and so forth' (p. 275) as embodiments of the threads of egoism, greed and glory in the constitutional make-up of the 'wondrous Manikin' (p. 174), Carlyle, in *Sartor Resartus* (p. 258), penetrates:

> through his wondrous Flesh-Garments, and his wondrous Social Garnitures; inwards to the garments of his very Soul's Soul, to Time and Space themselves! And now does the spiritual, eternal Essence of Man, and of Mankind, bared of such wrappings, begin in any measure to reveal itself?

What is revealing of a 'Carlylean' spirit in these matters of Creation and Human Expressivity is that the sense of 'wonder' appears to be genuine, a distinguishing trait of his Romantic – nay childlike, perhaps – sensibility, a fundamental dimension of the 'innocence' of his vision that matter matters in the ultimate scheme of things. Clothes were a ready-made metaphor for this panentheistic reverential dependency upon and regard for the 'ordinarily sacred' in the midst of our everyday lives. Whatever hardening of the spiritual arteries would occur in the elderly Carlyle as he grew more bilious and curmudgeonly with the years and lifelong dyspepsia (Campbell 1974/1993; Kaplan 1993), the Carlyle of *Sartor Resartus* was able to look upon the things all around him – and what better and more immediate than clothing – with a curious naïvety and an almost 'Blakean' eye for the 'Heaven in miniature', the 'eternal in the now'. It is this almost mystical, primitive spirituality that, on the one hand, distances Carlyle's 'clothes philosophy' from 'moderns' who have traversed the fiery brook of consumer culture, yet, on the other hand, demands of us a 'second naïvety' (Ricoeur 1973) if we are to look afresh on clothes in a larger 'Carlylean' sense uncluttered by conventional 'positivistic' and materialist assumptions. The 'clothes philosophy' embedded in *Sartor Resartus* provides an alternative 'horizon of expectation' (Gadamer 1975) to what clothes are 'normally' perceived to be. If nothing else, Carlyle helps us to see things – mere dress – differently as belonging to a wider context and deeper circle of significance. Such an intellectual option is invaluable within a field of study that would aspire to be pluralistic and open to old, new – and renewable – ideas.

No other great mind of his stature in his own day and, arguably, since, has applied itself so resolutely and with such scope, flair and genuine wit, to the study of the idea of dress as a matter of true substance and value. Where such other great Victorians as John Stuart Mill, Karl Marx, Lord Macauley, Jacob Burchkhardt, John Henry Newman, Herbert Spencer and the like were tracing the lineaments of such grand and worthy notions as the idea of Liberty, Equality, Progress, History, Civilization, Culture, a University and the like, Carlyle turned his brilliance upon the ostensibly somewhat more prosaic and humble subject of clothes. Both in his own day as ever since, it is Carlyle's more political projects such as those on Oliver Cromwell, Frederick the Great, Chartism, and, best remembered of all, the French Revolution and the hero figure in history, that have earned him his place in the pantheon of great works of nineteenth-century scholarship (Trela and Tarr (eds) 1997). While no less a luminary than his great contemporaries (Sanders and Clubbe (eds) 1976) – albeit never one to found a school or stir up a following – Carlyle, quill pen in hand, single-handedly plunged the first spade into the virgin soil of sustained enquiry and reflection on clothing. He is, however, rarely perceived today as a seminal, stimulating and still serviceable thinker whose profound and inspiring ideas on the import and impact of clothes on culture and society foreshadow the quest of contemporary scholars in search of solid intellectual foundations for the study of human dress. We can ill-afford to discard lightly the Carlylean mantle of ideas in this still massively under-covered area of enquiry into the infinity of ways in which clothes become employed in the social constitution and cultural construction of the human subject.

Of course, as a Victorian man of letters, he did not spin his erudite yarns of human dressways in terms suitable to our modern intellectual guises. His was not a recognizably social scientific style; nor one driven by modern-day technical obsessions. Certainly, his work in which we find no trace of a questionnaire, no hint of a correlation coefficient, would never pass muster with the methodological purists. *Sartor Resartus* is primarily the work of a littérateur and is certainly out-of-spirit with the emerging Comtean 'positivistic' orientation in the nascent sociology of his times (Manuel 1962; Pickering 1997). As Carlyle puts it (p. 72), his quasi-biographical composition has been 'philosophically-poetically written' and should be read accordingly. On the whole, dress studies remains committed to 'qualitative' rather more than 'quantitative' approaches. Before Simmel, Veblen, Barthes, Goffman, and so on, Carlyle, as it were, was there, charting the ground for an 'interpretative' orientation fitting to the subtleties and nuances of clothing as social symbolism. To take just one example, consider Carlye's anticipation (p. 140) of Goffman's celebrated 'dramaturgical' approach to 'the presentation of self in everyday life' in which dress 'props' play a most salient part in the sensitive and often volatile negotiations between the private 'backstage' and public 'frontstage' zones of life: '[S]ensuous life is but the small temporary stage (Zeitbühne), whereon thick-streaming influences from both these far yet near regions meet visibly, and act tragedy and melodrama.'

No mechanical scientific empiricist, Carlyle carries the hermeneutician's arts deep into the inexhaustible folds of dress culture and uncovers something of the mysterious rules, principles and processes operative therein. In bringing the present collection of essays under the suggestive title *Dressed to Impress: Looking the Part*, it is intended to convey a much wider sense of association between dress, body and culture than is conventionally addressed within the social psychology of dress (König 1973a; Kaiser 1985) or in the even more restrictive connotations of 'impression management' in the pop psychology of 'dress for success' manuals (Millman 1977; Molloy 1978). Carlyle's conception of clothing embraces a wider, fuller sense of its role and function as a marker of historical identities and cultural representations. Each of the studies in this book addresses dress within this more comprehensive frame of reference and it is in this regard that they can be considered 'Carlylean' in resonance if not in intention.

Moreover, Carlyle's profound sense of the complex paradoxicality of clothing – its power to simultaneously reveal and conceal; its solid matter-of-fact concreteness coupled with its metaphorical allusiveness; its ability to unite us with and divide us from our fellow (wo-)man; its deeply personal and intimate nature while resonant with the wider social 'habitus' and grander 'civilizing process' – is woven into these 'new dress studies'. We may find here discernible threads of Herr Teufelsdröckh's long-tailed philosophical coat deftly spun – perhaps with a lighter touch than '*the* Clothes Philosopher' himself – in order 'to expound the moral, political, even religious Influences of Clothes' (*Sartor Resartus*: 49). Through the medium of these essays, we are able to visit parts of the 'Orbis Vestitus', 'The World of Clothes', that the Founder himself would not have encountered directly but which, to be sure, he would have delighted in as 'splendiferous manifestations' of the dressways of humankind.

Dressed to Impress: Looking the Part provides a new look at the ancient yet ever new arts of 'looking the part' and shows how a variety of recognizable identities – political activist, ballerina, Muslim schoolgirl, erotic female, country gent, Mormon, 'vampire' – is achieved through dress representations and clothing imagery. Drawing upon a rich multidisciplinary seam of detailed scholarship at the cutting-edge of dress studies, this unique collection, indifferent to the somewhat artificial boundaries between anthropological, sociological and cultural studies approaches to the subject, provides an illuminating probe deep into the fascinating sub-worlds of 'dressways' where bodies, as the elemental canvas of the dress arts, are imprinted with potent social and cultural identities through the medium of clothing. Each separate contribution by a leading scholar in her or his field unpacks a different theoretical and substantive facet of the infinitely adaptable wardrobe of dress culture and provides a revealing glimpse of the particular ways in which clothes are utilised by social actors as identity props within specific institutional settings. Each chapter covers peculiarities of a distinctive dress tradition and puts on display the costume drama associated with a given community, sub-culture, social role or setting, or cultural identity. We are invited into the 'secular' dressworlds of nightclub, boudoir, dance studio and gents clothiers as well as the 'religious' dressworlds of Islam and Mormon Temple sanctuary and the 'quasi-religious' universe of political sectarians.

'Carlyle' remains an implicit but real presence in these chapters which provide for both general and specialist readers, undergraduate students and advanced researchers alike, a conspectus of just how far the Carlylean project of taking dress seriously has come since it was initially launched in *Sartor Resartus*. This Introduction aims to serve as a 'remembrancer' – lest we forget, as times change and academic as well as dress fashions and styles move on – of where we, as researchers, scholars and students of the dressways of humanity, are coming from, if we did but recognize our own deeper intellectual roots. By calling to mind our rarely acknowledged 'Carlylean' inheritance, a longstanding intellectual debt of some consequence may be, at least in some small measure, repaid.

Clothing Theorems

While written in the somewhat archaic stylistic conventions of nineteenth-century Victorian Scots belletrism, *Sartor Resartus: The Life and Opinions of Herr Teufelsdröckh* constitutes that *rara avis* in academic scholarship, a profound and sustained disquisition on 'the general wardrobe of the Universe' (*Sartor Resartus* 1869: 201), Carlyle's phrase for the myriad ways in which clothing – as matter and metaphor, substance and symbol – pervades language and culture. He makes a prescient point on what he called (ibid: 39)'the world in clothes': 'Clothes gave us individuality, distinctions, social polity; Clothes have made Men of us; they are threatening to make Clothes-screens of us.' Carlyle's original perspicacious insights into what might be called the fundamental principles of dress philosophy or theory brought together in this quotation under the triangular matrix of 'individuality, distinctions, social polity' can hardly be bettered as an outline of the fundamental foci of interest to the student of human clothing.

Herr Doktor Teufelsdröckh's 'theorems' – 'society is founded upon clothes' and 'I dress therefor I am' – are somewhat too metaphorical and deterministic for modern taste and convictions. Few today would wholeheartedly agree with his overly-triumphalist sartorial credo:

> Whatsoever sensibly exists, whatsoever represents Spirit to Spirit, is properly a Clothing, a suit of Raiment, put on for a season and to be laid off. Thus in one pregnant subject of CLOTHES, rightly understood, is included all that men have thought and dreamed, done and been: the whole External Universe and what it holds is but Clothing; and all the essence of all Science lies in the PHILOSOPHY OF CLOTHES.

However, serious writers on dress stray far at their peril from the Carlylean emphases on 'individuality', 'distinction' and 'social polity'. Outside these fundamental matters of 'the social bond' as refracted through and reflected in what we wear and how we wear it, there are few, if any, challenging and enduring issues of major intellectual substance in this vast and still largely uncultivated academic patch of dress studies. If the study of dress is to grow as a distinctive field, subject or discipline – a question of epistemological demarcation that need not preoccupy us at this juncture – then, arguably, it is around what might be called 'the Carlylean framework' and its critique that the reasonable likelihood of a coherent academic identity for dress studies promises to occur. An 'in-house' theoretical debate, exchange or conversation in which the 'Carlylean perspective' has its place can only be supportive of the further development and growth of dress knowledge.

That said, it must immediately be observed that this, at first light, seemingly restricted agenda does in fact cover a great body of potential historical, behavioural and social scientific enquiry with regard to dress, clothing and adornment. These three 'unit ideas' – individuality, distinction, polity – do, indeed, together, make up a considerable part of the conceptual backcloth of the human and cultural sciences. Dress not only provides empirical expression of these basic categories; but the three categories themselves are woven into what dress itself is and represents. We can say, indeed, that if the tripartite categorial arrangement 'individual-distinction-polity' represents the (idea of the) social framework in the abstract in regard to which the human, cultural and social sciences have their raison d'être and basic remit as descriptive and explanatory realms of enquiry, then 'society' makes itself manifest at every turn in the clothing forms worn everyday by persons and groups.

Carlyle was utterly persuaded that the eye of the mind could be trained to perceive, as he himself puts it in *Sartor Resartus* Book III, Chapter V, 'The World in Clothes'. As his contemporaries and near-contemporaries – Darwin, Bentham, J.S. Mill, Burke, Newman, Comte, Spencer, Marx – were busy laying their own ground plans for a characteristically modern approach to knowledge in the natural sciences, political economy, theology, social philosophy and sociology, Carlyle himself sought to discover in 'the Naked facts' of clothing, something about the constitution and character of the human subject as a creative, purposeful 'Tool-using animal' destined for a lifespan entailing a multiplicity of changeful, colourful and variously crafted 'habilatory endeavours' (p. 34). In his general approach to the social and cultural significance of the dress symbolic, Carlyle anticipated in broad terms by almost a century and a half, a number of late modern intellectual themes such as, for example, the modern 'constructivist' or 'constructionist' perspective (vide Berger and Luckmann 1966); the 'dramaturgical' or 'social interactionist' orientation (vide Goffman 1969); and the attention to the human body as a site of socio-cultural praxis (cf. Featherstone, Hepworth and Turner (eds) 1991; Frank 1988; Turner, 1996). *Sartor Resartus* engages with the dressed body as a social construction, a 'text' on which clothes impress distinctive cultural meanings which can be read by the acute observer of the human condition and its diverse, ever-shifting social milieux. 'How often,' remarks Carlyle (p. 232), 'does the Body appropriate what is meant for the Cloth only!'

Carlyle took his cue from Montesquieu whose *L'Esprit des Lois* (1748) had emphasized the value of a comparative understanding of the ways in which individual liberty was underpinned by respect for the diversity and separation of institutions and customs. Carlyle (p. 34) writes: 'As Montesquieu wrote a *Spirit of Laws* . . . so I could write a *Spirit of Clothes*; thus, with an *Esprit des Lois*, properly an *Esprit de Coutumes*, we should have an *Esprit de Costumes'*. However, Professor Teufelsdröckh suppresses this 'hypothetical, ineffectual, and even impertinent' idea in favour of the 'humbler and proper province' of 'naked Facts and Deductions drawn therefrom' (ibid: 35). *Sartor Resartus* is replete with wordplay of this sort which should not occlude the serious sociological import of his project to comprehend the human condition through the dress props that signal personal identity and group belonging and symbolize social and political power. As with Carlyle, each of the studies in this present collection is empirically and historically grounded. The observations and insights provided are evidenced-based, a data-driven approach that substantiates the claims made by the respective authors about the dress worlds in which they have been, as it were, temporary denizens.

The Carlylean Legacy

By entitling this present 'post-Carlylean' edition of dress addresses *Dressed to Impress* it is hoped that something of Carlyle's sense of the true and full measure of clothing as a veritable impress of the human subject can be indicated. Certainly, the essays here individually and together impact strongly on our sociological imagination with regard to the role of clothing in the identification and representation of human groups. As the sub-title *Looking the Part* also makes clear, it is by our dress we do much to stamp upon the social world around us an impression or image of who we are and what our role is likely to be. While not explicitly following the trail blazed some century and a half previously by Carlyle, the authors grouped together in this unique collection of dress studies all advance the 'Carlylean' frontiers of the subject. Each of the articles can be read as an independent, free-standing contribution to knowledge of dress and its connectedness with some particular area of human social life. Both substantively and in general scope, the essays presented here take forward the Carlylean attraction to and enthusiasm for the study of dress into empirical-historical and analytical-interpretative realms unexplored and probably unimagined in a Victorian context.

Yet, the spirit of Carlyle lives on in the creative energy and penetrating insight into dress as a marvellous and unparalleled palimpsest of the human social animal. Like Carlyle, each of the authors knows that clothes bear the indelible imprint of the individuals and societies which wear them. Dress as a social script or text tells us who we are, what we have been and what we are becoming. We are impressed on our dress just as our dress impresses itself on others and the world. Carlyle saw – foresaw – these social facts about clothing. He recognized that in dress the scholarly community had a superb register of the markings of human groups on the landscapes of time, civilization and culture. Surprisingly, therefore, that the academic community, particularly the social science 'tribe', with few honourable exceptions, has only belatedly come to follow the lead given so long ago by Carlyle in this now thriving realm of historical and sociological investigation.

History and society are inscribed on our mortal flesh through the 'text' of our dress – sometimes momentarily as with the disposable lightness of feathers, ribbons and lace; sometimes with the sheer solidity of the lifer's manacles and prison uniform. Carlyle had the courage and confidence to share his unique hermeneutic of the layered worlds of meaning within the material worlds of clothing even to a sceptical, high-minded, Victorian intellectual public. But it would be some time before the 'clothes philosophy' carefully designed in *Sartor Resartus* would become 'ready to wear' by a modern academic audience increasingly attuned to the dense material cultural signage surrounding us in every area of modern life. Late modernity or postmodernity constitutes that moment when a receptive reception community stands poised to embrace the hitherto strange, even uncomfortable world of Carlyle's dress observations and imaginings. Indeed, it has taken us almost the full span of modernity to truly appreciate the at once simple and at the same moment profound insight into the significance of clothing perceived initially by the great Scottish essayist, historian and social critic.

We live out our lives overwhelmingly for the most part, day and night, from the cradle to the grave, in times of poverty and prosperity, peace and war, in moments of obscurity and fame, whether we follow fashion or are left well behind by it, when we drape ourselves in the official uniforms of the collective or parade our unique individualities in garments created de nouveau for the purpose, in clothes.

Nakedness is exceptional, as foreign to the social being of the vast pre-ponderance of people down the ages, across the civilizations, as it was in the bedroom of respectable Victorian society. By and large, students of the social animal have conducted their studies in benign neglect of this apparently obvious sartorial truth about ourselves. Indeed, we seem more comfortable defining ourselves as the 'laughing' or 'tool-using' or 'language-using' species – attributes we in fact share with other species lower down the evolutionary chain – than we do with our, arguably, uniquely human characteristic as the 'dressing' species! Little wonder that Carlyle rings out (p. 263): 'Clotha Virumque cano [Of Clothes and the Man I sing] . . . to the whole World'!

Of course, dress is not *everything* about us; nor is it an infallible record of our comings and goings, inclinations and convictions. No symbolic code can fully cover something so infinitely malleable and changeful as the human being. However, dress is generally highly indicative of behaviour and belonging, social placement and taste culture membership. Maximally, clothing tells us all we want or need to know about persons or groups, whether, for example, the wearers are dangerous fascists, members of the opposing sports team, law enforcement officers or doughnut sales personnel. Minimally, they intimate possibilities and signal propensities as in the case of erotic or sexualised, military, religious and ethnic cultural displays. Dress is the best available prelude to action and reaction. It tells us, by and large, where bodies and selves belong in sociological terms. Carlyle was on to this question of the social semiotics of clothing long before the modern science of signs and symbols was conceived. He broke open the dress 'text' as a carrier of meanings and purposes and a vehicle for penetrating the mysteries of human association and commitment. He understood the iconic charge of clothing and its luminosity vis-à-vis the often partially concealed, sometimes barely glimpsed, gambits and stratagems of social intercourse.

In dress, as Carlyle taught us and as we are beginning to discover after generations of significant relative oversight, we live, move and have our social being. Carlyle served to make such self-evident realities intellectually significant by giving them the full attention they merit as facts of life fertile with significance about who we are and how we live out our span of life under different times and circumstances. Carlyle brought his unique eye to bear upon our dress condition and in *Sartor Resartus* left a treasury of insights and ideas which provide a rich seam for the exploration of dress worlds by contemporary students of the subject. While an interest in clothing has been a long-standing feature of literature and art and a passing feature of general social history, academic studies of dress today have moved on considerably from vague asides on sartorial status stereotypes based on notions of courtly profligacy, bourgeois sobriety, proletarian economy and peasant ingenuity. Dramatic images of such sartorial archetypes as the Elizabethan fop, the pin-striped accountant, the blue-overalled artisan and the besmocked son of the soil – the list is endless – linger on in the cultural imagination. These literary devices make veritable shortcuts through the thick, tangled *actualité* of real dress histories and complex clothing traditions. For popular histories, documentary films, television comedies, soap operas and other genres, a shallow, surface, impressionistic treatment of dress often prevails. For scholarship things are very different.

If there is one single, strong, didactic message running through *Sartor Resartus* it is that while we may be taken in by the allure and majesty of dress just as readily as we are by its shoddiness and unfashionability, the impression of dress that matters is its provocation of sympathy and fellow-feeling with the human being that lies underneath. However fine or forlorn our 'part' in the social pageant is displayed, our common humanity entitles us to mutual respect. This is the compassionate message Carlyle (p. 216) seeks to impress about clothes upon his readers:

[T]hey have no intrinsic, necessary divisiveness, or even worth; but have acquired an extrinsic one. Nevertheless through all these there glimmers something of a Divine Idea . . . Let but the Godlike manifest to sense; let but Eternity look, more or less visibly, through the Time-Figure (*Zeitbild*)! . . . the Godlike rendered visible.

Carlyle's vital contribution in *Sartor Resartus* was to take the intellectual consideration of dress to unprecedented new heights and depths long before it became necessary, even fashionable, to do so within what I have called the new dress studies to which a growing body of expert scholarship has contributed in recent years. While unsystematic cross-cultural surveys of exotic tribal adornments – resplendent feathers, nose-bones, lip and ear implants, scarification and the like – can make for exciting Sunday supplement and coffee-table visual impact, they fail to match up to the robust intellectual standards of modern social scientific ethnography and analysis. Likewise, merely charting the chronological changes in the cut and style of military uniforms or vaingloriously attempting an encyclopedic coverage of women's garments, occupational dress or ecclesiastical vesture is no match or substitute for what might be called 'the new dress studies', where the investigation of human dressways in brought within the ambit of the modern social sciences and social and cultural theory.

Carlyle, it can be argued, is the true founder of dress studies. There is, of course, a Carlylean 'pre-history' of the subject going back through nineteenth-century descriptive ethnographic and encyclopedic histories of dress, to missionary and travellers' reports on clothing customs and folklore, to religious reformers' moral tracts on vesture and virtue, to Renaissance and early modern books of manners and etiquette, to the sumptuary legislation of ancient society. Carlyle, however, was the first mind of any real weight to attend to the matter of dress with any sustained philosophical conviction and genuine intellectual confidence that here was an area of human life that fully deserved to be covered with all the resources of the modern empirical, analytical and theoretical mind. In contrast with Carlyle's conspectus of dress and the human condition, his predecessors' contributions remain fragmentary, inchoate and partial. Carlyle put the study of dress on a proper intellectual footing, giving it direction, purpose, shape and, above all, perhaps, its 'charter', *Sartor Resartus*, with which all subsequent work in defining the boundaries and scope of dress studies must needs contend.

Whether we agree or not with his approach, conclusions, style or 'voice', Carlyle's 'take' on dress as revelatory of *la condition humain* is a seminal one. It is precisely the recovery or rediscovery of this fundamental insight into dress, culture and society that lies at the heart of the new dress studies. Like him, we want to 'get at' the power and principles behind dress as a cultural sign and social force. Like him, we, too, wish to take the full measure of 'mere clothing' in the 'ever ancient, ever new' tale of 'the Scarecrow, as a Clothed Person' (p. 60), albeit, perhaps, a goodly distance down the modern road of patient, piecemeal scientific investigations on such matters, we undertake the task with somewhat greater scholarly diffidence and considerably less Carlylean *brio*. In the postmodern condition of heightened awareness of the power and presence of signs and symbols in the shaping, positioning and connecting of individual bodies in social space, Carlyle's willingness to take dress seriously is, if not prophetic, remarkably forward-looking.

We 'late moderns' do well not to overlook the sheer brilliance and courage of his lone voice as intellectual spokesperson for a subject area that – then and now – can all-too-readily and all-too-often be dismissed as incidental or trivial in relation to the mighty topics and significant themes of academic and intellectual life. With the publication of *Sartor Resartus*, the initial breakthrough was made from snobbery and disdain vis-à-vis dress as fitting subject matter for disciplined minds and developed imaginations. Carlyle showed what was possible. He by no means killed the prejudice against dress studies by traditional academics stone dead. It lingered on from his days to ours despite the work of a relative handful of pioneer workers in this particular corner of the academic vineyard. One thinks here of anthropological and ethnographic studies in particular which kept the embers of serious study of dress and adornment alight amidst the studied indifference to the subject around them within the ivory tower. Dress could be safely cordoned off amongst the exotic, bizarre and marginal practices of 'primitives', 'natives', 'sects', 'cults' and the like. For the most part, however, social sciences were oriented towards the human subject as a primarily 'cognitive' being inhabiting 'abstract' societies. In this 'mentalist' or 'intellectualist' world picture, physical bodies – especially dressed physical bodies – hardly figured at all. The corporeal was occluded; the somatic suppressed. Not a promising habitat for dress studies to flourish.

But, as dress studies today obtains a new lease of life as an attractive, relevant, highly illuminating field of enquiry, it behoves us at this point in cultural and intellectual history to acknowledge a debt to Carlyle as one who ploughed the initial furrow with all that that entails. In critique of R.K Merton's celebrated dictum: 'A Science which hesitates to forget its founders is lost', Alvin Gouldner (in Schneider 1976: vi) remarked: 'A Science ignorant of its founders does not know how far it has advanced nor in what direction.' From the classically-minded, theologically-grounded *belletrist* Carlyle, darling of the nineteenth-century Chelsea salon set, to the research scholars ensconced in globalized tertiary education institutions in the early decades of the third millennium is a considerable leap of mentality and context. Yet, if dress studies are to develop their potential as a robust and integrated realm of enquiry, it is precisely this fiery brook between Carlyle's 'world' and our own that has to be crossed. At the same time, it is essential if we 'late moderns' are to cultivate the subject area of 'the new dress studies' with intellectual depth and a sense of history, that we build on the legacy of our predecessors, Carlyle's magisterial contribution in particular. While we would wish not to become hidebound by the past, it is important that, wherever possible, contemporary and future contributors to the emergent academic field of dress studies cultivate a self-conscious tradition of in-depth philosophical reflection on their subject and subject matter.

Thus far, Carlyle's foundational work in this regard – archaic in its intellectual forms of expression and superseded by more systematic and 'scientific' approaches notwithstanding – has hardly been excelled. At the turn of the third millennium, following the 'cultural turn' within the social sciences, the times are propitious – as is the state of dress studies itself as an academic field – to acknowledge and even to celebrate Carlyle's pivotal position as the pantocrator and presiding genius of the intellectual study of clothing as a cultural form. In a real sense, dress studies is entering into that 'kind of maturity' referred to by Willis (2000) in his account of the contemporary development of cultural studies (and other disciplines before that, such as English and sociology). Such moments of self-definition and questing after academic recognition and 'establishment' (cf. Elias, Martins and Whitley (eds) 1982) are usually disputatious. In any inclusivist approach to the shaping of dress studies as a multidisciplinary intellectual field, Carlyle's *Sartor Resartus* fully deserves a place in the healthy mix of competing perspectives and methodologies focused on the same object of study – human dressways.

The aim here, in the context of an Introduction to a collection of highly individual studies of diverse facets of the dress worlds in which we live, move and have our social being, is to present Thomas Carlyle's *Sartor Resartus* as a 'charter' document for the area of dress studies within the cultural and social sciences. Though far from constituting a flawless sacred text beyond criticism, Carlyle's singular work provides a basis for engaging with the emergent academic study of the social and cultural life of dress as an attractive, fertile and exciting adventure of ideas with enormous scope for empirical and theoretical development. The essays gathered together here testify to the 'Carlylean' confidence we can have in the fecundity and intellectual challenge of dress studies.

Society in Dress, Dress in Society

Dress studies, we may suggest, is an emergent 'intellectual field and creative project' (Bourdieu 1971), an academic area in search of a scene-setting, pathbreaking Founder. Thomas Carlyle, it is claimed, is the rightful contender to this role. If dress studies is to develop as an identifiable, robust and coherent academic subject or discipline, it can ill-afford to neglect the seminal contribution of Carlyle. There have been, after all, few major thinkers of his intellectual power and public stature who have ventured with conviction into the area of dress. A combination of aristocratic and 'macho' disdain has all-too-frequently left clothes beyond the academic pale. It has been customary among academics and intellectual elites to snub dress as a surface, even superficial, aspect of culture and the human condition. There is, so the prejudice runs, something too obvious, quotidian, materialist, vain and self-conscious about dress, something altogether too unspiritual and uninspiring about clothes, to warrant serious-minded scholarly attention. Within this haughty traditionalist mindset, what we wear, how we look, why we dress the way we do are hardly matters of primary scholastic importance. One can – as yet – hardly begin to conceive of a Nobel Prize equivalent for dress studies! Clothing, in short, is infra dig for bona fide major intellection. Founder-finding, however, can help to raise the academic and public profile here as elsewhere in the history of human creative intellectual endeavour.

The dour, cantankerous, bilious 'Sage of Chelsea' breaks emphatically the negative stereotypical mould in which the subject of dress had languished. Carlyle's unique contribution to taking clothes seriously as a fitting subject of deep reflection and considered analysis still stands up in important respects as a useful framework for modern dress studies. Methods of investigation in the area of dress have taken a more systematic, even scientific turn (Steele (ed.) 1998), since Carlyle published his monumental study. However, 'the Carlylean paradigm', to coin a phrase, continues to provide a highly serviceable orientation to the investigation of the role, significance and value of human dress forms. Of contemporary theoreticians whose ideas have resonance with the Carlylean project on 'dress as culture, culture as dress', the ideas of Pierre Bourdieu seem to have the closest affinity albeit this is not a connection made by Bourdieu himself. Like Carlyle, Bourdieu focuses on ways in which cultural resources such as clothes empower and fit us for social position and placement. Clothes are part of the system of cultural stratification which holds individuals and groups in competitive, endogomous and self-perpetuating hierarchies of symbolic domination and control.

Dress styles unite and divide us into different taste 'classes'. Our clothes mark us out in social and cultural terms. To 'look the part' is to fit into a definable social niche. We impress by just how well our dress renders us comfortable and at ease in our habitus and for our social roles. Carlyle's rhetorical question (p. 232) remains unanswered: 'Who ever saw any Lord my-lorded in tattered blanket fastened with wooden skewer?' Clothes may not 'maketh the (wo)man' in 'moral' terms but they certainly shape our 'social' being in ways that nothing else can quite so immediately and palpably.

Bourdieu (1991) develops a wide-ranging sociology of symbolic power in which he addresses the complex relations prevailing in any society between cultural symbols, social stratification and power. Bourdieu (1993) does much to define and shape the 'culturalist' approach to understanding how symbols of social identity and belonging are not simply freely chosen by autonomous actors operating in a historical and cultural vacuum as 'rational choice theory' and 'psychologistic' and 'economistic' approaches suggest (Finkelstein 1991; Davis 1992; Jenkins 1996). For Bourdieu (1990a), by contrast, we do not interminably reconstruct ourselves. We do not, as it were, dress *de nouveau* every morning. Our wardrobe is culturally constructed, its 'contents' pre-defined and pre-selected to a considerable degree by our socially-produced sense of self (Bourdieu 1977; Lash and Friedman (eds) 1992). What we see in the mirror is, in no small measure, a reflection of the society we inhabit (Alexander 1987; Giddens 1991). Dress is key to the social construction of our image; our self-image.

In Bourdieu's terms, we inhabit a 'habitus', that is to say, a context of tradition, custom, evaluation and response which significantly shapes the symbolic selections we adopt and display. Our social presence in the form of cultural visibility and image recognition, together with the degrees of distinction and deference we attract, has much to do with the differential power of command over 'cultural capital'. Dress is one mode of 'symbolic capital' (Bourdieu 1993) and a significant part of the repertoire of cultural power goods available to us in our interactions with others. As such, clothes unite and divide at one and the same moment, making us members of this group but not that one, conferring upon us this sort of identity but not that one, indicating affiliations of this kind but not that kind.

In Bourdieu's 'general theory of the economy of practices', 'all practices' – in which we must include the cultural practices of dress(ing) – are 'aimed at maximizing material or symbolic profit' (Bourdieu 1990a: 209). For Bourdieu, building on Max Weber's multi-dimensional sociological model of class, status and power (Bourdieu 1990b), the struggle for social recognition is a fundamental aspect of all social life and one in which we all engage almost all of the time whatever our economic and social circumstances (Brubacker 1984). 'Cultural capital', like other forms of wealth, is socially stratified. But prince and pauper alike are unavoidably implicated in a complex and elaborate system of symbolic exchange and power relations in which clothing, alongside a myriad other modes of cultural capital goods – table manners and eating habits; educational background and credentials; scientific and religious associations; artistic, musical and sporting accomplishments and affiliations;

professional contacts and recognition; language itself; and so forth – are the currency. Who speaks, eats, associates and socialises, dresses etc. in the approved and proper manner has the advantage in the cultural power game. Who dresses 'best' – where this can be taken to mean not simply the economistic 'most expensively' or the aesthetic 'most tastefully', but the sociological 'most appropriately in role' – impresses most.

As a penetrating historian of cultures and civilizations and a sharp and informed observer of the mind and manners of the Victorian age, Carlyle's overt interest in dress was unusual for a man of his epoch, intellectual brilliance and social standing. His 'Meditations among the Clothes-shops' (p. 235) show the acuteness of Carlyle's 'Dickensian' interpretative or hermeneutical directness as a participant observer (Marauhao 1986) in the dress worlds he wrote about so vividly. His passionate social commentary beneath the steely critical gaze is reminiscent of the metropolitan flâneurs and urban 'strollers' made famous by Baudelaire and Benjamin (Benjamin 2000). Having earlier (p. 171) referred to his perigrinations 'in very early days . . . disguised . . . as a tavern-waiter', Carlyle writes (pp. 233–4):

> Often, when I sojourned in that monstrous tuberosity of Civilised Life, the Capital of England; . . . one lone soul amid those grinding millions; – often have I turned into their Old-Clothes market to worship. With awe-struck heart I walk through that Monmouth Street, with its empty Suits, as though through a Sanhedrin of stainless Ghosts. Silent are they, but expressive in their silence: the past witnesses and instruments of Woe and Joy, of Passions, Virtues, Crimes, and all the fathomless tumult of Good and Evil in 'the Prison men call Life.' Friends! Trust not the heart of that man for whom Old Clothes are not venerable . . . If Field Lane, with its long fluttering rows of yellow handkerchiefs, be a Dionysius' Ear, where, in stifled jarring hubbub, we hear the Indictment which Poverty and Vice bring against lazy Wealth . . . then is Monmouth Street, a Mirza's Hill, where, in motley vision, the whole Pageant of Existence passes awfully before us . . . the Bedlam of Creation!

Like so much else in the period – sex, death, diverse modes of social exclusion and intolerance – dress was, as it were, swept under the carpet. As a topic of public conversation, it was decidedly impolite in refined social settings and extremely embarrassing in impoverished ones to make explicit reference to clothing as a marker of personal identity and social belonging. A complex combination of biblical injunctions against vanity, the rampant embourgeoisement of good taste norms, and the sheer fear of being caught and thought out-of-fashion served to shroud dress matters in a mantle of dignified silence. In everyday life, particularly within contexts of polite society, in the realms of dress, one was expected to see and not to say, to form private judgement but not to articulate one's opinions, much less one's prejudices, within earshot beyond one's intimate, trusted circle of confidantes. When the tongue is mute, dress says it all.

Among the traditional landed upper classes, fine dress sense and sensibility, like connoisseurship of select wines and cheeses, came with good breeding. The aspiring middle classes endeavoured, with varying degrees of success, to cultivate this effortless aristocratic disdain for mere material personal display, albeit the nouveaux riches took pains to flaunt their conspicuous consumption in their dress and body adornment as elsewhere in their highly competitive, status-driven lifestyles. As ever, the less fortunate 'made do', many finding comfort in biblical 'samplers' reminding them of God's personal predilection for the birds of the air, the flowers of the fields, and the ubiquitous poor of the earth. The social class structure was, as it were, woven together within an elaborate system of implicit dress codes and clothing prejudices which remained particular, by and large, to each social strata who looked down or up on the adjacent 'dress class' with due, if privately reserved, disdain or deference. Something of that same Victorian taboo against the forthright expression of privatised dress discriminations persists today, though, happily, the more invidious features of dress stratification and clothing prejudice and exclusion are nowadays just beginning to be challenged and changed. Carlyle broke with convention in this matter and gave full rein to his views on the dressways of all manner of folk in his own time and from a diverse array of groups and societies further back in history.

Picking Up the Carlylean Thread

As the academic study of dress is poised for 'lift-off' in the context of the millennial 'cultural turn' where the human body and the things of the body become leading items on the intellectual agendas of many academic disciplines from anthropology to theology, the Carlylean project 'to look fixedly on Clothes . . . till they become transparent . . . look through the Clothes of Man . . . into the man himself' (p. 65) assumes, belatedly, one might argue, renewed point and purpose. Dress, we can suggest, has begun to loom especially significant in scholarly contexts at a time when fundamental ontological and phenomenological questions about human essence and identity come to the fore against the backdrop of anxieties regarding trans-genetic experimentation, cloning technologies and virtual reality. Clothing forms belong, at least in the Carlylean scheme of things, to the quintessentially human sphere and are ultimately tied up with questions of the mystery and sacrality of human expressivity and belonging. Come the cyborg revolution, questions will remain as to how to clothe the robotic humanoids. Society can stand only so much naked flesh, cold steel or raw plastic. Dressing is neither incidental nor incremental to the human project, but integral to its work of finishing Creation, rendering it acceptable – as when Adam delved and Eve span – in the sight of God and Society (Durkheim 1976).

Dress exposes us to social gaze while expressing something of – and only in part – who we are in our own eyes. Observer and observed – the onlooker and the 'on show' – play an artful game of guessing and second guessing how, where and when to get it right as to the correct 'look'. The interpretation is as much a science as an art form. In the context of mixed motives and changing fashions (Davis 1992; Craik 1994), conjecture has the final say and there is no final arbiter – no Archimedean vantage point – of taste and intention (Laver 1945; Bayley 1991). Thus, there is always ample scope for judgement and imagination on the matter of what clothes 'say' and little room for a final verdict of history in such matters. Carlyle's philosophical sociology of dress is conceived and executed with an artist's mind and eye. Taking one instance of this, Carlyle's invention of 'clothes classes', Wilson (1924: 230) remarks: 'The contrast in *Sartor* between Dandies and Drudges is as vivid as any piece of Rembrandt, and more convincing than anything written in economics before.'

The recent renewal of interest in the human body as a focus of sociological research and scholarship can be regarded as good news from the point of view of dress studies, just as the resurgence of academic works centred on dress can be viewed as good news from the standpoint of body studies. Unsurprisingly, dress and body studies (or body and dress studies) have a symbiotic relationship to one another (Gaines and Herzog (eds) 1990; Wilson 1992; Entwistle 2000), the 'good times' of the one heralding positive academic outlets and opportunities for, as well as theoretical and substantive reinforcements of, the other. A comment by Giddens (1984: 35), while addressing neither 'body' nor 'dress' explicitly, serves, perhaps, to set the wider context of significance in which we can locate the veritable flowering of body-dress studies in recent years: 'All social systems, no matter how grand or far-flung, both express and are expressed in the routines of social life, mediating the physical and sensory properties of the human body.' Giddens' recognition of the highly significant part played in social life by everyday bodily routines is a highly welcome development in the theorization of 'the constitution of society' and major contributions have been made in recent years to open up with considerable vigour the academic study of body and society (Featherstone et al. 1991; Falk 1994; Turner 1996; Mellor & Shilling 1997) and dress and society (Wilson 1985; Barnes & Eicher (eds) 1993; Eicher (ed.) 1995; Rubinstein 1995).

Each (overlapping) field of study has its own flagship academic journal – *Body & Society* and *Fashion Theory: The Journal of Dress, Body and Culture* – as well as being supported by a prolific volume of scholarly output from dedicated major publishing houses: Berg (in the case of dress studies), Sage (in the case of body studies). Whatever the fate of the institutional conduits through which scholarship in these areas passes in the future, the chances are high that opportunities to explore and exploit the theoretical and substantive 'commons' in which both parties have a stake are unlikely to be missed. Already there are signs that the complex of research issues and intellectual challenges surrounding the interlocking conceptual matrix of dress-body-society is the one that excites research workers and scholars such that 'body studies' are increasingly open to 'dress studies' and vice versa, a mutual exposure that can only help to advance knowledge and understanding in each area.

What Giddens leaves out of account, it is important to note, is what might be called the 'Carlylean' or 'symbolic-metaphysical' dimensions of bodily expression. Dress behaviours and bodily adornments most assuredly typify and represent the quintessential 'routines of social life'. Carlyle makes it plain that over and beyond 'mediating the physical and sensory properties of the human body' (which he examines in *Sartor Resartus* (1869: 37) under the prosaic functions of 'warmth . . . decency . . . ornament'), what really counts in his eyes (p. 261) are 'those pregnant considerations, ethical, political, symbolical, which crowd on the Clothes-Philosopher from the very threshold of his Science'. In the sense that our bodies, how they look, what we drape on and attach to them, are palpable, visible, physical and symbolic evidence of our place in society, history and culture, the equation holds true, generally speaking: 'society in dress; dress in society'. The one is dialectically, inexorably interwoven with the other.

There can be little that escapes the conceptual net of these interwoven strands of discourse about individual and group life. The part clothes play in self-presentation, status differentiation, and the material and symbolic arrangements made for communal life continue to be the staple fare of dress studies pursuant to a more modern scientific spirit of enquiry and mode of address. From whichever disciplinary background one engages with the multi-faceted subject of human clothing, investigations of the multifarious ways in which individuals and groups organise their dress 'ways' and deploy their dress 'options' come back in the end to Carlyle's original nineteenth-century project (p. 49) 'to expound the moral, political, even religious Influences of Clothes'. Moreover, Carlyle's prophetic intimation (born of recognition that at least since Solomon in all his splendour it was ever thus) of the power of dress 'to make Clothes-screens of us', can be taken as the leitmotif of contemporary critical studies of the fashion marketplace and the latter's ubiquitous impact on the commodification of the body-self.

All the essays in this present volume are implicitly 'Carlylean' in the sense of engaging with some or other aspect or parameter of his 'clothes-philosophy'.

Campbell (1993: 70) condenses this as follows: '[F]or the world is all appearances, like our clothes: the truth lies underneath.' Yet 'getting at' the 'truth' of dress is a complex, formidable enterprise in any given case or context. For the 'truths' of how and why we dress the way we do are far from obvious, even to the 'insider'. The full motivation and complete range of pressures to dress in this way rather than that are usually concealed from view – particularly of the dressed subject, perhaps – beneath complex layers of history and tradition, custom and habit, ideology and even self-deception. Indeed, we probably can never arrive at the final resolution to what Carlyle continually refers to as the 'mystery' of dress for any particular person or group. General 'theories' of clothing behaviours, decisions, tastes and customs are of heuristic value only and are generally pitched at the level of abstraction that loses sight entirely of the lived reality and experience of dress, its true habitus and context of significance. At a broader level still, observations regarding the dress codes of national cultures and civilizations remain essentially speculative and unfalsifiable (Popper 1963), useful as after-dinner conversational gambits or coffee-table popular history, but of limited use to the serious scholar of the subject.

All the contributors to this volume exhibit the trained social scientific observer's eye for significant cultural pattern and historical detail in relation to their own particular special field of dress study. In this regard, the subject of dress defies efforts to reduce it to cut-and-dried scientific method. There is always a 'remainder' after we have tried to provide a full description and explanation of why human beings dress as they do. Consequently, there is always scope for informed guesswork and insightful interpretation if we are ever to arrive at plausible and meaningful accounts of the innumerable dress ways that abound in human history and society. As with Carlyle himself, the enterprise of revealing the dress codes and mores of particular 'bodies' is approached in each instance with both intellectual rigour and humane sensitivity. None of the authors has sought cynically to debunk the dress values and beliefs of the communities whose distinctive dress ways form the subject matter of their enquiries. Each of the chapters advances our knowledge of a particular aspect of the vast world of clothes and provides a telling account of a dress 'story' that reveals something of the material and symbolic lives of those who live out their lives – some or all of the time – in specific defining garments. The collection of essays in the present volume is equally distributed between studies that focus on dress in both secular and religious contexts, a division that echoes Carlyle's own comprehensive sweep across this telling and, traditionally, dress-marked boundary.

When particular forms of dress come up against the 'limits' of tolerance and respect in particular periods or among specific groups, the analysts here continue to strive for detachment and value neutrality in their dealings with dress prejudice. While the authors maintain critical distance from their subjects as a means of providing objective accounts of dress behaviours and beliefs, the 'mystery' of the dress ways encountered here is never casually, carelessly demystified. In each instance, the integrity of 'their dress', to employ Bogatyrev's redolent category (Bogatyrev 1971) for the particular dress forms and customs of any group, is fully respected in its own quiddity as an expression or outworking of the mind or spirit of persons or sub-cultures. Carlyle (p. 34) writes of the close communion between the interior soul and its outward corporeal manifestations, including clothing: 'In all his Modes and habilatory endeavours, an architectural Idea will be found lurking; his Body and the Cloth are the site and materials whereon and whereby his beautiful edifice, of a Person, is to be built.'

Concluding Postmodern Stitch

Sartor Resartus, fittingly enough, perhaps, for its renewed 'postmodern' lease of life in the new dress studies, actually began life as something of a spoof text, a joke that its author himself believed for a time to have back-fired on him. The 'natural history' of *Sartor Resartus* is worth narrating in some fine detail at this point. Wilson (1924: 180–2) informs us that on 18 September 1830 Carlyle 'soliloquized with the pen' as follows: 'I am going to write – Nonsense. It is on "clothes". Heaven be my comforter!' The original title of the piece composed in 1830 and recalled by him in January 1831 was 'Thoughts on Clothes'. In an extract from his Journal in August 1830 (Froude 1882: 85; cf. *Sartor Resartus*: 59) we find Carlyle pondering as follows:

> What is a man if you look at him with the mere logical sense, with the under-standing? A pitiful hungry biped that wears breeches. Often when I read of pompous ceremonials, drawing-room levées, and coronations, on a sudden the **clothes** fly off the whole party in my fancy, and they stand there straddling in a half ludicrous, half horrid condition.

On 28 October of the same year (ibid: 92) he remarks: 'Written a strange piece "On Clothes". Know not what will come of it . . . Send away the "Clothes", of which I could make a kind of book, but cannot afford it.' Francis Jeffrey, the editor to whom Carlyle had sent his draft, indicates that he had previously frowned on the subject in a letter to Carlyle on 22 October 1828 advising him to extract the 'well-used joke' from Carlyle's study of the Scots poet, Robert Burns. Wilson (1924: 73) reports Jeffrey's rebuff as follows without apparently noting that it too commits with gusto the sin of which Carlyle stands solemnly accused:

> How can you dream of . . . that very simple and well-used joke of the clothes making the man and the tailor being a creator? It was condescension enough to employ such ornaments at first, but it is inconceivable to me that anybody should stoop to pick them up and stitch them on again, when they had once been stripped off. He who comes into a crowd must submit to be squeezed, and at all events must not think himself ill-treated if his skirts are crumpled or the folds of his drapery a little compressed.

The one-time Calvinist trainee ordinand and life-long dyspepsic Carlyle has the last laugh. An almost unavoidable pleasure (or pain, perhaps!) about dress studies is the daily discovery of the ubiquity of allusions to dress in human language and the well-nigh universal tendency of writers – in whichever genre they operate, be it popular press or academic scholarship – to import clothing references into their publications. Whether we write on clothing directly or on the institutional surrounds that cover and shroud our mortal flesh, dress metaphors of some description are almost unavoidable and remain immediately employable, readily recognizable and highly potent. Paraphrasing Carlyle, an inveterate spinner of dress metaphor and simile, Froude (1882: 130) uncovers the rich and allusive analogical imagination that underpins Carlyle's sociological dress sense:

> Customs, institutions, religious creeds, what were they but clothes in which human creatures covered their native nakedness, and enabled men themselves to live harmoniously and decently together? Clothes, dress, changed with the times; they grew old, they were elaborate, they were simple; they varied with fashion or habit of life; they were outward indicators of the inward and spiritual nature. The analogy gave the freest scope and play for the wilfullest and wildest humour.

Sartor Resartus, through Herr Teufelsdröckh's 'certain satirical turn, and deep under-currents of roguish whim' (p. 88), ironizes the foibles and frailties of fops, fetishists, fashion followers and fantasists to the point of Monty Pythonesque absurdity. It uncovers the private conceits and self-deceits shielded from public exposure by the armour of clothing. These postmodern ludic qualities are not to everyone's taste. Not for nothing does one biographer of Carlyle entitle his work *Moral Desperado* (Heffer 1995). There is an ammoral wit, a tolerant scepticism, at work in Carlyle's critique of the barriers we put up against one another, the defences we use to hide our common humanity from ourselves. Carlyle himself knew that his approach was risky and without guarantees of literary or academic success. In Volume 5 (p. 175) of his *Collected Letters* (Sanders et al., 1970–98) he pithily reviews his book in a letter to his brother, Jack: 'A very singular piece, I assure you! It glances from Heaven to Earth and back again in a strange satirical frenzy. Whether fine or not remains to be seen.' His wife, the formidable and talented Jane Welsh Carlyle (Campbell 1980), thought it 'a work of genius ... but of genius so original that a conventional world, measuring by established rules, could not fail to regard it as a monster' (Froude 1882: 161). She was right – arguably on both counts, certainly on the latter. *Sartor Resartus* was turned down by a succession of publishers, published piecemeal in *Frasers' Magazine*, and unfavourably reviewed by critics in the United Kingdom (Trela and Tarr (eds) 1997). The author himself takes a sardonic view of the negative reception of his work in his journal entries of 11 and 21 January 1834 (Froude 1882: 363):

> No one could tell what to make of it ... [It] excites the most unqualified disapprobation – à la bonne heure ... James Fraser writes me that 'Teufelsdröckh' meets with the most unqualified disapproval, which is all extremely proper.

By contrast, under the sponsorship of Ralph Waldo Emerson, who wrote a horatory Preface to the American edition, *Sartor Resartus* received favourable critical reviews in the United States where, it seems, there existed at that time less Victorian prudery and stuffinesss vis-à-vis bodily things and, perhaps, an emerging critical awareness of the cultural power of the material symbolic. In a Journal entry for 24 May 1834 (in Froude 1882: 410), Carlyle's verdict on the global response to his book was accurate, if terse: 'One spake up and the other spake down.' As like as not, that polarized opinion will remain the case today. That said, the following statement by Wilson (1924: 232-3) seems justifiable:

> [T]o anyone who feels called to open Sartor and reads it slowly, the best advice is like that of an early editor of Shakespeare – read it again and again, and again, and if at last you do not like it, you are in danger of not understanding it.

Carlyle's name choice for his own hero was itself a provocation. In his 'esoteric comedy' (Helmling 1988), Carlyle clearly enjoyed playing with fire and cocking a snook at high culture and respectable society of which he became in time, in the time-worn manner of the gauche Northern 'lad o' pairts' made good in Southern high society, a more relaxed and comfortable denizen (Fig. 1.3). Wilson (1924: 183) points out:

> [A]ssuredly the work is veiled autobiography. Diogenes Teufelsdröckh was Carlyle's ideal Carlyle ... The surname Teufelsdröckh is German for Asafedita, literally

Figure 1.3 Thomas Carlyle 1879, by Helen Allingham 1848–1926. Scottish
National Portrait Gallery, Edinburgh.

'devil's dung'. The drug so named was then familiar. It had a stink like garlic and
was a nerve tonic . . . the Scotch like the Germans called it 'the Deil's Dirt'.

These essays, provide living empirical and historical proof of the Ecclefechan
essayist's metaphysical conviction in his path-breaking work *Sartor Resartus*
(p. 262) that human beings, without violence to our social nature much of
the time, 'may be regarded as Cloth-animals, creatures that live, move and have
their being in cloth'. In diverse social contexts and under a variety of cultural
guises, the following chapters expose to view the full impress of this Carlylean
virtuoso practice of making sometimes unexpected interpretations of often
seemingly crude and trivial details of clothes: 'In a symbol there is concealment
yet revelation' (*Collected Works* 1: 175). If dress studies is to mature and progress
as an exciting field of academic studies while cultivating a vibrant intellectual
tradition enfolding the different generations of dress scholars, the successors
of Carlyle will do well to hold onto such Ariadne's threads from the Founder's
broad, inspiring mantle, *Sartor Resartus*. They help to lead us on beyond
matter and surfaces alone to the human substance within and the spiritual
loom beyond.

Notes

1. Unless otherwise attributed, all page references are to the 1869 edition of *Sartor Resartus*.

2. In an account of an international seminar on dress studies (de la Haye 2000: 235-40), Wilson is reported to have 'expressed surprise at the hostility generated by students of feminist theory towards fashion' in the UK context, with Gordon finding that 'a similar antipathy towards the subject existed within the USA'. One might argue that the more generic concept, 'dress studies', helps to neutralize the unfortunate and difficult-to-shake-off negative associations between fashion, faddishness and feminine ephemerality. But this question of 'naming the field' constitutes part of a prospective great debate that needs to take place alongside the whole project of mapping the subject area and engaging with its implicit and explicit empirical-historical, cross-cultural, conceptual and ideological boundaries. It is the contention here, of course, that Carlyle's deeply textured discourse in all this should be more than merely vestigial.

3. The considerable collaborative labour of compiling an up-to-date bibliography and references guide to dress studies in general and in relation to its many sub-fields is a key task that remains to be undertaken by scholars in the field across continents and language groups. Rather than expand an already sizeable References section here, readers are directed to the bibliographies in Joseph (1986), Barnes and Eicher (eds) (1993), Eicher (ed.) (1995), Rubinstein (1995), Barnard (1996), and Warwick and Cavallaro (eds) (1998), for example, and the detailed references pages in successive volumes of *Fashion Theory: The Journal of Dress, Body and Culture*. Berg Publishers' new *Fashion and Dress* catalogue is an excellent resource for identifying recent contributors to the sizeable critical mass of publications developing in the area of dress, body and culture.

References

Abler, T.S. (1999), *Hinterland Warriors and Martial Dress. European Empires and Exotic Uniforms,* New York and Oxford: Berg.

Alexander, J.C. (1987), 'Action and Its Environments', in J.C. Alexander, Giesen, B., Münch, R., and Smelser, N.J. (eds), pp.289-318, *The Micro-Macro Link*, Berkeley: University of California Press.

Arac, J. (1979), *Commissioned Spirits: The Shaping of Social Motion in Dickens, Carlyle, Melville, and Hawthorne,* New Brunswick, NJ: Rutgers University Press.

Archer, M.S. (1988), *Culture and Agency: The Place of Culture in Social Theory,* London: Cambridge University Press.

Arnold, R. (2000), *Fashion, Desire & Anxiety,* London: I.B. Tauris.

Arthur, L.B. (ed.) (1999), *Religion, Dress and the Body,* Oxford and New York: Berg.

—— (ed.) (2000), *Undressing Religion: Commitment and Conversion from a Cross-Cultural Perspective,* New York and Oxford: Berg.

Ash, J. and Wilson, E. (eds) (1992), *Chic Thrills: A Fashion Reader,* London: Pandora.

Ashton, R. (1994), *The German Idea: Four English Writers and the Reception of German Thought, 1800-1860. Coleridge, Carlyle, Eliot, Lewes,* London: Libris.

Barnard, M. (1996), *Fashion as Communication,* London and New York: Routledge.

Barnes, R. and Eicher, J.B. (eds) (1993), *Dress and Gender: Making and Meaning,* Oxford, Providence: Berg.

Barthes, R. (1967), *Elements of Semiology,* translated by A. Lavers and A.C. Smith, London: Jonathan Cape.

—— (1983), *The Fashion System,* Berkeley: University of California Press.

Baudrillard. J. (1987), 'Modernity', *Canadian Journal of Political and Social Theory,* XI (3): 63–72.

Bayley, S. (1991), *Taste: The Secret Meaning of Things,* London: Faber and Faber.

Becher, T. (1989), *Academic Tribes and Territories,* Oxford: Oxford University Press.

Becker, H. and Barnes, H.E. (1961), *Social Thought from Lore to Science,* New York: Dover Publications. Original 1938.

Bell, Q. (1992), *On Human Finery,* London: Allison & Busby.

Benjamin, W. (2000), *The Arcades Project,* translated by H. Eiland and K. McGlaughlin, Cambridge: Harvard University Press.

Bentley, E. (1940), *The Cult of the Superman: A Study of the Idea of Heroism in Carlyle and Nietzsche, with notes on other hero-worshippers of modern times,* New York: Smith Peter.

Berger, P.L. (1963), *Invitation to Sociology. A Humanistic Perspective,* New York: Anchor Books.

—— and Luckmann, T. (1966), *The Social Construction of Reality: A Treatise in the Sociology of Knowledge,* Garden City, N.Y.: Doubleday.

Blumer, H. (1968), 'Fashion', in *International Encyclopedia of the Social Sciences,* New York: Macmillan.

Bogatyrev, P. (1971), *The Functions of Folk Costume in Moravian Slovakia,* translated by R.G. Crum, The Hague, Paris: Mouton. Original 1937.

Bourdieu, P. (1971), 'Intellectual Field and Creative Project', in M.F.D. Young (ed.), *Knowledge and Control: New Directions for the Sociology of Education,* London: Collier-Macmillan.

—— (1977), *Outline of a Theory of Practice,* London: Cambridge University Press.

—— (1984), *Distinction: A Social Critique of the Judgement of Taste,* translated by R. Nice, London: Routledge & Kegan Paul.

—— (1990a), *The Logic of Practice,* Oxford: Polity.

—— (1990b), *In Other Words: Essays Toward a Reflexive Sociology,* Cambridge: Polity.

—— (1991), *Language and Symbolic Power,* edited by J. Thompson, translated by G. Raymond and M. Adamson, Cambridge: Polity Press.

—— (1993), *The Field of Cultural Production: Essays on Art and Literature,* translated by R. Johnson, Cambridge: Polity Press.

—— (1997), 'The Forms of Cultural Capital', in J.G. Richardson (ed.), *Handbook of Theory and Research for the Sociology of Education,* New York and London: Greenwood Press.

—— and Passeron, J.-C. (1990), *Reproduction in Education, Society and Culture*, translated by R. Nice, second edition, London: Sage.

Brantley, R.E. (1993), *Coordinates of Anglo-American Romanticism: Wesley, Edwards, Carlyle, and Emerson*, Florida: University Press of Florida.

Brubacker, R. (1984), *The Limits of Rationality: An Essay on the Social and Moral Thought of Max Weber*, London: Allen and Unwin

Campbell, I. (1974/1993), *Thomas Carlyle*, Edinburgh: The Saltire Society.

—— (1980), *Thomas and Jane*, Edinburgh: Edinburgh University Library.

Carlyle, T. (1966 ed.), *On Heroes, Hero-Worship and the Heroic in History*, edited by C. Niemeyer, Nebraska: University of Nebraska Press.

—— (1869), *Sartor Resartus: The Life and Opinions of Herr Teufelsdröckh in Three Books*, London: Chapman and Hall.

—— (1987), *Sartor Resartus*, edited by K. McSweeney and P. Sabor, Oxford: Oxford University Press. World Classics Series.

—— (2000), *Sartor Resartus: The Life and Opinions of Herr Teufelsdröckh in Three Books*, Introduction and Notes by R.L. Tarr, Berkeley, Los Angeles: University of California Press.

Chaney, D.C. (1994), *The Cultural Turn: Scene Setting Essays on Contemporary Cultural History*, London; Routledge.

Connerton, P. (1989), *How Societies Remember*, Cambridge: Cambridge University Press.

Craik, J. (1994), *The Face of Fashion: Cultural Studies in Fashion*, London: Routledge.

Crane, D. (1972), *Invisible Colleges: Diffusion of Knowledge in Scientific Communities*, Chicago: University of Chicago Press.

Crawley, E. (1931), 'Sacred Dress', in T. Besterman (ed.), *Dress, Drink and Drums*, London: Methuen. Original 1912.

Dale, P.A. (1977), *The Victorian Critic and the Idea of History: Carlyle, Arnold, Pater*, Cambridge, Mass.: Harvard University Press.

Davis, F. (1992), *Fashion, Culture and Identity*, Chicago: Chicago University Press.

de la Haye, A. (2000), 'Articulating Dress Studies: A Workshop on Research and Teaching, 11th June 1999', *Fashion Theory* 4(2): 235-40.

de Solla Price, D. J. (1969), *Little Science, Big Science*, New York: Columbia University Press.

Durkheim, E. (1976), *The Elementary Forms of the Religious Life*, translated by J. W. Swain, London: Allen & Unwin.

Eicher, J.B. (ed.) (1995), *Dress and Ethnicity: Changes Across Time and Space*, Oxford, Washington DC: Berg.

—— and Roach-Higgins, M.E. (1993), 'Definition and Classification of Dress. Implications for Analysis of Gender Roles', in Barnes, R. and Eicher, J.B. (eds) (1993), *Dress and Gender: Making and Meaning*, Oxford, Providence: Berg.

El Guindi, F. (1998), *Veil: Modesty, Privacy and Resistance*, New York and Oxford: Berg.

Eliade, M. (1954), *The Myth of Eternal Return*, Princeton, NJ: Princeton University Press.

—— (1959), *Cosmos and History*, New York: Harper Row.

Elias, N. (1978), *The Civilizing Process*, Oxford: Basil Blackwell. Original 1939.

——, Martins, H. and Whitley, R. (eds) (1982), *Scientific Establishments and Hierarchies,* London: D. Reidel.

Entwistle, J. (2000), *The Fashioned Body: Theorizing Fashion and Dress in Modern Society,* Cambridge: Polity.

Evans, J. and Hall, S. (eds) (1999), *Visual Culture: A Reader,* London: Sage.

Falk, P. (1994), *The Consuming Body,* London: Sage.

Featherstone, M. (1990), *Consumer Culture and Postmodernism,* London: Sage.

——, Hepworth, M and Turner (eds) (1991), *The Body: Social Process and Cultural Theory,* London: Sage.

Fentress, J. and Wickham, C. (1992), *Social Memory,* Oxford: Blackwell.

Fielding, K. J. and Campbell, I. (eds) (1997), *Thomas Carlyle. Reminiscences,* Oxford: Oxford University Press.

Finkelstein, J. (1991), *The Fashioned Self,* Cambridge: Polity.

Frank, A. (1988), 'Bringing Bodies Back In: A Decade Review', *Theory, Culture and Society* 1: 131–62.

Friedmann, G. (1947), *Problèmes humains du machinisme industriel,* Paris: Gallimard.

Froude, J.A. (1882), *Thomas Carlyle. A History of the First Forty Years of His Life. 1795–1835,* London: Longmans, Green & Co.

Gadamer, H-G. (1975), *Truth and Method,* New York: Seabury Press.

Gaines, J. and Herzog, C. (eds), (1990), *Fabrications: Costume and the Female Body,* London: Routledge.

Garber, M. (1992), *Vested Interests: Cross-Dressing and Cultural Identity,* London: Routledge.

Giddens, A. (1984), *The Constitution of Society: Outline of the Theory of Structuration,* London: Polity Press.

—— (1991), *Modernity and Self-Identity: Self and Society in the Late Modern Age,* Cambridge: Polity Press.

Goffman, E. (1969), *The Presentation of Self in Everyday Life,* London: Allen Lane. Original 1959.

Gottdiener, M. (1995), *Postmodern Semiotics: Material Culture and the Forms of Postmodern Life,* Oxford, UK & Cambridge, USA: Blackwell.

Griggs, C. (1998), *S/he: Changing Sex and Changing Clothes,* New York and Oxford: Berg.

Gronow, J. (1997), *The Sociology of Taste,* London and New York: Routledge.

Hall, S. (ed.) (1997), *Representation: Cultural Representations and Signifying Practices,* London: Sage.

Haynes, M.T. (1998), *Dressing Up Debutantes. Pageantry and Glitz in Texas,* New York and Oxford: Berg.

Hebdige, D. (1979), *Subculture: The Meaning of Style,* London: Methuen.

Heffer, S. (1995), *Moral Desperado. A Life of Thomas Carlyle,* London: Weidenfeld and Nicholson.

Helmling, S. (1988), *The Esoteric Comedies of Carlyle, Newman and Yates,* Cambridge: Cambridge University Press.

Hobsbawm, E. and Ranger, T. (eds) (1983), *The Invention of Tradition,* Cambridge: Cambridge University Press.

Hollander, A. (1993), *Seeing Through Clothes,* New York: Avon.

Jenkins, R. (1996), *Social Identity,* London and New York: Routledge.

Jessop, R. (1997), *Carlyle and Scottish Thought,* London: Macmillan.

Johnson, K.P. and Lennon, S.J. (eds) (1999), *Appearance and Power,* New York and Oxford: Berg.

Joseph, N. (1986), *Uniforms and Non-Uniforms: Communication Through Clothing,* Westwood, Conn.: Greenwood Press.

Kaiser, S.B. (1985), *The Social Psychology of Clothing,* New York: Macmillan.

Kaplan, F. (1993), *Thomas Carlyle: A Biography,* California: University of California Press.

Keenan, W.J.F. (1999a), 'Of Mammon Dressed Divinely: The Profanization of Sacred Dress', *Body & Society,* 5 (1): 73–92.

—— (1999b), 'From Friars to Fornicators: The Eroticization of Sacred Dress', *Fashion Theory,* 3 (4): 389–410.

—— (2000), '"Clothed with Authority": The Rationalisation of Marist Dress Culture', in L.B. Arthur (ed.) *Undressing Religion: Commitment and Conversion from a Cross-Cultural Perspective,* pp. 83–100, Oxford and New York: Berg.

Kelman, J. (1924), *Prophets of Yesterday and Their Message Today. Thomas Carlyle, Matthew Arnold, Robert Browning,* New York: Ayer.

Kidwell, C.B. and Steele, V. (eds) (1989), *Men and Women: Dressing the Part,* Washington, DC: Smithsonian Institute Press.

King, M.D. (1971), 'Reason, Tradition and the Progressiveness of Science', *History and Theory,* X (1): 3–32.

König, R. (1973a), *A La Mode: On the Social Psychology of Fashion,* New York: Seabury Press.

—— (1973b), *The Restless Image: A Sociology of Fashion,* London: Allen and Unwin.

Kuhn, T.S. (1970), *The Structure of Scientific Revolutions,* second edition, enlarged, Chicago: University of Chicago Press.

Lakatos, I. and Musgrave, A. (eds) (1970), *Criticism and the Growth of Knowledge,* London: Cambridge University Press.

Lash, S. and Friedman, J. (eds) (1992), *Modernity and Identity,* Oxford and Cambridge: Blackwell.

Lash, S. and Urry, J. (1994), *Economies of Signs and Space,* London: Sage.

Laver, J. (1945), *Taste and Fashion: From the French Revolution to the Present Day,* London: G.G. Harrap.

Levin, M. (1998), *The Condition of England Question: Carlyle, Mill, Engels,* London: Macmillan.

Lurie, A. (1992), *The Language of Clothes,* London: Bloomsbury. Original 1981.

Lyotard, J.-F. (1984), *The Postmodern Condition: A Report on Knowledge,* translated by G. Bennington and B. Massumi, Minneapolis: University of Minnesota Press.

Machlup, F. (1962), *The Production and Distribution of Knowledge,* Princeton: Princeton University Press.

MacIntyre, A. (1982), *After Virtue,* London: Duckworth.

Manuel, F. (1962), *The Prophets of Paris,* Cambridge, Mass.: Harvard University Press.

Marauhao, T. (1986), 'The Hermeneutics of Participant Observation', *Dialectical Anthropology*, X: 291–309.

Martin, B. (1981), *A Sociology of Contemporary Cultural Change*, Oxford: Blackwell.

Mauss, M. (1973), 'Techniques of the Body', *Economy and Society*,2 (1): 70–89. Original 1934.

Mayo, J. (1984), *A History of Ecclesiastical Dress*, London: B.T. Batsford.

McDowell, C. (1997), *The Man of Fashion. Peacock Males and Perfect Gentlemen*, London: Thames and Hudson.

McVeigh, B. (2000), *Wearing Ideology: The Uniformity of Self-Presentation in Japan*, New York and Oxford: Berg.

Mellor, P.A. and Shilling, C. (1997), *Re-forming the Body: Religion, Community and Modernity*, London: Sage.

Merton, R.K. (1968), 'The Matthew Effect in Science', *Science*,159: 59–63.

Milbank, J., Ward, G. and Pickstock, C. (1999), 'Introduction: Suspending the material: the turn of radical orthodoxy', in J. Milbank, C. Pickstock and G. Ward (eds), *Radical Orthodoxy. A New Theology*, London and New York: Routledge.

Miller, D. (1987), *Material Culture and Mass Consumption*, Oxford: Basil Blackwell.

Millman, M. (1977), *The Women Dress for Success Book*, Chicago: Follett Publishing.

Mills, C.W. (1959), *The Sociological Imagination*, New York: Oxford University Press.

Molloy, T. (1978), *Dress for Success*, New York: Warner Books.

Muggleton, D. (2000), *Inside Culture: The Postmodern Meaning of Style*, Oxford: Berg.

Nisbet, R.A. (1976), *Sociology as an Art Form*, London: Heinemann.

Oliphant, M. (1892), *The Victorian Age of English Literature*, New York: Dodd and Mead.

Perani, J.M. and Wolff, N.H. (1999), *Cloth, Dress and Art Patronage in Africa*, New York and Oxford: Berg.

Perrot, P. (1994), *Fashioning the Bourgeoise: A History of Clothing in the Nineteenth Century*, Princeton: Princeton University Press.

Pickering, M. (1997), 'A New Look at Auguste Comte', in C. Camic (ed.). *Reclaiming the Sociological Classics: The State of Scholarship*, pp. 11–44, Oxford: Blackwell.

Polhemus, T. (1994), *Streetstyle: From Sidewalk to Catwalk*, London: Thames and Hudson.

Poll, S. (1962), *The Hasidic Community of Williamsburg*, New York: Free Press.

Popper, K.R. (1963), *Conjectures and Refutations*, London: Routledge & Kegan Paul.

—— (1974), *Objective Knowledge: An Evolutionary Approach*, London: Oxford University Press.

Ricoeur, P. (1973), 'The Hermeneutical Function of Distantiation', *Philosophy Today*, 17: 112–28.

Ritzer, G. (2000), *Sociological Theory*, New York: McGraw-Hill.

Roach-Higgins, M.E., Eicher, J.B. and Johnson, K.K.P. (eds) (1995), *Dress and Identity*, New York: Fairchild Publications.

Roche, D. (1994), *The Culture of Clothing: Dress and Fashion in the 'Ancien Regime'*, translated by J. Birrell, Cambridge: Cambridge University Press.

Roe, F.W. (1969), *The Social Philosophy of Carlyle and Ruskin,* London: Kennikat Press.

Rouse, E. (1989), *Understanding Fashion,* Oxford: BSP Professional Books.

Rubinstein, R.P. (1995), *Dress Codes: Meanings and Messages in American Culture,* Boulder, CO & Oxford: Westview Press.

Sanders, C.R. and Clubbe, J. (eds) (1976), *Carlyle and His Contemporaries,* Durham, N.C.: Duke University Press.

Sanders, C.R., Fielding, K.J., de L. Ryals, C., Campbell, I., and Christianson, A. (eds) (1970–1998), *The Collected Letters of Thomas and Jane Welsh Carlyle,* 26 Volumes, Durham, N.C.: Duke University Press.

Schneider, L. (ed.) (1976), *Classical Theories of Social Change,* New York: Wiley.

Schwartz, B. (1982), 'The Social Context of Commemoration: A Study in Collective Memory', *Social Forces,* 61 (2): 237-56.

Seigel, J.P. (1995), *Thomas Carlyle: The Critical Heritage,* London: Routledge.

Shelston, A. (ed.) (1971), *Thomas Carlyle: Selected Writings,* London, Harmondsworth: Penguin.

Shilling, C. (1993), *The Body and Social Theory,* London: Sage.

Simmel, G. (1957), 'Fashion', *American Journal of Sociology,* 62: 541–58. Original 1904.

Sklair, L. (1973), *Organized Knowledge. A Sociological View of Science and Technology,* St. Albans, Herts: Paladin.

Steele, V. (1985), *Fashion and Eroticism,* New York: Oxford University Press.

—— (1996), *Fetish: Fashion, Sex and Power,* Oxford: Oxford University Press.

—— (ed.) (1998), *Fashion Theory: The Journal of Dress, Body & Culture,* 2 (4), Special Issue on Dress and Methodology, New York and Oxford: Berg.

—— (ed.) (1999), *Fashion Theory. The Journal of Dress, Body & Culture,* 3 (4), Special Issue on Fashion and Eroticism, New York and Oxford: Berg.

Stone, G. (1962), 'Appearance and the Self', in M.E. Roach and J.B. Eicher (eds), *Dress, Adornment and the Social Order,* New York: John Wiley and Sons.

Symons, J. (1952), *Thomas Carlyle: The Life and Ideas of a Prophet,* New York: Ayer.

Tarr, R.L. (1989), *Thomas Carlyle: A Descriptive Bibliography,* Oxford: Clarendon Press.

Trela, D.J. and Tarr, R.L. (eds) (1997), *The Critical Response to Thomas Carlyle's Major Works,* New York: Greenwood Press.

Tseëlon, E. (1992), 'Is the Presented Self Sincere? Goffman, Impression Management and the Postmodern Self', *Theory, Culture and Society,* 9 (2): 115–28.

—— (1995), *The Mask of Femininity: The Presentation of Women in Everyday Life,* London: Sage.

Turner, B.S. (1996), *The Body and Society: Explorations in Social Theory,* London: Sage.

—— (1999), *Classical Sociology,* London: Sage.

Vale, V. and Juno, A. (eds) (1989), *Modern Primitives: Tattoo, Piercing, Scarification: An Investigation of Contemporary Adornment and Ritual,* San Francisco: Re/Search Publications.

Vanden Bossche, C.R. (1991), *Carlyle and the Search for Authority*, Ohio: Ohio State University Press.

Warner, W.L. (1975), *The Living and the Dead: A Study of the Symbolic Life of the Americans*, New Haven, Connec: Yale University Press.

Warwick, A. and Cavallaro, D. (eds) (1998), *Refashioning the Frame: Boundaries, Dress and the Body*, New York and Oxford: Berg.

Weber, M. (1949), *The Methodology of the Social Sciences*, translated by E.A. Shils and H.A. Finch, Glencoe, Illinois: The Free Press.

Willis, P. (2000), 'Foreword' to Barker, C., *Cultural Studies: Theory and Practice*, London: Sage.

Wilson, D.A. (1924), *Carlyle To 'The French Revolution' (1826–1837)*, London: Kegan Paul, Trench, Trubner & Co. New York: E.P. Dutton & Co.

Wilson, E. (1985), *Adorned in Dreams: Fashion and Modernity*, London: Virago.

—— (1992), 'The Fashioned Body' in J. Ash and E. Wilson (eds), *Chic Thrills: A Fashion Reader*, London: Pandora.

Yerushalmi, Y.H. (1982), *Zakhor: Jewish History and Jewish Memory*, Seattle: University of Washington Press.

Yoder, D. (1969), 'Sectarian Costume Research in the United States', in A. Fife and A. Fife, with H.G. Glassie (eds), *Forms Upon the Frontier: Folklife and Folk Arts in the United States*, Logan: Utah State University Press.

2

A Comparative Exploration of Dress and the Presentation of Self as Implicit Religion[1]

Eileen Barker

Dressing up was always fun when we were children. Indeed, that might have been one of the reasons why I decided that I wanted to be an actress – to be paid to dress up and hide under the clothes that could present my alter egos to the world. Years later I was to become a sociologist of religion, studying the weird and wonderful worlds that are inhabited by others, but it was some time before I was to recognize the extent to which my training and experience in dressing up might have been sensitizing me to what the American sociologist, Erving Goffman (1959), wrote about as *The Presentation of Self in Everyday Life*.

This chapter was kindled by a paper that I had concluded with 'a grossly over-sketched caricature' which compared the apparel and mannerisms of different groups of persons whom I was studying at the time (Barker 1979a). I want to emphasize the methodological point that I had written the descriptions long before making any attempt to analyze them, and I am not at all sure that I would ever have entertained the arguments that follow had I not been forced to think about the concept of implicit religion.[2] I had recorded my descriptions without any clear awareness that they were testing any particular explanation or theory – it was only much later that I started to make explicit that which had been implicit. I am stressing this point because I, for one, would be highly suspicious of what follows if I thought the descriptions had resulted from the search. I am still slightly suspicious, but think that there might be enough in what follows at least to form the basis for further discussion.

The Wider Study[3]

The study from which most of the caricatures are drawn ought perhaps to be introduced in general terms before turning to their implicit religion. It was a study that was, very broadly speaking, concerned with science and religion (both being widely defined). More precisely, my thesis was that the pluralism of ideological positions in modern society had created an embarras de choix in which just about the only expert who is officially sanctioned for his (or, occasionally, her) true, independent knowledge is the scientist. A 'consumer demand' for scientific sanctioning of a wide range of ideological beliefs had been met by a 'production supply' of a new priesthood of scientists who are ready to provide supporting proof, or at least permission, for such diverse beliefs – all in the name of science.

The priests of science and the organizations that employ and promote their particular pronouncements can be classified into five Ideal Types (in the Weberian (1949: 89ff) sense). The classification depends primarily on attitudes towards the truth or falsity of the Bible with respect both to the particular details and to the general spirit. The labels given to the types are meant to do no more than suggest a recognizable placement in an ideological spectrum. It is important to stress that, in what follows, there is no suggestion that people other than those whom I was studying would present themselves in like manner – even when similar labels are applied to them.

The Types

My first type, *Fundamentalists,* believe in the literal truth of the Bible as the revealed word of God. Creation occurred as described in Genesis, Chapter I, and the scientists' job is to establish the falsity of evolution and proclaim the truth of the Bible as a scientific textbook. Next, *Liberals* have the task of showing that the Bible and science are concerned with different areas and consequently neither can be seen as threatening to the other; each deserves to be celebrated in its own right. The third type, *Modernists,* see the world in strongly evolutionary terms; for them, it is through an enlightened and enlarged science that we can learn the way forward – science must not restrict itself to reductionist materialism, but explore the spiritual, the ineffable, the 'more than . . .'. Fourthly, *Agnostics* offer a secular version of Liberalism and are concerned with balancing science with a humanistic ethic that might rest upon a traditional (though factually dubious) religious morality. And finally, *Atheists,* like Fundamentalists, believe that science and religion must be seen as competing in a straightforward way but, in their case, science proves that religion is false. In its place is put a scientific ethic, or perhaps a political ideology, supported by science. In order to simplify matters somewhat, I take a Marxist group which I studied as my sole representative of the Atheist category.

Noticing the Groups' Collective 'Presentation of Self'

I suppose that it was because I was studying an unusually wide range of ideological positions that I was pushed into thinking about the diverse 'presentations of self' more than I might otherwise have done. When, for example, I had to visit two different groups on one day I found myself unsure of what I ought to wear. What would be suitable for one group would stick out like a sore thumb in another group. But while this initial interest was really to avoid making myself too noticeable, it was also related to the years I had spent working in the theatre. I began to notice that, while involved in participant observation of the different groups, I had been subconsciously observing and adopting different styles of speech and different ways of sitting and holding my body. All this became recognized at a fairly low level of awareness during the less interesting hours that I spent with each group. I had not at that point contemplated an attempt to relate the differences to the respective ideologies.

The Descriptions

Let me now present my caricatures, or, to put them on a more legitimate-sounding basis, the ideal typical representations. At Fundamentalist meetings, men wear off-the-peg suits or slacks with either Fair Isle sweaters or hand-knitted cardigans. Women seem to buy their sensible clothes at C and A or Marks and Spencer (British clothing stores broadly equivalent in the United States to, say, J C Penney). Hair is controlled. Members sit with their feet together. Everywhere they go they carry well-thumbed Bibles. During lectures they take copious notes on Winfield notepads. Conversations are punctuated with appreciative 'Praise the Lord!'s.

At the opposite end of the ideological spectrum, Marxists wear jeans which end in sneakers or boots. On top, voluble T-shirts are covered by combat jackets or epauletted overcoats which are long and thick enough to protect their wearers from the ravages of a Siberian winter. Hair is in abundance. Marxists sit with their legs apart, grunt, use 'like' and 'see' in most sentences. They carry *Private Eye* and an unpublished report from the World Federation of Scientific Workers in their pockets. They seldom take notes during lectures. They wear dark glasses – indoors – during winter months.

Turning to the middle of my somewhat wobbly continuum, we find that Modernists have the widest range of styles. They also vary quite considerably in demographic terms, including, most noticeably, the young (of both sexes) who embrace the counterculture and the old (upper-middle class and usually women) who cling to 'progressive ideas'. But despite, or possibly because of, this range, it is still possible to isolate a style which excludes both Fundamentalist and Marxist styles. Modernists are carefully absent-minded about their apparel, which tends to be expensively expensive or expensively cheap. Men wear polo-neck sweaters. Dog collars are either abandoned or worn with abandon. Female garments, be they kaftans or fisherman's smocks, have a kind of 'flow' about them. Modernists achieve a style that Marxists studiously avoid and which Fundamentalists might occasionally emulate but either cannot or dare not achieve in their worthy respectability. Modernists carry the *Guardian*, the *West Sussex Gazette* or poems by a Zen Buddhist either under their arms or in a copious carpetbag. They do not use pockets. During lectures they take the odd note on the back of an envelope with a foreign stamp. Modernists will talk in either County or Trans-Atlantic accents of their experiences in Africa, the Far East and the East End.

Theologically separating the Modernists from the Fundamentalists on the one side and the atheistic Marxists on the other, we have the Liberals and the Agnostics. Both Liberals and Agnostics avoid excess. The Liberal will be less formal than the Agnostic in dress, but neither would be likely to cause the other sartorial embarrassment. The Liberals might have a slightly dusty appearance and sport leather patches at the elbow; the Agnostic might have a slightly polished appearance and sport a furled umbrella. While the Liberal could have *The Crucible* in his pocket, the Agnostic would have the *Financial Times* in his briefcase. Both make selected notes, the Agnostic in an electronic organizer or on the yellow pages of a filo-fax with a Parker, the Liberal at the back of a diary with a Pentel.

If jewellery is worn at a Fundamentalist meeting, it will be a small gold cross or unobtrusive pendant around the neck of a young girl or, perhaps, a small lapel brooch on an older woman. Liberal women also wear unobtrusive jewellery but it will probably be more valuable, possibly something left to them by their maternal grandmother. Agnostic jewellery is expensive and could come from Bond Street. Modernist adornment comes from Habitat, an Eastern craft shop or a Victorian attic. It might consist of large, chunky rings or fertility symbols dangling on leather thongs. Marxists wear badges.

Underneath the outer apparel one can discern that Fundamentalist women have a neat, though flattening uplift. Liberals merely contain; Agnostics have enlarging support and Modernists a careless, lopsided support. Marxist women spurn any support at all.

Fundamentalists do not smoke. Liberal men may suck at pipes, Agnostics at cigars. Modernists smoke Gauloise, Black Sobranie, or herbal cigarettes – or, more frequently, have given up. The Marxists pass round pot.

Marxists wear dark colours – black and dark blues. Fundamentalists wear bright colours but these are non-startling and monochromatic. Liberals and Agnostics wear subdued colours, the Agnostics tending more towards greys with the Liberals going more for autumn tweeds, browns and greens. Modernists wear any colour but usually several colours at once. The effect may well be startling. Modernists excel at being attired in a gestalt of colour.

While Fundamentalists whisper to you confidentially as at a vicarage tea party, Marxists mumble to you with their heads turned away as in an American B film. While Agnostics declaim solemnly as at a Board Meeting, Modernists give you the impression that they are talking to the person behind you at an intense Hampstead cocktail party.

It is not merely styles of talking but also patterns of speech and the use of words that differentiate the various groups. But before looking at this in further detail I would like to pause in order to begin to assess the descriptions to see how far the various presentations of self can be interpreted as being consistent with – or having some consonance with – the ideological positions of the different types. In doing this, I hope to do more than focus on the 'internal' beliefs, opinions and orientations to the prevailing social scene – as it might be conceived by the members of each type. After all, saying what one is *not* is as important a defining characteristic as saying what one *is*.

Aligning Presentations of Self with Ideological Positions

Fundamentalists in both theology and presentations of self enjoy a correct conservatism. Their approach, like their source of revelation, is direct and unambiguous. This is a closed approach in that it is not open to other outside influences. It is straightforward and uncluttered by alternatives. In dress there is little or no attention paid to the latest craze of fashion, a respectable attire which survives minor and passing variations is adhered to. There is no confusion through colour, merely modest enjoyment of it. The self is clean, controlled and 'correct'. There is no hint of sexual provocation. Reliability and acceptance of the traditionally given reign supreme. It is easy to see how dirt would, in Mary Douglas' phrase, be matter out of place (1966).

Staying for a moment with the vision of Mary Douglas (1970), one can see in both the Fundamentalists and the Marxists an expression of the 'strong group/weak grid' syndrome. For both, the Them/Us distinction is clear and their respective ideologies embrace the concomitant dualisms of good and evil, Godly and Satanic, elect and damned – or of oppressed and oppressor, worker and bourgeoisie. In both cases, the boundary separating insiders and outsiders is strengthened not only by distinctive presentations of *self* but also by a group presentation of '*us*'. There is, for example, the laughter which is evoked to ridicule non-believers. Although both the Fundamentalists and the Marxists have an explicit message to tell the world, neither group actually communicates freely with non-members. Fundamentalists, cosily and confidentially, whisper to their fellow believers; Marxists, darkly and conspiratorially, murmur to theirs. The outsider does not overhear the inner truths. (Of course the outsider *can* overhear merely by going to the relevant meetings. What I am suggesting, however, is that, in discussing the higher gnoses, the *manner* suggests that these *are* higher gnoses which separate the knower from the unenlightened.)

Perhaps it seems strange to look for similarities between the Fundamentalists and the Marxists. On first acquaintance they could not seem to be more different from each other. Among the Marxists there is apparently a completely *un*controlled presentation of self. Dirt, it might almost be said, must be matter *in* place. Yet, if one looks a bit more carefully, it is not difficult to see the Marxists' presentation of self as rather tightly controlled uncontrol (this is more transparently so if one compares them with Modernists). Differences between the Marxists and the Fundamentalists seem, above all, to reflect the difference between a conservative and a revolutionary ideology. Marxists conform to their own group in rejecting the wider society of which they are a part. Their clothes and hair are statements of rejection. They reject the upright posture of the Fundamentalist for an aggressively uninvolved slouch. They will smoke the outlawed pot. Their dark glasses and dark clothes make them conspicuously inconspicuous and 'away from it all'. Their manner is as inclusive/exclusive as that of any other sectarian, but it is the bourgeois conventionalism of capitalism, rather than the lax immorality of modernity, from which they are separating themselves. The Marxist is presenting a stand against oppressive order, the Fundamentalist is presenting a stand against permissive disorder.

While both Fundamentalists and Marxists obviously await their respective Armageddons, their ideologies are in practice more oriented towards a past or a present than a future, tending to focus on Biblical traditionalism or contemporary evils. It is with the Modernists that one finds an implicit religion of teleology stated in the presentation of self. In conversation, bodies lean forward and voices are thrown beyond the person they are talking to for all – and the future – to hear. Their dress is uncontrolled by the present conventional fashion but, like the wearer, flows ahead. Modernists are eagerly 'with it' and 'beyond it' as they seek out the newest thing in their newest thing (which, perhaps not altogether paradoxically, could be the oldest thing but newly reincarnated). There are no restrictions except on restrictions. If they can be placed anywhere on Mary Douglas' schema, it is in the 'strong grid/weak group' box. Anything and everything is explored. Nothing is rejected. It is only by trying out all possibilities that one can hope to find the way forward and discover the hidden secrets and directions of the future, unbounded by the constraints of the past or, especially, present.

As with their ideological positions, Liberals and Agnostics occupy a middle ground between Modernism on the one hand and Fundamentalism and Marxism on the other. They are more 'modish' than the latter two and less 'way out' than the Modernists. Agnostics are 'with it' in the sense that they *are*, socially speaking, 'it'. They speak as though they expect to be listened to. They are the providers of the future – not in the enthusiastic, possibly irresponsible, way of the Modernist who tries everything out on principle, but in a steady, judicious way asserting that this is the tried and proven way ahead. Their clothes *will* last, their jewellery *is* made by the best jeweller. The Liberals are perhaps slightly less forward looking. They are anxious to protect what is good and tried from the past, their clothes *have* lasted, their jewellery *was* made by craftsmen. Liberals do not live in the past, but they preserve a thread of continuity with the past in a manner roughly equivalent to the Agnostics' thread of continuity between the present and the future.

But while both Liberals and Agnostics express in their ideologies and self-presentation a belief in the rightness of a certain continuity over time, they differ from the other three types in that they also express a *dis*continuity between *contemporary* areas of life. They, it will be remembered, were defined as the two categories that carefully separated religion and science into different compartments, each being more or less complementary to the other. There are other possible explanations, but it is curious that it is the Liberals and the Agnostics who are most likely to distinguish between appropriate manners of presentation of self according to the particular occasion it happens to be. Marxists are nearly always formally informal, Fundamentalists, on the other hand, tend to be informally formal. Modernists could be either in dress, but this is not necessarily tied in any predictable way to the occasion. It would not be surprising for a Modernist to change into a safari suit to go to the theatre having just returned from buying decaffeinated coffee at the supermarket in a long skirt and embroidered blouse. For the Liberals and Agnostics, however, diversity of occasion, like diversity of knowledge, is acknowledged and celebrated as diverse and met with the socially appropriate response.

Implicit Distaff Ideologies

To end this descriptive section on what I hope will not be considered too fanciful a note, I would like to indicate a second-order ideology to be found within the first-order beliefs that I have discussed so far. I do this, I admit, as a not entirely liberated feminist.

Women are treated and, indeed, see themselves in a different light according to the sort of group with which they are connected. At Fundamentalist meetings the women are usually wives or girlfriends. Very rarely does a woman contribute to the debate. On only one occasion did I hear a lecture from a woman. Women are, on the whole, women; and a woman's place is in the home. A good woman is someone's wife. She is not confused with men; *she* does not confuse her role. God created Eve *for* Adam, *out of* Adam.

Liberal women are allowed to make intellectual contributions and are respected as being capable of thinking like men. They are, however, still women and, although one accords them equal status at times of intellectual discussion, one also offers them seats and assumes that they will be a different kind of person in the home.

Agnostics, like Liberals, tend to divide up the way women are treated. They too are allowed to be academic, but outside the work situation the Agnostic man will tend to retire to his club while the Liberal will tend to retire to his home. Women, when it is appropriate to regard them as women, are marriage partners for Liberals but either mothers or 'bits of alright' for Agnostics.

Women in Marxist groups are theoretically on equal terms all round with the men. They lecture, they chair and they organize sessions. But somehow one gets the feeling that it is *because* they are women that they, like blacks, are encouraged to perform. They are really there as the big men's Molls. Their proper function is their animal function – but they must, of course, be liberated animals.

The Modernists is the only group which seems genuinely to ignore sex differences as an important defining characteristic. Women are just as likely – or unlikely – to take office as men. The difference between the sexes is not denied in the way that the Marxists would deny it, but the difference is accepted as a fact of nature which is of little relevance outside the realm of purely biological functions – and these are celebrated as such and forgotten about for the other purposes. It is not the neat division into separate categories which the Agnostics and, to a lesser extent, the Liberals, employ. To be a woman in a Modernist group is to be liberated from the necessity of socially defining oneself in female terms. The biological definition is performed by one's genes and there is little need to think about the matter further. There are other, more important, things to think about.

No-one would be likely to turn a hair if a woman started to suckle a baby at a Modernist meeting – that would be the natural thing to do. It would not be so much the natural thing to do as a gesture at a Marxist meeting. Women do not turn up to Liberal and Agnostic meetings with their children – they belong elsewhere. Fundamentalists do bring their children. It is a family meeting and the older children sit through the lectures; if babies have to be fed, their mothers take them to a place where there is privacy. And then they return to their husband's side.

It is possible, I would argue, to recognize an implicit religion in these attitudes. It is further possible, I believe, to see an implicit expression of these in the description I gave earlier of the different uses of bras (burning included). I shall return briefly to an exposure of implicit religion in the presentation of the breast later, but do not wish to pursue the point any further at the moment. Let us, rather, turn to the alignment of belief and practice at a more theoretical level.

From Practice to Theory

To recapitulate the practices described thus far: it has been intimated that we might find links between the ideological beliefs of the five different types of groups and the presentations of self that were offered by the members of the respective groups. I am, in other words, arguing that the practice is praxis – a living out of the theory in action: Fundamentalists as monistically conservative in their unambiguous return to the Bible; Marxists as monistically revolutionary in their rejection of the present society; Liberals and Agnostics as dualistically separating the complementary functions of science and religion, the Liberals forging a link between the present and the past, the Agnostics between the present and the future; and Modernists as uniting all knowledge and being pluralistically future-oriented, experimenting, exploring and enthusiastically attempting to transcend all man-made barriers. What the members of the groups wear, how they wear it, how they sit, stand and talk, how they think of and treat women, how they orientate themselves to time and to society reflects, in some recognizable ways, their religious views – their praxes do, in short, exemplify their implicit religions.

What now has to be asked is what are the theoretical assumptions that would seem to underpin, and that might be drawn from, the alignment of these practices. What generalizations can be made that might be of relevance to sociological theory?

Obviously, the main underlying assumption must be that of some kind of consistency. Social psychology has a considerable literature based on experiments exploring consistency not only in the laboratory but also in 'real life' situations – even religious ones (see, for example, Festinger, Rieken and Schachter 1955). There are also respectable schools in sociology and anthropology that rely heavily on an assumption of consistency between different areas of social life. Indeed one could almost say that the whole practice of sociology relies on some postulate of consistency. But this in itself does not get us very far. It is patently obvious that human beings are capable of gross inconsistency. Social life is, moreover, full of tensions and conflicts. It is as easy to argue that social life depends on tensions and conflicts as much as, if not more than, it does on complementarities and consistencies. Where, the question then becomes, is one more likely to find consistencies, and consistencies between what? And when are there likely to be tensions and when complementarity between tensions and consistencies?

Before proceeding further, it must be acknowledged that there is already a problem rising out of the use of the word consistency. It would, however, be counter-productive to go into too nice a definition of what is meant by the term. This is because we are concerned not with an explicit consistency which can be logically or even psychologically verified or refuted, but with the kind of consistency that only works through its covert implications. It is a consistency that lies in an ability for the people involved to be able, at some acknowledged level, to recognize things as 'fitting' (and *being* fitting) – of two or more phenomena enjoying what Sorokin has called logico-meaningful integration – which produce a seamless web, a whole without a break. In its tightest manifestation, consistency can imply sameness; in its most loose, it is harmony, lack of discord.

It must not, however, be thought that it is a psychological question with which we are concerned – not even, perhaps not especially, in the Levi-Straussian sense of the universal mind recognizing and in some way resonating with the deep structure of a myth. What we are concerned with now is to ask what social practices are most likely to demand, to produce or to allow the assumed psychological comfort of consistency – and what functions these perform for all concerned.

To repeat, I do not assume that individuals are consistent. It is not difficult to find the most glaring inconsistencies in most of our beliefs and practices. Indeed, I have frequently argued that it is a characteristic of those people who, according to society at large, hold the most incongruous beliefs that they are actually the ones who are far *less* inconsistent in their beliefs and practices than the rest of us. In this category I would include both Creationist scientists (those who do not accept evolution but work to show, scientifically, that Genesis Chapter One is literally true (Barker 1979b)) and members of new religious movements that I have studied (Barker 1984; 1989). Yet what

I want to consider here is not the degree of internal consistency (or inconsistency) to be found *within* a set of beliefs but the fit *between* a set of beliefs and a set of practices (presentations of self) carried out by a group of persons sharing those beliefs. I would want, furthermore, to argue that this is a socially induced consistency, and that, ceteris paribus, this type of consistency increases (a) the more the set of beliefs is rejected by the accepted beliefs of the wider society and (b) the more the set of beliefs itself rejects the accepted ideology of the wider society.

At the risk of over-stressing the point, let me reiterate that I have been discussing the social presentation of self in relation to members of a particular ideological group who are defining themselves or being defined *as* members of that group. The argument is not tautological because the members of the group are only *explicitly* defining themselves or being defined as holding a particular ideology – the presentation of self, through its consistency, is the *implicit* statement of their beliefs. It is implicit because (a) it is not consciously recognized as such *but* (b) it can be unconsciously (or subconsciously) internalized. Furthermore, if an individual's presentation of self is not consistent with the implicit mores, this *is* recognized as 'something wrong' and can be taken as a warning that the individual may not be wholly committed to the group's ideology.

It can be argued at this point, and I would agree, that I am referring only to a very special instance of implicit religion. There must be an enormous range of implicit religion which is in no way tied to any explicit religion in the way it is with the groups at which I have looked. There will be also those who hold an explicit religion who do not restate it in an implicit form. There are also those who compartmentalize their religion from all other aspects of life and could be complete Jekylls and Hydes. All this I freely acknowledge. But while I believe that there are things that can be said about such cases, I am not attempting to do so now. I merely want to try to consider the simpler case which I have laid out. That is fraught with enough methodological problems as it is, and I certainly do not wish to embrace more than necessary the problem of intuiting what an implicit religion implies for the believer. But, having hinted at some of the methodological difficulties, I shall now forge ahead, trying to keep qualifying statements to a minimum by referring to less contentious illustrations in order to attempt more contentious hypotheses.

When people decide to join an ideological group as a public statement of faith they are expressing a desire to align themselves with one lot of people rather than with another. The group may in the first instance accept all sorts, but once one is an integral part of the group there are certain things which one is *not* that one might have been before. The more the group excludes or is excluded by society or even sections of society, the more clearly will there be a visible boundary between 'them' and 'us'. Definitions are made and identities are established. Boundary maintenance is preserved in various ways, but one common way is through the presentation of self as a particular type – or, more forcefully, as not another type.

The process by which this works for initiates is fairly simple socialization. They do, after all, want to be accepted as part of the group. If a young man has just received Jesus into his life he will not blaspheme as he used to when he stubs his foot against the door, but there will be other, more subtle changes that he will learn to make – and if the young man had long hair when he converted to the group, he is unlikely not to have noticed that his hirsute appearance is at odds with that of his new co-religionists. The neat trim he receives could almost be an implicit *rite de passage* into the community. There will however be other changes that he will have to make in his self-presentation which may not be so obvious at first. Sometimes he will be explicitly told, sometimes he will just pick it up as he realizes that his behaviour is no longer *'fitting'*. I received a gentle lesson in what was fitting – or, in this case, unfitting – even before I started to study the Unification Church on a formal basis. I was a 'visiting academic' who knew very little about the movement apart from the fact that they were the notorious Moonies. Out of curiosity, I had accepted an invitation to chair a Round Table on science and religion at their London headquarters. A Unification artist sat in a corner during the proceedings and at the end of the session I was presented with the portrait he had drawn of me. It was a hot day and I had been wearing a somewhat low-cut dress. The portrait showed a dress in which the neckline had moved a good four inches towards the neck. It was not, however, until I started to learn something about the *Divine Principle* (Unification Theology) that I noticed this and realized how unfittingly I had been clad – in what an Unprincipled way I had presented myself.

By using the concept of implicit religion in describing the group-negotiated presentation of self what is added is that it is not just that each group draws boundaries which establish and preserve the similarities between the members and differences from non-members, but that the similarities and differences also make a statement about, and reinforce, the *kind* of ideology that is being held by the members. I do not want it to be thought that I am suggesting that the process is a unidirectional affair with the line of causation going always from ideology to practice. I am, however, arguing that this is certainly one way it can go as my study did actually start from religion as the independent variable. We still have to ask why people join the groups, of course, but the point here is that after they have joined they are taught by the group how to express their religion implicitly through their presentation of self. The fact that I have seen a large number of people join a group and *then* change their appearance in a quite radical way could be taken to indicate that they were just changing with their converted beliefs – that is that it was the working out of a psychological consistency at the individual level that was being observed. But I don't think so.

I am, in fact, arguing that it is very much a *social* workout; that there is a dialectical process of negotiation that goes on between the group as a whole and the individual members. Changes within the movement do occur and these can reflect changes in relation to the society at large, or (just as in the children's 'whispering' game) variations occur as different members interpret the 'correct' presentation with slightly different emphases, thus shifting the group norm over time. There is, however, always a process at work which blocks the introduction of behaviour that would go too much against the ideology. It is as though what Jacques Monod (1972) has called a teleonomic filter were at work, allowing through those practices that have been thrown up (perhaps by chance) and which can be adapted to the ideological environment, but not allowing through those practices which too blatantly deny it. The individual by him or herself is unlikely to provide as efficient a filter as the group working together. Let me give an illustration.

It was a Marxist meeting in the upstairs room of a London pub. The subject was the role of the scientific worker in the revolution. Most of the participants were research workers or teachers in some institution of higher learning. As usual, there were a lot of jeans and hair. The meeting had just got under way when a man entered and joined the group. He was closely shaven with short-back-and-sides and was wearing not only a clean shirt and tie but also a suit. I sat through the introductory lecture fascinated as he busily scribbled into a spiral notebook. Was he a journalist, I wondered – but surely a journalist would know better than to turn up to a such a meeting looking like a bourgeois, capitalist spy? Perhaps he *was* a bourgeois capitalist spy. I began to feel worried. Some of what the lecturer was saying was pretty hot stuff. Did he know every word he was saying was being taken down and could be used against him once the (Fascist) police state took over? I noticed one or two curious glances in the man's direction but nothing was said, and after the lecture was over the usual discussion on the role of the workers ensued with fervent and intellectual ardour. The man continued to note everything that was said, then suddenly he broke into the discussion. 'I'm sorry I was late', he began in a thick cockney accent. 'I had to go home and clean up after my shift finished.' I listened with astonishment. He was a *real* worker. Moreover, he was, I realized, the first one I had come across at any of the Marxist meetings.

Although it was quite apparent that he shared the Marxist ideology of the other members of the group, the man's presentation of self was completely different – so different, in fact, that I felt pretty certain that he would either feel so uncomfortable that he would not come again or he would acquire a pair of jeans before he put in another appearance. He had made the 'mistake' of assuming he was to identify with 'intellectual/establishment' rather than 'revolutionary/rejector'.

From Outside In

At drama school, we were presented with two theoretical positions that had to be juxtaposed with each other in our preparation for the greater glory of representational creativity. One was the Stanislavski/Method approach – from the inside out; the other was what could perhaps be called a behaviourist approach – from the outside in. To develop the first, we would contemplate deeply on inner feelings and meanings, sublimating ourselves into the inner life of a cornflakes packet if necessary. To develop the second, we would learn to breathe in and exhale on a laugh, sit down gracefully in a crinoline and instantly adopt any dialect or accent demanded of us. Although most of us favoured the first approach, our teachers were wise and they insisted that we learned our technical tricks carefully. Later, while earning my living on the stage, I was profoundly grateful. I found that in order to get 'into' a part quickly the most efficient way I could do it was not to sit down and contemplate what the deep reality of the character was, but to rehearse in the right pair of shoes. That helped me to 'feel' (not just 'present' superficially) more than anything else. The externally applied presentation of self assisted in the creation and confirmation of the character's inner life. I suspect that, as well as differentiating members of a religious or ideological group from non-members, and reaffirming the ideological position of the group, it is possible that group pressure to present oneself in a particular way can actually *increase* and make more meaningful an individual's religious or ideological position.

Tipping off the Sociologist?

Thus far, I have argued that one can detect an implicit religion expressed in the presentation of self and that this is socially negotiated so that it is sufficiently recognizable at an unconscious level to have positive functions in terms of identity, ideological affirmation and reinforcement for both the group and the individual. Might the recognition of this implicit religion also have a positive function for the sociologist?

It has already been indicated how insensitivity to this implicit religion might produce problems for those involved in participant observation, but I would also like to suggest that an awareness of its existence could alert us to notice something we might otherwise have been unaware of. If, for example, the male members of a group cease to wear ties in public, might this be a clue that the movement is moving away from a sectarian towards a more denominational approach to the world?

On the assumption that sociologists – in fact, all scientists – probably learn more from their mistakes than from their routine confirmation of hypotheses, and as this is already a rather anecdotal paper, let me end with an illustration of how, by making a mistake, I became aware of something at a conscious level that I had known only implicitly before. Again, I draw an example from my study of the Unification Church. James Beckford, who was also researching the movement (but from the perspective of those outside rather than inside the movement) and I were both giving papers at a conference in Strasbourg. We were sitting next to each other just before the session was due to start and began to wonder whether any Unificationists would turn up to hear us talk. I looked round the audience. By that stage in my research I felt fairly confident I could tell a Church member from a common-or-garden sociologist of religion. 'There's only one possibility,' I whispered to Jim. 'That man at the end of the third row.' Jim looked and laughed. 'That's the second in command of the *anti*-Moonie organization in France,' he told me.

The point of this story is that although in one way I could not have been more wrong, in another way I was hitting a theoretical nail on the head. I was 'picking up' more than the fact that the man was one of the few non-sociologists in the room. It emerged quite clearly during my research that the values and beliefs of those who are most violently opposed to the Unification Church are often only a very short ideological distance from the Church members themselves. Young people frequently join the Church not because they are *rejecting* their parents' values (as both they and their parents suppose) but because they have internalized them too successfully (Barker 1984). The motivating force that had led the man at the meeting to become involved in an anti-Church organization was that his brother had become a Moonie. Had I been thinking about it (which I must admit I was not) I should not have been surprised to find that I could make such a mistake.

Concluding Remarks

It has been argued that it is possible to observe a consistency between a group's ideological position and the way in which the members of the group 'dress up' or present themselves and adopt certain secondary positions such as attitudes to women or society at large. This I have called their implicit religion.

The consistency is particularly marked when the group ideology either rejects or is rejected by the society as a whole. The consistency can take the form of consistent inconsistency – as in the case of the Modernists where there is inconsistency between ideologies and between practices, but consistency between the ideology of inconsistency and the practice of inconsistency.

The process by which a particular manifestation of implicit religion is adopted is a social one. To dress oneself is not merely to keep oneself protected from the elements – it is to make a statement that evolves into a shared statement through a process of more or less explicit socialization. The practice of this implicit religion functions most markedly with the less socially 'normal' ideologies to identify the group and offer a sense of identity to the individual member; it also functions to reaffirm and strengthen the ideological position of the group. Sensitivity to the expression of the correspondence between social behaviours and religious beliefs might, moreover, alert the sociologist to matters of which he or she might otherwise have remained unaware.

Perhaps this paper could conclude with three not unrelated questions. First, under what situations might one expect an implicit religion to be in tension with an explicit religion? Next, is a case of 'anything goes' actually a case of 'everything goes'? And finally, if the implicit becomes the explicit, might we lose sight of what we had sight of only because we had not sight of it?

Notes

1. This chapter is a slightly adapted version of a chapter of the same title which was first published in Helen Sasson and Derek Diamond (eds), *LSE on Social Science: A Centenary Anthology,* London: LSE Books, 1996: 195–215.

2. There are a number of different concepts that are used in the sociology of religion, such as 'invisible religion', 'common religion', 'customary religion', 'folk religion', 'popular religion', 'civil religion' and 'implicit religion' – all of which describe different aspects of non-official religion. My adoption of 'implicit religion' in this context is due to the insights of Edward Bailey (1997), who was responsible for my original thoughts along these lines when he invited me to give a talk at one of his conferences on the subject.

3. The research was funded by the Nuffield Foundation, to whom I would like to express my gratitude.

References

Bailey, E. (1997), *Implicit Religion in Contemporary Society*, Kampen & Weinheim: Kok Pharos.

Barker, E. (1979a), 'Thus Spake the Scientist: A Comparative Account of the New Priesthood and its Organizational Bases', *The Annual Review of the Social Sciences of Religion,* 3: 79–l03.

—— (1979b), 'In the Beginning: The Battle of Creation Science against Evolutionism' in R. Wallis (ed.), *On the Margins of Science*, Keele: Keele University Press.

—— (1984), *The Making of a Moonie; Brainwashing or Choice?* Oxford: Blackwell. Reprinted by Gregg Revivals, Aldershot, 1993.

—— (1989), *New Religious Movements: A Practical Introduction*, London: HMSO.

Douglas, M. (1966), *Purity and Danger: An Analysis of Conceptions of Pollution and Taboo*, London: Routledge and Kegan Paul.

—— (1970), *Natural Symbols: Explorations in Cosmology*, London: Barrie & Rockliff.

Festinger, L., Rieken, H. and Schachter, S. (1955), *When Prophecy Fails*, Minneapolis: University of Minnesota Press.

Goffman, E. (1959), *The Presentation of Self in Everyday Life*, New York: Doubleday.

Monod, J. (1972), *Chance and Necessity*, London: Collins.

Weber, M. (1949), *The Methodology of the Social Sciences*, translated and edited by E. Shils and H. Finch, New York: Free Press.

3

An 'Informalizing Spurt' in Clothing Regimes: Court Ballet and the Civilizing Process

Norman R. Gabriel

Introduction

The aim of this chapter is refine the model of long-term social processes proposed by Elias (1994) in the *Civilizing Process* by concentrating on one particular development in the early history of ballet, the transition from court to romantic ballet during the eighteenth and nineteenth centuries in France. According to Carter (1998), dance historiography has suffered from a veneer of glamour, myth and mystery: she argues that the focus on the history of stars and the self-promoting mythologization of the performer-choreographer relationship has resulted in a rather rosy perception of dance heritage.

Ballet history has tended to concentrate on individual moments of innovation, where particular women performers have 'rebelled' against restrictive clothing: for example, a number of standard texts (Au 1988) point to the occasion when Marie Camargo (1711–770) raised her skirts in order to perform beaten steps known as cabrioles. Such inquiries into the technical aspects of individual ballet performances can prevent a more adequate understanding of the wider relationship between the evolution of ballet costume and historical changes in clothing. Why, for example, did particular forms of ballet costume, such as the tutu originate at a particular stage of social development and gradually become absorbed into the accepted canon of dress in romantic ballet?

This chapter will move beyond explanations of the history of ballet which are based on an unstructured or fortuitous accumulation of virtuosic performances in order to explain how wider social developments provided a framework for changes in ballet clothing and style that occurred during the eighteenth and nineteenth centuries. Elias (1996) has suggested that particular historical periods should be investigated for the changing balance of formality and informality that effect the regulation of behaviour in society. My main argument is that in a relatively autonomous area of artistic production, there may have occurred an 'informalizing spurt' in the transformation of external restraints into internal compulsions, one that brought about a lessening of the highly restricted clothing styles associated with court ballet. Within this historical context, I will also discuss how changes in ballet clothing enabled performers a greater freedom and individual expression of body movement.

Social Conventions of Court Ballet

Courtly dancing may have begun with the *estampie*, a couple dance favoured by the poet-musicians of the late Middle Ages. Under their influence, male and female dancers, previously dispersed around a communal circle, were reorganised into heterosexual pairs to reflect the Provençal songs of romantic love (Rust 1969). According to Skiles (1998), the movements of courtly dancing were an important component of aristocratic self-fashioning that positioned each person within a social hierarchy. The physical danger derived from warfare under feudalism was redirected from an external foe toward the self, as the subject tried to secure control over his or her body. In a society in which every outward manifestation of a person had special significance, courtiers needed to know how to adjust their features, their words and their movements exactly to the rank of the people they met (Elias 1983).

During the reign of Louis XIV, the early development of ballet was characterized by a measured artificiality of gesture demanded by the social conventions of court life. With the perfect deportment taught by the dance master and suitable clothing chosen for each occasion with taste and skill, French men and women acted out their role with the precision and grace of a minuet (Ribeiro 1995). To maintain their position at the court of Louis XIV, the upper classes spent a large amount of their money on the splendours of formal costume: for women the expensive and lavishly trimmed *grand habit* and for men the *habit à française* was a necessary expenditure in the struggle for status and prestige. Another important instrument in the maintenance of upper-class status was the enactment of sumptuary laws. Finkelstein (1991) and Hunt (1996) have argued that these laws not only regulated the visible appearance of relationships by allowing individuals to identify the power and social position of higher ranks, but also prohibited particular items of dress and ornamentation. For example, Louis XIV granted a few favourite courtiers the wearing of a jerkin similar to his own – blue mire lined in red and embroidered with silver. These privileged courtiers received a warrant authorizing them to wear their jerkin at all times except during periods of deep mourning (Saint-Simon 1874).

In eighteenth-century France, these refinements of impression were an important factor in the cultivation of appearance and gestures that distinguished court ballet from romantic ballet. Bows were often made so frequently in company that walking and standing seem only occasionally to have interrupted them. During this stage in the development of ballet, the steps and movements reflected the increasingly self-imposed restrictions that were placed on the court nobility. The inclination of the body in a bow and the bending of the knees in a curtsy depended on the rank of the person and the solemnity of the occasion. Steps and movements were derived from social dances in the ballroom, which emphasized decorum rather than strength or agility. Ball dances conformed to these social codes – to move impulsively or exuberantly was a breach of etiquette (Cohen 1974). Manuals were devised to explain the rules and intricate steps: because dance protocol reflected the performers' social rank, hosts would research the background of each guest to determine who would open the ball and what order each guest would step out onto the floor. According to Hilton (1981), the procedure for ballroom dances followed an established pattern of a hierarchical society: the highest social rank danced first, beginning in a straight line and moving toward the presence, the person of highest rank seated in the centre at one end of the room. Although the choreographers were professionals, they were primarily employed to teach the nobility: simple steps were arranged to form complex floor patterns, an intricate array of geometrical shapes that formed, dissolved and reformed to display a tantalising variety of designs (Cohen 1974).

Stylised Movements in Restricted Clothing

From this highly imposed structure of self-constraint, distinctive styles for female and male dancers emerged. For ladies, Rameau (1728) stressed the need for modesty and lack of affectation in social demeanour. He believed that their steps should not be bold as the gentlemen – they must walk smoothly so that their skirts did not bob up and down. In performing a bow, a lady had to turn her legs outward and bend, then straighten her knees while lowering and raising her gaze. The court dresses that moulded the female silhouette at costume balls were heavy, uncomfortable and regimented: the huge hoops and large patterns of the dress fabric, often with attendant trimmings, made women appear like 'state beds on castors' (Ribeiro 1995). As a result, women needed lessons from a dancing master in order to learn how to give the little kick required to move the yards of fabric when, after curtsying low several times, they had to retreat backwards from the royal presence without becoming tangled up in their train. John Villiers (1789: 270) noted how ridiculous court dress appeared at Versailles: 'their long trains, as they walked through the courts, were supported by pages, and their monstrous hoops, rising on each side, seemed destined to defend their ears from the never-ending nonsense and impertinence of their beaux'.

Because women's ensembles were primarily designed to impress spectators with their opulence and inventiveness, their range of movement was severely limited. Their costumes consisted of the following characteristics: a closed, very rigid, whale-boned bodice which cut into the upper arms, reinforced in the front by a long steel strip that narrowed the waist, raised the bust and forced the shoulders back. A skirt spread over immense panniers, often with a circumference of more than 3m 60cm. And a train, known as a *bas de robe*, which was hooked to the waist at the back and whose length was proportionate to the rank of its wearer (Delpierre 1997). A picture of one of the eighteenth-century's well-known female dancers, Marie Camargo (1710–1770) reveals that she is wearing the conventional dance dress of the period: her waist is tightly corseted, her sleeves puffed and her skirts and panniers swing out like giant bells. With pinched elegance, the only free parts of her body are her ankles and feet which peep from underneath her skirt (Minden 1996). During her performances in the early eighteenth-century at the Paris Opera, another famous dancer Marie Salle (1707–1756) was so displeased with some of the stilted clothing and tedious aspects of court ballet that she quarrelled with the director (Migel 1972). Dancing the role of the statue, she tried to give greater veracity to Pygmalion (1734) by dressing in simple Greek robes rather than the corset, petticoats and panniers more commonly worn by female dancers. Nevertheless, some of the dancers refused to consider any changes to their elaborate costumes, even when they were incompatible with their roles. As Migel (1972: 20) aptly remarks: 'the taller the coiffures and feather head-dresses, the more voluminous the skirts and panniers, the more glittering with sequins and jewels, the better pleased they were'.

In their short hooped skirts or tonlets male dancers had considerable more freedom to move and display their ornamental virtuosity. In one of the most elevated of the eighteenth-century's three balletic styles – the *genre noble*[1] – distinguished male exponents like Auguste Vestris (1760-1842) brought a supreme elegance and beauty to the stage through their majestic performance of the adagios. Guest (1980) points to the prerequisites of the danseur noble: the solemn elegance and gracefulness of his attitudes and arabesques, together with the added nobility achieved through the slow deliberate preparations and majestic developments of his arms and legs. According to Garafola (1993), no-one embodied more than the danseur noble the courtly origins of ballet, its aristocratic manner and the masculinity of a refined, leisure society. Although these virtuosic jumps and steps became part of the rhythmic flow of the music, they were not considered as important as the mastering of the arm motions. An accomplished dancer was one who could articulate the complex movements of the arms, relating to style, phrasing and nuance (Hilton 1981). Professional dance instruction was considered to be one of the best methods to acquire the social graces necessary for a gentleman: they were expected to dance at least a minuet with good grace, and be well-versed in the etiquette of polite society. Lord Chesterfield gave the following advice to his son:

> Remember that the graceful motions of the arms, the giving your hand, and the putting on and pulling off your hat genteely are the material parts of a gentleman's dancing. But the greatest advantage of dancing well is that it necessarily teaches you to present yourself, to sit, stand, and walk genteely: all of which are of real importance to a man of fashion. (quoted in Hilton, 1981: 50)

Brief Interlude: Ballet d'action

Before I discuss the main differences between court and romantic ballet, it is important to briefly describe a transitional development known as *ballet d'action*, a form of dance that replaced the narrative functions previously taken by poetry or song. Innovative ballet theoreticians like Noverre (1727–1810) argued that ballet should move beyond the formal symmetry and constraints of decorum that had dominated court ballet on the stage of the Paris Opera by developing the dramatic potential and expressive movement of dance. He criticised the wearing of women's panniers and men's abbreviated hoop-skirts, suggesting instead that dancers should be dressed in light fabrics that facilitate ease of movement. And he protested against the use of masks, because he believed that a dancer's facial expressions reinforced gestures and heightened emotions that were being communicated to the audience.

On the eve of the French Revolution, ballet dancers were beginning to benefit from significant changes in theatrical costume: the panniers that women wore were replaced by flowing diaphanous dresses and tunics and men were beginning to wear knee-breeches and stockings. The French actor Talma recalled that one of his predecessors, Henri-Louis Lekain, had tried to make some improvements to the antique dresses worn on stage. But 'the simplicity of it was lost in a profusion of ridiculous embroidery . . . would he have dared to risk naked arms, the antique sandals, hair without powder, long draperies and woollen stuffs?'(Ryan 1825). Talma was referring to his appearance as Proclus in Voltaire's Brutus, performed in November 1790: wearing a short tunic with no breeches underneath, Mademoiselle Vestris reproached him for his indecency. He replied that the Romans never wore such garments. During this period of revolutionary change, important technical innovations in ballet footwear also enhanced the movement of male and female dancers: around 1790, the dancers' heeled shoes were replaced first with a flat-heeled cothorn or open-work sandal, then by a flat-soled glove-fitting slipper worn by men and women. These type of slippers had been worn by circus riders, acrobats and rope dancers for at least a decade earlier, when they did not wear extremely supple leather boots moulded to the foot (Winter 1974).

An 'Informalizing Spurt' in Clothing Regimes

For court-aristocratic upper-classes, conspicuous differences in clothing served an important role as symbols of social membership and exclusion: in the hierarchical society of the Ancien Regime, aristocratic dress performed a socio-political function – self-affirmation for some and subordination to others (Perrot 1994). But in the latter half of the eighteenth-century in France, the rising bourgeoisie began to challenge the dominant clothing codes of the ruling court-aristocracy. In the French Revolution, the elegant clothing styles of the Ancien Regime were overthrown by a convention which declared that each person was 'free to wear such clothing or attire of his sex that he chooses' (Steele 1988). After the dethronement of royal absolutism, the bourgeoisie rejected the multi-coloured splendour of fabrics and finery identified with aristocratic idleness: as an ideal the sumptuously clad aristocrat was supplanted by the gentleman austerely dressed in black or discreetly striped fabrics (Perrot 1994). Described by Flugel (1950) as 'the great renunciation' – a reduction of male sartorial decorativeness which took place at the end of the eighteenth-century – men demonstrated their practical relationship with the commercial world through the sombreness and severity of cut in their clothes. In the abandonment of display and colour, the triumph of black dress embodied the social legitimacy of the male bourgeoisie: clothing reaffirmed modesty, propriety, reserve, and self-control (Perrot 1994). Men's clothing was tailored in an angular, square mode using stiff, sturdy and durable material which allowed a great deal of physical movement (Finkelstein 1991). As men renounced beauty and the pleasures of adornment to become useful providers, they 'gave up their right to all the brighter, gayer, more elaborate, and more varied forms of ornamentation, leaving them entirely to the use of women' (Flugel 1950: 110–11).

Female clothing in the early nineteenth-century was beginning to move towards greater luxury from the politically motivated austerity of the French Revolution (Ribeiro 1995). By the beginning of the 1820s there was a gradual trend towards more decorated costume in France, which made it easier to distinguish between different types of dress. An amalgamation of textures, ornaments and accessories created a frivolous effect that drew attention to specific parts of the body. In the prose devoted to ballerinas, spectators like Gautier, one of the most important romantic French commentators of the nineteenth century, found the paradox of a real woman playing an incorporeal nymph a sensual experience. For him, the main attraction in ballet was the grace and curves in the motion of the dancers' bodies, and the development of flowing lines which were a delight to the eye. In his descriptions of ballerinas, he lingered erotically over the adorned clothes with trimmings of ribbings, lace and pieces of jewellery that concealed and covered their hips, breasts, legs and feet:

> She comes forward in a basquine skirt of pink trimmed with wide flounces of black lace; her skirt, weighted at the hem, fits tightly on the hips: her wasp-like figure is boldly arched back, making the diamond brooch on her bodice sparkle; her leg, smooth as marble, gleams through the fine mesh of her silk stocking; and her small foot, now still, only awaits the signal from the orchestra to burst into action. (Guest, 1980: 152)

One of the main arguments in this chapter is that these developments in romantic ballet can be structurally related to an 'informalizing spurt' which occurred from the 1820s to 1850s, one that may have been connected with a greater leniency in the expression of clothing styles. In opposition to the rigid observation of form which dominated artistic activity in the eighteenth century, a relaxation in clothing codes may have paved the way for the thin floating frocks of Romantic ballet. The fluid lines of the romantic style were created not only by the drifting white tulle skirts, softly puffed sleeves and transparent wings, but also by the less regimented corseting which allowed the dancers to bend more freely in the torso (Minden 1996; Jowitt 1998). Unlike the pre-Revolutionary corset, the 'Ninon' corset that appeared around 1810 was considerably shortened and only slightly stiffened. It was designed to be more hygienic and aesthetic, to strengthen a weak anatomy and enhance its privileged aspects (Perrot 1994).

According to Garafola (1993), the tastes of a new bourgeois public transformed the social relations of ballet from a courtly aristocratic art to an entertainment geared to the marketplace: the danseur noble, with his measured dignity and old-fashioned dress was gradually edged from the limelight by the ballerina. In her long white tutu, starkly simple compared with the ornate costumes of the previous century, the romantic ballerina represented idealized feminine purity and virtue. As a reflection of contemporary fashion, the sylphide costume was 'nothing unusual in its cut or style' (Guest 1980: 117). The development of the bell-shaped skirt was gradual, reaching its maximum circumference in the Second Empire. In *La Sylphide* the ballerina is the ideal but unattainable woman who lures the Scotsman James away from his peasant sweetheart into the misty highlands, where he seeks in vain to tame her evasive flights. This plot introduced to French ballet the symbols of lost love and unrealized dreams; a spirit falls in love with a mortal, epitomizing the romantic quest for the infinite and unattainable (Guest 1980). As ballerinas like Marie Taglioni (1804–1884) reduced the man to the occasional lifter, they rendered more obsolete the classical style of the *dance noble*, with its mannered poses, constricted clothing style and stereotyped smiles. Jules Janin (1832) openly welcomed the response to Taglioni's 'new artistic performance':

> All the danseuses noble, after seeing how she is applauded, have clipped off some of their nobility, just as their ancestors cast off their panniers. They have been using their arms and legs like ordinary mortals, they have even risked splitting their satin corsets by bending their bodies more, while they bend their arms much less since Taglioni. (Guest, 1980: 116)

In her performance of *La Sylphide*, Taglioni was one of the first dancers to show how the pointes could be used to convey an illusion of weightlessness and to express an ethereal spirituality which was romantic (Guest 1980). When she rose on pointe, the female dancer entered the realm of spirit and otherworldly grace (Minden 1996). Weaving the use of pointes into the fabric of dance technique, she gave the ballerina a fairy-like quality. Such leading female dancers rose to the ascendancy through their display of virtuoso dancing: their characters helped to balance the drama and integrate the plot. Expanding physical achievement required a new level of body responsiveness and skill. In the large group classes which dancers attended, training procedures were standardized sequences of exercises to which all bodies had to conform (Foster 1996). The development of intensive training was accelerated by the needs of the romantic choreographers, who required dancers with strength and control to realize their characterizations (Cohen 1974). Albert and Filippo Taglioni devised a syllabus which included new methods of gruelling length that developed the lungs, gave the legs a new-found mastery and prepared the body for complex movements (Guest 1980).

Romantic Ballet: Gendered Styles of Dress?

Au (1988) has drawn attention to two major strands in the development of romantic ballet: first, a sharpened sense of the historical past and an attraction to exotic locales reflected a highly developed trait in Romantic art and literature (see also Guest 1980). Second, the predilection of the mystical and the irrational, as manifested in ballet themes concerned with supernatural, feminine creatures, such as sylphides and water nymphs. For Foster (1996) a principle of distinct vocabularies was developed in romantic ballet: as 'useful accessories', men were expected to guide and support the ballerina in her performance of dainty and complex pointe work. In its choreographic focus, the steps of the female dancer mirrored the tension between mobility and strenuous precariousness. The legs and feet of the ballerina, detached from the rest of the body and sheathed in nylon from hip bone to pointe shoe, required an astonishing straightness, length and flexibility of the hip and thigh muscles. However, Garafola (1993) has argued that this aesthetic and gendered division is misleading. First, because it ignores the position of the female dancer in the social order of ballet – her working-class origins and sexual impropriety as a demi-monde. Young corps dancers were keen to secure wealthy benefactors or husbands: *abonnes*, regular opera subscribers, were their protectors. From their meagre salaries, they had to pay for classes, obtain practice clothes and scheme for advancement (Jowitt 1998). Alberic Second (1844) has described the simple practice costume worn by women:

> their arms are bare, and their waists confined in a tight bodice. A very short, very bouffant skirt made of net or striped muslin reaches to the knees. Their thighs are chastely concealed beneath large calico knickers, impenetrable as a State secret. (Guest 1980: 24)

The demi-monde's social and material existence required her to push everything to excess. She became a decorative status symbol whose function was to flaunt her lover's accumulation of capital (Veblen, 1967). Young female dancers were a source of sexual titillation and even gratification. In *Les Petits Mystères de L'opéra* (1844), Alberic Second's satirical description of the backstage world of the Paris opera, one *petit rat*[2] wears a capacious pocket under her sylph costume into which she packs useful objects including a pack of cards, five or six cigar butts, a squeezed half-lemon, some cheese, a scrap of soap and a necklace. This bulging pocket is supposed to give her a 'Spanish shape', pleasing to the gentlemen in the stalls. The same girl relates how the dancing master Cellarius lures coryphées to come to his place three times a week when they are not performing and partner gentlemen who are learning to waltz – five francs to dance with a chair, ten to dance with a figurante at the opera (Jowitt 1998). Under the new commercial management at the Paris Opera, the elect of its paying public were offered entry to the *Foyer de la Danse*, a large room lined with barres and mirrors just behind the stage. Before and after the performance, it operated as a private seraglio for the commercial exchange in dancers' bodies (Garafola 1993; Guest 1980).

Second, Garafola (1993) has also raised doubt about the gendered division in ballet performance by suggesting that the travesty dancer was a 'troubling third' who challenged the feminine images of romantic ballet. For example, in Gautier's description of Fanny Elssler's performance as a young officer in the ballet *Le Diable Boiteux* (1836), we discover his fascination with the transition between the two sexes:

> Although she is a woman in the full acceptance of the term, the slender elegance of her figure allows her to wear male attire with great success. Just now she was the prettiest girl, and here she is the most charming lad in the world. She is hermaphrodite, able to separate at will the two beauties which are blended in her. (Guest, 1980: 151)

Dressed as a shipboy, sailor, hussar or troubadour, the travesty dancer was designed to eliminate the male dancer as a possible obstacle to sexual license – no male could disrupt the peace of their private harem. Wearing breeches and skin-tight trousers that displayed her shapely legs, slim corseted waist, rounded hips, thighs and buttocks of the era's ideal figure, she invoked the bordello underside of romantic ballet. A prominent feature in the portrayal of licentious public balls was the wearing of trousers by women. One nineteenth-century French print shows a woman getting dressed for the Opera or Carnival Ball: wearing skin-tight black pantaloons, she gazes into the mirror saying, 'I look good' (Steele, 1988). Because trousers and short skirts were associated with sexual impropriety, it became difficult for respectable bourgeois women to adopt either mode of dress. When these associations were not overtly sexual, they tended to be infantile or working class – apart from young girls, the only people seen wearing short skirts were young boys, working-class women and ballet dancers (Steele 1988).

Love in an Intolerable World

I now want to turn to some additional comments made by Garafola about the significance of a particular traverse ballet, *La Volière*. For Gautier one of the advantages of this ballet was the absence of male dancing and the long duet dances of the Elssler sisters, Fanny and Theresa. He states that 'there is nothing more delightful or harmonious to the eye than this dance, which is both rapid and precise' (Guest 1980: 169). According to her, this duet hinted at an ideal attainable only in the realms of art and enacted in the privacy of the imagination. Although ballet's travesty pas de deux gave public form to private fantasy, it ultimately had to be kept within the bounds of decorum. Why? In contrast to the monotony of bourgeois respectability, the world of ballet had become a last asylum: Aschengreen (1974) argues that romantic ballet became an art form that at once both entertained the middle classes and provided a means of escape. As the scope for the manifestation of feeling becomes narrowed to special areas in private life, leisure pursuits provided an imaginary setting which can imitate real-life situations without its dangers and risks (Elias 1994). Bourgeois men, enticed by the deliberately raised skirts and the prolonged exposure of the lower legs, fell in love with beautiful dancers, enduring their punishments of neglect and begging for their rewards of intimacy (Hanna 1988). They enjoyed illicit liaisons with some of the leading members of the female corps of dancers: the Marquis de la Valette, for instance, had two affairs with Pauline Guichard and Pauline Duvernay, both of whom had children by him (Migel 1972). When he was not abroad on diplomatic assignments, the Marquis sat in the *loges infernales*. This seating arrangement of the Paris Opera was hierarchically arranged so that the male members of the exclusive jockey club sat in boxes three deep on either side of the proscenium, watching at eye level the female dancers' legs.

However, even though romantic ballet offered to a mainly bourgeois male audience the prospects for escape in an intolerable world, its ultimate realization was restricted by a more long-term extensive regulation of behaviour. According to Elias (1983), the rising standard of affect-control manifests itself in the postponing of the enjoyment of love and a melancholy satisfaction in painful joys. He argues that these romantic tendencies are symptoms of a major advance in the development of self-constraint through the romantic love ideal. This ideal is usually based upon a passionate emotional bond between an unmarried woman and man that can find fulfilment only in marriage. These relationships are associated with an ethos that requires the subjugation of the lovers to social norms imposed on them by their own consciences, particularly the fidelity of the man to the woman. Did the sylphide really exist, or was she a symbol of the unrealizable aspirations that divided his soul (Foster 1996)?

Aspects of these romantic ideals and attitudes are enacted in the romantic ballet *Giselle*. The personal conflict that Giselle and Albrecht display may evolve from romantic tendencies in dual-front classes.[3] Elias (1983) argues that such conflict is derived not only from the hierarchical distribution of power in society, but also from the self-imposed constraints which form an integral part of an individual's personality. Albrecht, as a representative of court nobility, wishes to retain the advantages and privileges of his superior civilization. But at the same time he wants to discard these negative restrictions by pretending to be a peasant, longing for a lost rural and natural homeland and the relative simplicity of country life. For him, Giselle represents the spontaneity of innocence untainted by the tedious codes of aristocratic civilization. However, the leading couple fail to unite: Giselle realizes the impossibility of achieving union across class or blood lines, and Albrecht suffers the agony of the antagonism between social proprieties and deepest desires. In this conflict of romantic forms of experience, people who seek to escape civilizing pressures through their ideals are unable to do so without undermining the social order which secures their own dominant position:

> The peculiarly romantic light in which this bathes the past, the light of an unrealisable longing, an unattainable ideal, a love that cannot be fulfilled, is the reflection of the conflict . . . of people who cannot destroy the constraints from which they suffer without destroying the foundation and the distinguishing mark of their high social position, what gives their life meaning and value in their own eyes without destroying themselves. (Elias 1983: 223)

Conclusion

This chapter has argued that the historical development of ballet dress can be used to test an important element of Elias's theory about the changing balance of formal and informal behaviour-regulation in a transitional society. In eighteenth-century French court ballet, there was comparatively little distinction between the steps of the ballroom and the stage. Theatrical dances created for court reflected the mannerly and decorous behaviour expected from ladies and gentlemen – nobility, precision, grace and lightness. Court ballet occurred within an illusion of stasis: poses and rests signified the virtue of respectability and conveyed a notion of propriety. Women pulled back against their corsets as they held in their stomachs and lifted in their rib cages (Hanna 1988). What was performed shared the same measured deliberation of structure that was characteristic of court life: every detail in the intensive elaboration of etiquette, ceremony and dress served as an ever-ready instrument of power in the struggle for prestige. Competencies in these fields were not only amusements enjoyed by individuals, but vital necessities of social life (Elias 1983).

However, in a relatively short period after the French Revolution, the stylish certainties of the Ancien Regime were altered. In place of the sumptuary clothing rules of the eighteenth-century, based on an immutable system of privilege and luxury, a new dressing code emerged in the world of professional ability and industry. With the development of the capitalist economy, there was an initial 'democratic' shift in women's dress towards simplicity and cheaper fabrics, and a greater uniformity in the clothing of men was required to elicit a sense of trust and co-operation from prospective clients. Ribeiro (1995) has argued that, by the 1820s a formal-informal dress hierarchy was re-established, even though it was not as complicated as the previous dress codes of the eighteenth-century, nor the one that was to appear by the middle of the nineteenth-century.

During this stage of development, it has been argued that an 'informalizing spurt' occurred in the clothing style of society, one that was closely associated with the sexual elaboration of the relationships between female and male dancers in romantic ballet. In the attempt to refine Elias's general thesis about the emergence of self-restraint in the *Civilizing Process*, I have suggested that it is important to investigate the degree of relaxation in formal dressing codes that were permitted in the erotic art of romantic ballet. Spectators experienced the sensation of existing in, and at the same time, fleeing from the rapidly increasing social and economic change of the Industrial Revolution. With the eroticization of sexual relationships in romantic ballet, the predominantly male recipients and consumers of ballet began to view the aristocratic, stately refinements of male dancing as unmanly. Instead what they desired were performances in costumes that displayed parts of the dancing female body, especially the erotic pre-eminence of their legs (Foster 1996). In her alluring white tutu, the female dancer represents the impossibility of resolving a passionate conflict: an otherworldly creature responsible for the crystallization of genuine desires but who also becomes a conjuration of torment-filled fantasies.

These historical changes in ballet may also be a useful point from which to illustrate another important aspect of Elias's model of the 'civilizing process' which has somewhat been overlooked: the development of a more adequate understanding of how romantic tendencies are related to structural shifts in particular social classes. Some of these tendencies were discussed through the tragic fate of women dancers, and the impossible love between man and sylph in romantic ballets such as *Giselle*. Although the increased armouring of impulses by elevated classes may have reduced their scope for the realization of spontaneous desires, they were still able to find enjoyment in the 'beautiful danger' of romantic ballet. Romantic performances provided an imaginary environment in which sections of the bourgeoisie preserved the privileges of their own 'civilized' culture, without jeopardizing their position of authority.

Notes

1. The two other main styles were the *demi-caractère* and the *comique* (Guest 1980: 19).

2. This term referred to child dancers. Roqueplan (1855) comments (in Guest (1980: 44–6): 'The real *rat* ... is a little girl of between six and fourteen, a ballet pupil, who wears cast-off shoes, faded shawls and soot-coloured hats, who warms herself over smoky oil-lamps, has bread sticking out of her pockets, and begs you for ten *sous* to buy sweets.'

3. These classes are 'exposed to social pressure from above by groups possessing greater power, authority and prestige than themselves, and to pressure from below by groups inferior to them in rank, authority and prestige, but nevertheless playing a considerable role as a power factor in the overall independence of society' (Elias 1983: 262).

References

Aschengreen, E. (1974), 'The Beautiful Danger: Facets of the Romantic Ballet', *Dance Perspectives 58*.

Au, S. (1988), *Ballet and Modern Dance*, London: Thames and Hudson.

Carter, A. (1998), 'Introduction to Part V – Locating dance in history and society,' in A. Carter (ed.), *The Routledge Dance Studies Reader*, London: Routledge.

Cohen, S.J. (ed.) (1974), *Dance as a Theatre Art: Source Readings in Dance History from 1581 to the Present*, London: Harper and Row.

Delpierre, M. (1997), *Dress in France in the Eighteenth Century*, New Haven: Yale University Press.

Elias, N. (1983), *The Court Society*, Oxford: Blackwell.

—— (1993), *Mozart – Portrait of a Genius*, Oxford: Polity.

—— (1994), *The Civilizing Process*, Oxford: Blackwell.

—— (1996), *The Germans – Power Struggles and the Development of Habitus in the Nineteenth and Twentieth Centuries*, Oxford: Polity.

—— and E. Dunning (1986), *Quest for Excitement: Sport and Leisure in the Civilizing Process*, Oxford: Blackwell.

Finkelstein, J. (1991), *The Fashioned Self*, Oxford: Polity.

Flugel, J. (1950), *The Psychology of Clothes*, London: Hogarth Press.

Foster, S.L. (1996), 'The ballerina's phallic pointe,' in S.L. Foster (ed.), *Dancing Knowledge, Culture and Power*, London: Routledge.

Garafola, L. (1993), 'The Travesty Dancer in Nineteenth-Century Ballet,' in L. Ferris (ed.), *Controversies in Cross-Dressing*, London: Routledge.

Guest, I. (1980), *The Romantic Ballet in Paris*, Second Edition, London: Pitman and Sons.

Hanna, J.L. (1988), *Dance, Sex and Gender: Signs of Identity, Dominance, Defiance, and Desire*, Chicago: University of Chicago Press.

Hunt, A. (1996), *Governance of the Consuming Passions: A History of Sumptuary Law,* London: Macmillan.

Jowitt, D. (1998), 'In pursuit of the sylph: ballet in the Romantic period', in A. Carter (ed.), *The Routledge Dance Studies Reader,* London: Routledge.

Hilton, W. (1981), *Dance of Court and Theatre: The French Noble Style 1690–1725,* London: Dance Books.

Mackrell, J. (1997), *Reading Dance,* London: Michael Joseph.

Migel, P. (1972), *The Ballerinas – From the Court of Louis XIV to Pavlova,* New York: Macmillan.

Minden, G. (1996), *A History of Pointe Shoes and Pointe Technique,* Located at http://www.dancer.com/Hist.html.

Noverre, J.G. (1951), *Letters on Dancing and Ballet,* translated by C.W. Beaumont, London: Beaumont. Original 1760.

Perrot, P. (1994), *Fashioning the Bourgeoisie: A History of Clothing in the Nineteenth Century,* New Jersey, Princeton.

Rameau, P. (1728), *The Dancing Master: or, the Art and Mystery of Dancing Explained . . . done from the French of Monsieur Rameau,* by J. Essex, Dancing Master, London: J. Essex and J. Brotherton.

Ribeiro, A. (1995), *The Art of Dress,* New Haven: Yale University Press.

Rust, F. (1969), *Dance in Society,* London: Routledge.

Ryan, R. (ed.) (1825), 'Talma's Reflections on the Theatrical Art', in *Dramatic Table Talk,* London.

Saint-Simon, Louis de Rouvroy, Duc de. (1874), *Memoires,* Paris.

Skiles, H. (1998), *The Politics of Courtly Dancing in Early Modern England,* Amherst: University of Massachusetts.

Steele, V. (1988), *Paris Fashion – A Cultural History,* Oxford: Oxford University Press.

Veblen, T. (1967), *The Theory of the Leisure Class,* New York: Viking Press.

Villiers, J. (1789), *A Tour through Part of France,* London.

Winter, M.H. (1974), *The Pre-Romantic Ballet,* London: Pitman.

4

Land of Hip and Glory: Fashioning the 'Classic' National Body

Alison Goodrum

Introduction

The fashion brand Burberry with its signature check fabric has recently been labelled as the 'spinster of the high-street' (*Independent on Sunday* August 1998: 3). As an iconic British fashion label, such an association has far-reaching implications since this famous Burberry check, as a national symbol, is viewed as representing all that is backward-looking, stuffy and prim. From this, we see that representing 'Britishness' through the medium of clothes is a problematic task. The politics and pluralities of the globalizing high street and the fin-de-siècle catwalk mean that national style is currently experiencing a period of transition. Britain's identity, both in sartorial and political terms, is in flux and this has profound consequences for all brands trading in a British 'look'.

According to a recent report by Demos (Leonard 1997: 13), an independent think-tank involved in strategic political research, British national identity is up for renewal and the fashion industry is poised to play a crucial part in this make-over:

Britain has a new spring in its step. National success in creative industries like music, design and architecture has combined with steady economic growth to dispel much of the introversion and pessimism of recent decades. 'Cool Britannia' sets the pace in everything from food to fashion. Yet around the world Britain continues to be seen as backward-looking, hidebound and aloof. The world's business community ranks Britain's industries as less innovative and committed to quality than our competitors, while the world's tourists view Britain as a worthy – but dull – destination.

Here, amidst the negative tone of global perceptions, British fashion is promoted as a booming forum and as becoming the country's flagship industry (see also for example, *The Times* October 1997: 46; *Independent on Sunday* February: 1998). Such an emphasis on creative industry and on the superficiality that characterizes clothing and style provides an intriguing commentary on the state of the nation. Whilst British national identity has traditionally been built around a powerful Protestant ethic which militates against show and excess (de la Haye 1996), fashion with all of its spectacle and façade is, quite paradoxically, being heralded as the lifeline for a flagging national image. Likewise, a similar tension is found when the aspirational images of 'classic' British labels are juxtaposed against the gathering momentum of street style with its coining of 'Cool Britannia'. These competing portraits of Britain and 'Britishness' call into question the definitive claims to the nation previously made by long-established British labels and their marketing campaigns. Imperious marketing, for example, has frequently assumed 'Britishness' to refer to a vision solely of (the south-east of) England. Thus, in the rapidly mobilizing cap-italist world of the 1990s, what actually makes British fashion *British* is at long last up for reconsideration.

In view of this climate of change, this chapter examines the gendered nature of the national fashion industry in an attempt to problematize longstanding conceptualizations of 'Britishness'. The ways in which our bodies have been employed by iconic British clothing labels to represent feelings of national togetherness are unpacked in order to disrupt hegemonic androcentric accounts of nationhood. In particular, this chapter plugs into the use of masculine dress symbols and discusses the creation of the British country gent in clothing imagery. In dressing the body to achieve a particularly 'British' look, the national fashion industry has been responsible for projecting a partial and heavily gendered version of the nation to audiences not only within the con-fines of the British Isles but also to export audiences overseas. Whilst 'traditional' images of 'Britishness' continue to provide extremely powerful vignettes, the success of overseas trade and fashion export initiatives mean more plural notions of national identity are ever more difficult to ignore. As identities are picked and mixed around the globe, the notion of a static and settled national community pedalled by 'classic' British labels becomes increasingly problematic to sustain. In consequence, the country gent, as an icon of British style in herringbone and tweed, needs to be interrogated for the multi-cultural nation.

(Ad)Dressing the Body

Dress constitutes one of the most basic methods through which we are able to place ourselves and others in the social world. Clothes socialize the body into a cultural being. This socio-cultural production and reproduction of the body contributes to a highly politicized series of definitions through which our individual and collective identities are mapped and ascribed meanings. Therefore the clothed body may be viewed as a cultural product central not only to a sense of self, but also crucial in the creation of conformity, a feeling of shared belonging and in fostering a national identity.

The body, as a site of cultural production and consumption, underpins and characterizes much of the fashion industry and its anti-foundationalist sentiment. Here, the body is considered as a surface to be inscribed upon, transformed and manipulated by various hegemonic and institutional régimes. The signs of late twentieth-century capitalist society are not reflected, but rather discursively produced and contested across the canvas of the body. The body, together with the clothes that we dress it in, become meaningful products and representations. As Corrigan (1997: 152) explains, 'in order to sell commodities such as fashionable clothing, cosmetics, and the like, the body must be seen as something that floats about the world signifying things . . . What matters about the body here is its capacity to act as a sign, as an element in a language: the body here is representation, rather than lived reality.'

Such mechanisms of representation are powerful and pervasive forces in both commodity culture and identity politics. Likewise, the notion of embodiment as representation also forms the touchstone of the contemporary fashion industry in which identities are continually being made and remade via the processes of aestheticization. Lifestyles, including the leisured, sporting way of life associated with the wealthy 'county set', are commodified, in part, through various representations of the clothed body. It is this commodification and the discourses and knowledges infused within it that nominates the fashion industry as a crucial agent in the production of culture and cultural identities. The Burberry check has come to be a true fashion *statement* about the style of the person who dons it. This deliberate inscription of fashionable images with meanings and associations is a characterizing feature of the clothing system since fashion is purpose-built to secure certain effects. Techniques of fashioning the body are a visible form of acculturation in which identities are created, constructed and presented through the habitus of clothing (Bourdieu 1986; Craik 1994; Mauss 1973).

Nowhere are the struggles over identity more evident than in the fashion industry. In looking at the imagery surrounding 'country' style and the 'gentlemanly look' it is evident that the clothed body is peculiarly positioned to commentate on identity politics at a variety of scales from the proximate nature of personal style to transnational debates over images of collective community. Clothing is neither purely functional nor a symbolic, superficial gloss disguising the 'true' nature of the body. Rather, fashion systems are shaped by and, in turn, shape social conduct. As such, the relationship between our bodies, their clothes and the manifestation of identities is a complex matrix of exchanges and interchanges within the social world. Therefore clothing as a cultural sign-post may be characterized as a potent zone of limnality across which the various knowledges of everyday life may be engraved, enforced and contested. This intrinsic ambiguity of the clothed body is commented upon by Wilson (1985: 2–3):

> Clothing marks an unclear boundary ambiguously, and unclear boundaries disturb us . . . If the body with its open orifices is itself dangerously ambiguous, then dress, which is an extension of the body, yet not quite part of it, not only links that body to the social world, but also more clearly separates the two. Dress is the frontier between the self and the notself.

Fashioning the Nation, Fashioning Gender

The emergence of 'lifestyle' as the definitive mode of consumption has profound implications for the body and its cultural representation. The transformation to a post-Fordist era with its flexible production and segmented consumption has led to the 'lifestyling' (du Gay 1997) of everyday goods and activities. Here, specific niche consumer groups can, quite literally, go 'lifestyle shopping' in the pursuit of particular cultural identities with specific dictates on how the body should be coded and performed (Shields 1992). In dressing as a country gentleman, for example, is also to assign ourselves a definite set of social markers commentating on ethnicity, class, sexuality and nationality.

Following this, national identity and more specifically, the cultural pro-motion and propagation of British identity, assumes a contentious role in the designing and styling of the body in a sartorial context. The culturally manu-factured concept of 'Britishness' is a highly marketable phenomenon that emerges repeatedly at the upper end of the ready-to-wear clothing sector. Nationalistic discourses characterize this particular niche of the fashion industry where iconic British clothing brands (for example, Aquascutum, Barbour, Mulberry and Burberry) assume sovereignty over images of the body and the narratives infused within them. It is here, within the aesthetics of the fashion industry, that national identity has become commodified.

The nation itself is a cultural construct located in social memory and popular sentiment. In the clothing industry this 'imagined community of the nation' (Anderson 1991) is bolstered through carefully crafted branding strategies which articulate the character of the nation and define the criteria of collective identity. Nationalism and national identity are built as much on powers of exclusion, than on belonging, solidarity and inclusivity. McClintock (1995: 353) articulates this sentiment when defining the nation as a relationship between the two poles of limitation and legitimization: 'Rather than expressing the flowering into time of the organic essence of a timeless people, nations are contested systems of cultural representation that limit and legitimize peoples' access to the resources of the nation-state.'

In crafting a wearable and therefore actualized British lifestyle, it may be suggested that the clothing industry assumes a vantage point from which to represent the nation in its own image and according to its own agenda. The national clothing industry, with its fondness for the 'country look', is afforded the power of envisioning and embodying the nation. The ideas of national identity that are reproduced and represented through the images of iconic clothing organizations are fundamentally connected to ideas of gender, race and sexuality. Representations of nationhood employed and endorsed by clothing companies throughout their corporate identities present visions of ideal national subjects and citizens. This citizenship defines the ideal relationship between individuals and the state by rigidly delimiting the roles and identities of subjects according to gender and other such variables. In effect, this means that the stability of the nation relies upon very particular gender roles and sexualities and the continual enforcement of these ideals by such cultural protagonists as those found throughout the various strata of the ready-to-wear industry.

Gender is crucial to the discourses of nationalism. Nationalism cannot begin to be understood without first subscribing to a theory of gender power. Cynthia Enloe (in McClintock 1995: 353) remarks that nationalisms have typically sprung from 'masculinised memory, masculinised humiliation and masculinised hope' and all too often within these male nationalisms, the gender difference between women and men serves to symbolically define the limits of national difference and power. This sentiment is captured by many writers (for example, McClintock 1995; Yuval-Davis and Anthias 1989), suggesting all nations depend upon powerful constructions of gender difference which subsequently amount to its sanctioned institutionalization. Nowhere is this gender difference more evident than in the contemporary clothing industry. Just like nationalism itself, fashion is obsessed with gender and the continual defining and redefining of gender boundaries and identities (Wilson 1985). Craik (1994: 44-63) for example suggests that if 'sex is determined by biology, then gender is learned and acquired as a set of social trainings about how female bodies behave . . . Social and sexual identity is lodged in the way the body is worn. Gender – especially femininity – is worn through clothes.' Thus, dress is a powerful weapon of control and supremacy that represents dominant cultural values. Normatively (and problematically) fashion has been viewed as a female domain. The rhetoric of men's fashion is merely a set of denials rejecting fashion and its associated cultural baggage. Craik (1994) identifies a six-strand index which accounts for such male denials of fashion. This index asserts that:

- there is no male fashion
- men dress for fit and comfort rather than style
- women dress men and buy their clothes
- men who dress up are peculiar
- men do not notice clothes
- men are not duped into the pursuit of fads.

This rationale for the fracture between masculine and feminine identities in fashion underscores the reliance on binary reproductions of gender found at the core of the clothing industry. With women, this binarism means their fashion revolves around a particular 'look' to be admired, whilst the male appearance enhances male social roles and positions. Similarly, this 'woman as spectacle' scenario also privileges the male gaze and in doing so, women become objectified and relegated to simple objects of that male gaze. It is this polarity, which is visibly played out in the fashion world and which sanctions and augments gender difference, that is a problematic presence in debates to do with the nation and identity. The ideological investment in the notion of popular unity found throughout representations of 'Britishness' is open to interrogation. Ideas of equal membership together with the narration of the nation in terms of cultural homogeneity defies the imbalances which are the essence of its foundation (Bhabha 1991).

Such binary oppositions are crucial to the maintenance of mainstream perceptions of the nation at a variety of levels. The Cartesian legacy is heavily gendered and dualisms denote systems of domination (Grosz 1989; Longhurst 1997). As Lloyd (1993: 2) observes, 'from the beginnings of philosophical thought, femaleness was symbolically associated with what Reason supposedly left behind – the dark powers of the earth goddesses, immersion in unknown forces associated with mysterious powers'.

The symbolic force of the nation is culturally reinforced through the careful utilization of these dualisms. Whilst the nation is not created through an originary moment or culturally distinct essence, the discourses of naturalness, authenticity and preordained authority which anchor national identity, inculcate such essentialist sentiments. As a result, the nation has come to be constituted through gender-distinct representations and ritualizations and these are perpetuated by the nature of fashion and the fashion industry.

Designing and Delimiting 'Britishness': the Case of 'The Cutting Edge'

The reproduction of 'essential' identities is traceable throughout the fashion industry. Although there is no single British identity per se in clothing, certain 'looks' have been nominated as embodying a sense of 'Britishness' and of authenticity more so than others. In particular, certain players (advertisers, designers, press agents) are appointed as 'cultural intermediaries' and occupy privileged positions with the freedom to identify and delimit national images without question. These cultural intermediaries are responsible for producing a sartorial portrait of the nation which is based on essentialist stigma.

Ideas of nationhood, just like ideas of gender itself, are constituted by the 'naturalizing' of certain emblems. As Butler (1990) asserts, gender is encoded via the repeated stylization of the body and of action within a rigid frame. The rendering of national identity shares a similar post-structural genealogy. Both are produced by repetition. As Sharp (1996: 98) writes, 'like national identity, gendered identity takes on its apparently "natural" presence through the repeated performance of gender norms. In the performance of identity in everyday life, the two identifications converge. The symbols of nationalism are not gender neutral but in enforcing a national norm, they implicitly or explicitly construct a set of gendered norms.'

This repetition and ritualistic commodification of a gendered national identity manufactures and manifests not only a national 'us', but also a national 'them'. Gender is crucial to this exclusionary story. As Cynthia Enloe writes, it is gender that is employed 'to fashion a national community in somebody's, but not everybody's image' (1993: 250). With reference to the fashion world, it is the cultural intermediaries of the clothing system who are liable for inventing these images of 'Britishness'. These images have distinctly bounded and delimited parameters with an assertively androcentric agenda.

A particular example of the parameters to British identity in the fashion world emerges in an exhibition titled 'The Cutting Edge: Fifty Years of British Fashion 1947–1997', held at the Victoria and Albert Museum, London, from March to July, 1997. This exhibition made attempts to encapsulate the development of a distinctive British fashion identity. The following excerpt from the accompanying exhibition catalogue (de la Haye 1996: 11–12) formulates a vision of the nation and in doing so, lays its own claims to 'Britishness':

high fashion has been Britain's most successful visual art form since the Second World War... The Britishness of British fashion determines its inspirational role, sets it apart and establishes its identity. British fashion is peculiar to itself... many facets of British culture would appear to be antipathetic to the idea of high fashion. The powerful Protestant ethic traditionally militates against show and excess . . . This partly explains why the British have never fully recognized, in the way that others have, the commercial potential and cultural cachet of the High-fashion industry . . . Fashion is a mirror of socio-cultural trends, reflecting nuances of the culture from which it emerges. Whether inadvertently absorbed or fully exploited by fashion designers, national identity offers a route to product differentiation and makes good business sense . . . From the 1870s, when Britain's role as the 'workshop of the world' was undermined, the British have increasingly projected a national identity dominated by history and custom . . . Britain's profile was created not by looking to the future, but to its illustrious past: when the present is unstable the past is an obvious refuge . . . the past is reworked and re-presented as the future.

Whilst it has already been established that the symbiotic relationship between bodies, clothes and identities is in constant motion and subject to change, 'The Cutting Edge' exhibition, in its role as an authoritative and empowered 'cultural intermediary', succeeds in countering these relationships. 'The Cutting Edge' exhibition is split into four sub-themes (Fig. 4.1) and goes about pigeon-holing the development of a British fashion identity into discrete topic areas. The tidily compartmentalized themes of, 'Romantic', 'Tailoring', 'Bohemian' and 'Country' place 'Britishness' into manageable boxes. Whilst it is unfair to be critical of categorization per se, these boxes do deny the subtleties of nation-hood, and by extension, reinforce the restrictive, essentialist groupings that succeed in consolidating the insider-outsider dictate of dominant nationalist sentiment.

In addition, the exhibition dislocates and disembodies lived identity and nationalist experience in ways other than this rigid compartmentalizing. The use of mannequins in the display of clothes and accessories throughout the exhibi-tion introduces a further debate on the relationship between fashion and the body and the methods employed for its display and representation. Clothes are activated by wearing them, just as bodies are actualized by the clothes they wear. However, this reciprocity is ignored in such cultural representations as 'The Cutting Edge' exhibition, since there is a 'strangely eerie' quality of clothes on mannequins rather than living bodies (Wilson 1992: 15 in Ash and Wilson 1992). As Wilson (1985: 1) comments: 'clothes are so much part of our living, moving selves that, frozen on display in the mausoleums of culture, they hint at something only half understood, sinister, threatening; the atrophy of the body, and the evanescence of life'.

In this exhibition, the body of the nation is *dis*embodied. The 'inner body' is deemed negligible in preference to the meaningful emblems of nationhood which adorn the aesthetic outer being, (Featherstone 1991). When considering symbols of British identity, the body in its physicality and as corporal reality

Figure 4.1. British sartorial identity is delimited in 'The Cutting Edge' exhibition by the four themes, Romantic, Tailoring, Bohemian, Country (reproduced with kind permission from V&A Picture Library).

is deemed unimportant and undesirable. Thus, 'The Cutting Edge' exhibition instils an idea of 'Britishness' that is a partialized cultural negotiation. This clothed representation of national identity is one of the many traditions that we draw on as part of our 'geographical imagination'. Hence these partial representations have enduring and problematic implications for the way in which we know, order, understand and interpret the world and our individual and collective identities within it.

'Britishness' and 'Blokeyness': Representations of the Burberry Ideology

As intimated in 'The Cutting Edge' exhibition, notions of the 'countryside' have become synonymous with ideas of the nation. Quite paradoxically, in spite of its pioneering industrial past, many determining images of 'Britishness' in the twentieth century have been closely associated with the rural world and with an imaginary 'rural idyll' (Daniels 1993). Burberry is a by-word for a British middle-class style which draws upon the mythical golden age of rural living and cultural values. Hobsbawn and Ranger (1983), Porter (1992) and Samuel and Thompson (1990) have reflected upon the reasons behind this nationalist investment in rurality. They explain that our sense of past evolves not just as a datum or as an innocent snapshot, but rather as the product of cultural negotiation, expressive of present needs. Thus, 'Britishness' and its references to the countryside, are an invention to meet the (fashion world's) challenges of modernity. Recall for example, the excerpt from 'The Cutting Edge' catalogue disclosing 'Britishness' as offering a route to product differentiation and as making good business sense, as well as providing a convenient refuge from the modern world (de la Haye 1996). This passage is testimony to the relationship between rurality and British identity as a carefully constructed reaction, providing reassuring, national vignettes, otherwise coined as 'placed identities for placeless times' (Robins 1991). As Porter (1992: 1) writes: 'those who appeal to bygone ages for the way, the truth and the life, are often those who know least about them. The past thus seems to be up for grabs, a chest of props and togs ready-to-wear in almost any costume drama, available to fulfill all manner of fantasies.'

Many iconic ready-to-wear clothing organizations are intent on investing in this portrait of a particularly rural nation with all of its gender distinctions and hierarchy. Particularly in the post-war period, fashion is among the many media to have reflected and reinforced this special relationship between the British and the countryside. Images of place, together with relations of gender, sexuality, class and ethnicity are central to ideas of nation. As Massey and Jess (1995: 1) argue with reference to the English landscape:

> nowhere else is the landscape so freighted as legacy. Nowhere else does the very term suggest not simply scenery and genres de vie, but quintessentially national virtues . . . when we think of, or imagine cultural identity, we tend to see it in a place, in a setting, as part of an imaginary landscape or 'scene'. We give it a background, we put it in a frame, in order to make sense of it. Can we think of 'Englishness' without seeing, somewhere, in our mind's eye, England's 'green and pleasant land'?

The legacy of feudal ownership which underpinned the British establishment and their associated country estates and leisured lifestyle has come to be a leit-motif of Britishness. This legacy has been consolidated, ritualized and naturalized by the aspirational representations asserted at the elite end of the ready-to-wear clothing industry. In particular, the clothing organization Burberry of London provides a specific example of these elite and aspirational associations via its construction of the British country gent as a recognizable identity achieved through its corporate imagery. Not only is this 'Britishness' heavily gendered but it is also class specific in its depiction of members of the nation as monied, wealthy landowners.

Thomas Burberry opened his clothing business in Hampshire in 1856 to cater for a very specific niche of clientele. Burberry was interested in developing specialist clothes for sportsmen of the leisure classes and aristocracy and set about developing protective, innovative clothing for country sportsmen. Burberry patented his specialist clothes from 1888. By 1900 the company had become so successful that the first Burberry shop opened in the Haymarket in London and currently continues to trade as the company flagship store (de la Haye 1996). Today, Burberry is seen as occupying a niche at the upper end of the ready-to-wear market and alongside all of its aspirational baggage, Burberry, as an inherently British company continues to promote a very biased portrait of the nation. In particular, Caryn Franklin (1996: 17) articulates the androcentric ethos of Burberry by branding this organization as propagating a particularly 'blokey' look. She writes that:

> Burberry export a uniform of the country squire hinting at outdoor pursuits like hunting, shooting and fishing. It's a particularly blokey look, reminiscent of the days of Empire. The female equivalent of this attire is drab and completely lacking in individuality, almost like army uniform with gleaming buttons and natural colouring. The women's styles play a supportive role, lieutenant to the revved-up commanders of the male style.

Burberry promotes itself as an arbiter of British identity in many different ways and on many different levels. Throughout the entire corporate identity, Burberry instructs its clientele on how to live a privileged British country lifestyle. To cite a particular example, the idea of 'belonging' to the nation is played out and performed in a literal sense by the themes of surveillance and of censorship that are infused in the Haymarket store. Here, an overt attempt is made to filter out those clients who are not considered suitable for the Burberry lifestyle. A doorman wearing military-style uniform is stationed at the entrance to the Burberry shop. Via this censorship Burberry invests itself with the power of veto and even further still, with the power of authorship.

Certain groups are afforded a sense of place in this British space, whilst others are branded as 'outsiders'. This censorship directly relates to the constitution of the nation since Burberry has a selective gaze, editing the identity of the nation from a superior standpoint. As such, this attempt at purification echoes the 'destructive gemeinschaft' (Sennett 1986) borne out of the collective personality of the community. The preoccupation with boundaries and exclusion inherent to national identity is also evident at the very threshold of the Burberry corporation.

Burberry's version of nationhood and of who belongs to the nation is deeply invested with gender politics. Just as nineteenth-century department stores were founded on the socially perceived need for appropriately gendered spaces of consumption, the actual spaces of the Burberry organization similarly reflect its own gender ideology (Craik 1994; Domosh in Wrigley and Lowe 1996). The Haymarket store is festooned with boating and cricketing paraphernalia. Hunting trophies and 'Oxford Blue' oars are emblems of success and achievement, encoded with associations of privilege, elitism and of rugged masculinity. When we enter the Haymarket store, we enter a male domain. Military uniforms and battle canvases reinforce the 'traditionally' masculine values of courage, of national pride and of a pluckiness that is inherently British. Burberry construct their London branches as a 'kind of British experience for tourists' (*Independent on Sunday* Magazine 1996) and in extension, the notion of 'imperialist nostalgia' (Rosaldo 1993) is deeply embedded in this portrait of 'Britishness'. Burberry exudes an imperial culture throughout its store and the notion of a golden age of empire is evoked, in part, through the strictly divided gender distinctions manifested in the spatial negotiation of the consumption site itself.

The interior of the Burberry Haymarket store is highly textualized. The aggressively masculine decor of the ground floor is significant in that this is what we first encounter when we enter the store. This is the public and prioritized face of Burberry which succeeds in demoting the ladies' department to a secluded cloister tucked away in the private recesses on the first floor. The feminine is made peripheral. Burberry dictates the feminine to be an afterthought and marginalized in preference to the 'up front' and domineering British Burberry gent. Even further, Burberry's construction of femininity is inscribed throughout the fixtures and fittings of the ladies department. Here, intricate and elegant crystal chandeliers hang from the ceilings whilst paintings of butterflies and flowers invoke notions of beauty and fragility. These images are in direct contrast to the militaristic and imposing landscapes of Burberry man found downstairs and as such, these spatial representations reinforce the gendered fracture that is crucial to essentialist portrayals of the nation.

From this, we begin to see that Burberry sets up an image of the nation operating between the dichotomy of men as active members of the nation and women as passive symbols of the nation. The mind, masculinity, rationality and Sameness have been given priority over the body, femininity, irrationality and Otherness. Burberry's assertion of 'Britishness' is androcentric. Men are seen as the active agents of national modernity according to Burberry. Men are placed in forward thrusting and in enterprising roles to do with imperial projects and of 'pushing back the land' in colonial conquest, (in the Burberry Centenary Exhibition, several display pieces around the Haymarket store caricatured the Burberry gent as, for example, the 'Sportsman'; 'Aviator'; 'Polar Explorer' and even as the 'Country Gentleman' himself). In short, Burberry man is seen as the negation of everything signposted as feminine. Masculinity, then, does not derive from any intrinsic character of men, but from what men are supposedly not (Blomley in Wrigley and Lowe 1996; Segal 1990).

The juxtaposition between male and female representations in Burberry's promotional strategies underscores the assymetric binary logic of nationhood. Mind is privileged over the body, just as men are privileged over women. Whilst men actively construct the nation, women are seen as the authentic body of the nation. Burberry women are passive, inert and backward looking and from this, the subordination of women in the national story begins to emerge. As Kirby (1992: 12–13) writes:

> although it is granted that Man has a body, it is merely as an object that he grasps, penetrates, comprehends and ultimately transcends. As his companion and complement, Woman is the body. She remains stuck in the primeval ooze of Nature's sticky immanence, a victim of the vagaries of her emotions, a creature who can't think straight as a consequence.

Such discourses of neo-imperialism are also refracted in Burberry's promotional literature. Pictures taken from the Burberry Autumn and Winter catalogue, 1996, (Fig. 4.2 and Fig. 4.3) are testimony to the enduring influence of imperial culture and its marketability as a desirable and sought-after identity even at the fin de siècle. The importance of landscape re-emerges as a characterizing feature of 'Britishness' since the landscape tradition inherent to British national identity draws on gender and the body in legitimating masculine dominance. Women's bodies as terrain and as natural, submissive and even exotic landscapes to be mapped and appropriated are common metaphors in nationalist and geographical discourse (for example, Nash 1993; 1996; and Rose 1992; 1993). The gendered logic of the gaze dictates that both the feminized landscape and the female body are portrayed as sites to be mapped, appropriated and colonized. Rose (1993: 98–9) writes that the masculine gaze:

> sees a feminine body which requires interpreting by the cultured knowledgeable look; something to own, and something to give pleasure. The same sense of visual power as well as pleasure is at work as the eye traverses both field and flesh: the masculine gaze is of knowledge and desire.

Figure 4.2 Representations of the Burberry gender ideology – Burberry man, Autumn and Winter catalogue, 1996 (reproduced with kind permission from Burberry of London).

Once again, the fashion industry is amongst many media to cast such a proprietorial gaze over the landscape. Landscape is woman according to Burberry. The power of cultural intermediaries to appropriate the natural world for their own means remains unchallenged and further still, it may be argued that this appropriation and manipulation of the female body contributes to the

Figure 4.3 Representations of the Burberry gender ideology – Burberry woman,
Autumn and Winter catalogue, 1996 (reproduced with kind permission
from Burberry of London).

very crux of the fashion system with its preoccupation with the 'gaze'. The
power of men to stare at women reinforces their objectification and in doing
so the 'monarch-of-all-I-survey' (Pratt 1992) narrative is inscribed across the
(material, cultural, physical and corpo-real) landscape.

These distinctive national and gendered discourses are highlighted in Fig. 4.2 whereby the idea of the Burberry gent as an agent of conquest, authority and empowerment is played out against a wild and feminized rural backdrop. The country gent is symbolized in this image through the clothes that he is dressed in. The once utilitarian country garb comprising water-resistant brogues and hard-wearing tweed has been appropriated by Burberry to evoke a specific way of life. The classical associations embodied through the clothes of the country gent point to a British identity which looks to the past. Meanwhile Fig. 4.3 shows Burberry woman in the security of a domestic setting, outside the home and accompanied by a child. In opposition to masculine characteristics, the Burberry woman lacks individuality with her clothes being black and neutral in colour. In this catalogue pose she is pictured as the symbolic bearer of the nation. However other than playing this supportive role, Burberry woman is not afforded any direct relation to national agency. Thus the gendered fissure of national citizenship is manifested between the pages of Burberry's promotional literature. As such, these sorts of images and these promotional strategies point to a highly exclusive and exclusionary portrait of Britishness emerging. Further still, in endorsing these branding strategies the motives and even the wisdom of endorsing any single national image may be called into question and subjected to critical interrogation.

Mobilising Gender: Reconfiguring Places

It is Felix Driver who poses the question, 'when does the 'age of empire' begin and end?' (Driver 1993: 615). Whilst it is easy to assume that we are living in a *post*-colonial era, the legacy of imperialism still pervades much of the ready-to-wear clothing sector and similarly continues to shape our understanding of 'Britishness' via its heavy investment in the discourses of 'imperial camp' (Driver 1993). The maintenance of this powerful imperial presence throughout the present-day national fashion forum is indicative of the supremacy apportioned to certain national vignettes in preference to others less enduring. For example, whilst there are many British fashion identities, the 'country' look (with its gender narrative) dominates global perceptions of 'Britishness'.

On a global scale, the imperial tropes of the fashion industry are influential in serving up a world view that has been coined as the 'European-dictator model of fashion' (Craik 1994) characterized by its 'trickle-down' effect. In this view, the static, singular, and imperialistic story told by the upper end of the ready-to-wear industry and embodied by the Burberry gent is identified as being determined, dictated and disseminated 'downwards' by a social and a male elite. Therefore the fashion of popular consciousness is revealed as being not only androcentric but also as Eurocentric in design.

The processes of globalization are increasingly an identifying characteristic of the present-day fashion industry. In examining these processes and in viewing the interplay of different cultures inherent to them, the skewed account of the 'Burberry nation' may be posited into a wider, more inclusive frame. A call for this mobilization of national culture is made in the report by Demos (Leonard 1997: 10). Here, the key task in renewing Britain's identity is seen in the emphasis of its place:

> as a hub, an importer and exporter of ideas, goods and services, peoples and cultures; Britain's history as a hybrid nation; our traditions of creativity and non-conformism . . . Together these add up to a new vision of Britain as a global island, uniquely well placed to thrive in the more interconnected world of the next century.

From this, the significance of globalization as a crucial factor in the development of national identity politics begins to emerge.

Globalization manifests itself in many different ways throughout the world of fashion. Braham (1997: 122) states that globalization is extremely relevant to fashion since the clothing system is an exemplar of the 'new international division of labour', the existence of the 'global corporation', and also of the power relationships that depict and delimit fashion identities. Braham goes on to assert that the portrait of standardization frequently conveyed by global practises may be questioned and that equally, the cultural diversity of globalization is continually underestimated. This assertion is important when considering the changing face of fashion. When globalization is explained in terms not of sameness but of hybridity and of local uniqueness, British fashion begins to transcend the Burberry check to become a multitude of fashions.

The interconnectedness of the many fashion systems that are simultaneously jostling for position across the global style arena suggests that rather than conceptualizing fashion identities as bounded and as static in format, we should approach them as fluid and constantly evolving. This idea can be applied directly to the Burberry corporate identity. The notion of 'Britishness' propagated by this organization in the form of the 'country gent' is almost a memorial to the past with its rigidly defined boundaries and singular viewpoint. The version of national identity found here is a relic suspended in time and place and as such thwarts the claims for a mobilization of identity attested by the global fashion scene and in particular, its export practises.

Fashion has no absolute or essential meaning. Rather, fashion might be viewed as operating at many different spatial scales in ways appropriate to particular contexts. Therefore, 'rather than seeking some essential explanation of fashion, we must look for more localised rationales' (Craik 1994:10). In view of this, the inspiration and influences, designs and dictates of fashion do not 'trickle-down' in a linear motion as intimated in the European-dictator model of fashion and endorsed by Burberry in it's masculine dress identity. Instead, (British) fashion is seen as a polycentral system that is historically nuanced and that contains various 'tribes' each borrowing and developing personalities through the convection of cultural identities (Maffesoli 1996). Massey and Jess (1995: 1) write about the changing dynamics precipitated by globalization whereby:

> contacts, chains of command, personal interlinkages and relations of social power and domination are increasingly stretched out around the surface of the planet. And in the midst of this global connectedness, places and cultures are being restructured; on the one hand, previous coherences are being disrupted, old notions of the local place are being interrupted by new connections with a world beyond; on the other, new claims to the – usually exclusive – character of places, and who belongs there, are being made.

Here, the mobility inherent to globalization and to fashion export practises, is made apparent. The picking and mixing of cultures that goes hand in hand with British exports around the globe accounts for the renegotiation of identities. As such the neatly delimited and essentialist portrait of 'Britishness' painted by the clothing industry is more difficult to reconcile as Eurocentric elitism gives way to post-colonial pluralism. The claims to an authentic vision of the nation made by Burberry fails to acknowledge the multitude of other identities and nationalities simultaneously running across the style circuit. As Burberry export 75 per cent of their entire annual production overseas to places as far-flung as Singapore; the USA; Japan and Sweden (*Independent on Sunday* Magazine, 1996), 'Britishness' is translated into a host of local scenarios. Thus, the exchanges between different local cultures inevitably leads to a disruption of long-standing symbols and signs. The British country gent does not exist in isolation and as detached from the globalizing national story.

The rigid definition of 'Britishness' concocted by certain ready-to-wear organizations only gives a snapshot of the nation and its members. In spite of its problems however, this gendered version of the nation is not in need of total dissolution. Indeed, to render the existence of the country gent obsolete would be to deny its cultural kudos, its authority over the collective geographical imagination, and also its commercial prowess and economic profitability. The country gent is a distinct symbol and powerful presence in the fashion industry and offers a fascinating 'take' on national identity politics. Most significantly, an exploration into the discourses that go to make up the 'gentlemanly look' highlights the current 'crisis of representation' in British fashion and the importance of dress in structuring the local and global imagination.

References

Anderson, B. (1991), *Imagined Communities: Reflections on the Origins and Spread of Nationalism,* London: Verso.

Ash, J. and Wilson, E. (eds) (1992), *Chic Thrills: A Fashion Reader,* London: HarperCollins.

Bhabha, H. (1991), *Nation and Narration,* London: Routledge.

Bourdieu, P. (1986), 'The biographical illusion', in *Actes de la Recherche en Sciences Sociales,* pp. 62–72.

Braham, P. (1997), 'Fashion: unpacking a cultural production', in P. du Gay (ed.) *Production of Culture/Cultures of Production: Culture, Media and Identities,* London: Sage.

Butler, J. (1990), *Gender Trouble: Feminism and the Subversion of Identity,* New York: Routledge.

Corrigan, P. (1997), *The Sociology of Consumption,* London: Sage.

Craik, J. (1994), *The Face of Fashion: Cultural Studies in Fashion,* London: Routledge.

Daniels, S. (1993), *Fields of Vision: Landscape Imagery and National Identity in England and the United States,* Cambridge: Polity Press.

de la Haye A. (ed.) (1996), *The Cutting Edge: 50 years of British Fashion,* London, V&A Publications.

Driver, F. (1993), 'Editorial – Imperial camp', *Society and Space,* 11: 615–17.

du Gay, P. (ed.) (1997), *Production of Culture/ Cultures of Production: Culture, Media and Identities,* London: Sage.

Enloe, C. (1993), *The Morning After: Sexual Politics at the End of the Cold War,* Berkeley: University of California Press.

Featherstone, M. (1991), 'The body in consumer culture', in M. Hepworth & B. Turner (eds), *The Body: Social Process and Cultural Theory,* London: Sage.

Franklin, C. (1996), *Franklin on Fashion,* London: HarperCollins.

Grosz, E. (1989), *Sexual Subversions: Three French Feminists,* Sydney: Allen and Unwin.

Hobsbawn, E. & Ranger, T. (eds) (1983), *The Invention of Tradition,* Cambridge: Cambridge University Press.

Kirby, V. (1992), 'Addressing essentialism differently . . . some thoughts on the corporeal', Hamilton: University of Waikato, Dept. of Women's Studies. Occasional Paper Series 4.

Leonard, M. (1997), *Britain: Renewing Our Identity,* London: Demos.

Lloyd, G. (1993), *The Man of Reason: 'Male' and 'Female' in Western Philosophy,* London: Routledge.

Longhurst, R. (1997), '(Dis)embodied geographies', *Progress in Human Geography,* 21 (4): 486–501.

Maffesoli, M. (1996), *The Time of the Tribes: The Decline of Individualism in Mass Society,* London: Sage.

Massey, D. & Jess, P. (eds) (1995), *A Place in the World: Places, Cultures and Globalization,* Oxford and Milton Keynes: Oxford University/Open University Press.

Mauss, M. (1973), 'Techniques of the Body', *Economy and Society,* 2 (1): 70–87.

McClintock, A. (1995), *Imperial Leather: Race, Gender and Sexuality in the Colonial Context,* New York: Routledge.

Nash, C. (1993), 'Embodying the nation: the west of Ireland, landscape and Irish identity', in M. Cronin & B. O'Conner, *Tourism and Ireland: A Critical Analysis,* Cork: Cork University Press.

—— (1996), 'Reclaiming vision: Looking at landscape and the body', *Gender, Place and Culture,* 3(2): 149–69.

Porter, R. (ed.) (1992), *Myths of the English,* Cambridge: Polity Press.

Pratt, M-L. (1992), *Imperial Eyes: Travel Writing and Transculturation,* London: Routledge.

Robins, K. (1991), 'Tradition and Translation: National culture in its global context', in J. Corner & S. Harvey (eds), *Enterprise and Heritage: Crosscurrents of National Culture,* London: Routledge.

Rosaldo, R. (1993), 'Imperialist nostalgia', in *Culture and Truth,* London: Routledge.

Rose, G. (1992), 'Geography as a science of observation: Landscape, the gaze and masculinity', in G. Rose & F. Driver (eds), *Nature and Science: Essays on the History of Geographical Knowledge,* Cheltenham: Historical Geography Research Series.

—— (1993), *Feminism and Geography: The Limits to Geographical Knowledge,* Cambridge: Polity Press.

Samuel, R. & Thompson, P.(eds) (1990), *The Myths We Live By,* London.

Segal, L. (1990) *Slow Motion: Changing Masculinities, Changing Men,* London: Virago.

Sennett, R. (1986), *The Fall of Public Man,* London: Faber & Faber.

Sharp, J. (1996), 'Gendering Nationhood: A feminist engagement with national identity', in N. Duncan (ed.), *Bodyspace: Destabilizing Geographies of Gender and Sexuality,* London: Routledge.

Shields, R. (ed.) (1992), *Lifestyle Shopping: The Subject of Consumption,* London: Routledge.

The *Independent on Sunday* Magazine, 4 February 1996, 'Burberry's'.

The *Independent on Sunday* 'Real Life' Magazine, 9 August 1998: 3 'Born-again Burberry.'

The Times, 27 October 1997, 'British at Forefront of Designer-led Revolution'.

Wilson, E. (1985), *Adorned in Dreams: Fashion and Modernity,* London: Virago.

—— (1992), 'Fashion and the postmodern body' in J. Ash & E. Wilson, *Chic Thrills: A Fashion Reader,* London: HarperCollins.

Wrigley N. & Lowe, M. (eds) (1996), *Retailing, Consumption and Capital: Towards the New Retail Geography,* Essex: Longman.

Yuval-Davis, N. & Anthias, F. (eds) (1989), *Women-Nation-State.* London: Macmillan.

5

Multiple Meanings of the 'Hijab' in Contemporary France

Malcolm D. Brown

Joanne Eicher (1995: 1) points out that: 'Dress is a coded sensory system of non-verbal communication that aids human interaction in space and time.' As such, it is not only a cultural symbol, facilitating the *Erlebnis* ('lived experience') of a given (or chosen) identity, but is also a display, a statement of that identity, and has an important political significance. This undermines the cosy academic division of labour which attributes responsibility for the investigation of dress to cultural studies, while a traditional sociology concentrates on 'more serious issues' of power and resistance. This chapter is written by a sociologist, and shows that the *hijab* (Islamic headscarf) is an item of dress with immense political-sociological importance, as well as coded cultural significance.

More specifically, this chapter problematizes the contemporary debate in France about the wearing of the *hijab,* taken in the French Muslim context here to refer to the headscarf only rather than Islamic dress covering in general (El Guindi 1999), in state schools. As we shall see, much of the French debate about the *hijab* has been premised on its having a single meaning, or code, with the concomitant assumption that there is a simple conflict between French secular republican values on the one hand, and those of Islam, or what is referred to as 'Islamic fundamentalism', on the other. In order to problematize this debate, it is necessary to show that the *hijab* means different things to different people, on all sides of the debate. Some prominent French academics and politicians, for example Michel Wieviorka, Danielle Mitterrand and Lionel Jospin, are cited in this chapter as having associated opposition to the *hijab* with xenophobic reaction or exclusion. Also, some Muslim theologians and leaders, like Soheib Ben Cheikh, the Grand Mufti of Marseilles, have argued that the Qur'anic injunction on women to veil themselves should not be taken literally, and today should be understood as prescribing education for women. Most importantly, some Muslim women and schoolgirls see the *hijab* as liberating and affirmative of their identity, while others refuse to wear it, or wear it reluctantly. In breaking down homogenizing assumptions about Islam, the position of women in Islam, and the relationships between Islam and the West, it becomes possible to understand this issue in a more sophisticated and less Eurocentric way.

As well as using written sources from books, journals and newspapers, this chapter draws on fieldwork in the Lille area of northern France, carried out in 1996 and 1997, which was part of a doctoral research project on the construction of Muslim identities in the United Kingdom and France.[1] Some ethnographic material is presented, and the responses of a few interviewees are cited. The chapter begins with an introduction to the so-called *affaire du foulard* (headscarf affair), followed by a discussion of the twin contexts of relations between Islam and the West, and the significance of the *hijab* in Islam. Then, arguments for and against the *hijab* are presented, before concluding with some comments about the complexity and wider significance of the debate.

The *affaire du foulard*

The *affaire du foulard* first came to prominence in the autumn of 1989, shortly after France had celebrated the bicentenary of the Revolution, when three Muslim schoolgirls in the town of Creil, not far from Paris, were expelled for wearing the *hijab*, and refusing to remove it. In so doing, they were judged to have infringed secular Republican principles, or, more accurately, the principle of *laïcité*, which had been developed from the ideas of the Revolution, and was held to be an important guarantor of religious and civil liberties, and even of democracy itself. The debate had the appearance of dividing France in two: one part of France saw the *hijab* as an attack, either on French values or the universal value of *laïcité*; the other part saw its ban as a negation of those same principles, which implied tolerance, religious liberty, and the welcome of other people's cultures and ideas. It was compared to the Dreyfus affair (see Gaspard and Khosrokhavar 1995: 11), which had polarized France with an even greater intensity, and had highlighted the centrality of religious intolerance in France, but, ironically, the Dreyfus affair was an important factor in the institutionalization of *laïcité*, which was being used against those and other Muslim schoolgirls.

The understanding and application of *laïcité* has been central to this affair. Notwithstanding the etymology of the word (which refers to the laity, as opposed to the clergy), *laïcité* is essentially a juridical principle, and this distinguishes it from secular principles. It dates from the law of 1882, which separated the Catholic Church from public education, the Jules Ferry law of 1905, which separated Church and state, and Article II of the 1958 Constitution: 'France is a Republic, indivisible, *laïque*, democratic and social. Equality of all citizens before the law, without distinction on the grounds of origin, race or religion, is assured. The beliefs of all are respected.' They are respected, but within the framework of *laïcité* as established in 1905. This framework was clear: 'the Republic neither recognizes, pays the salaries of, nor subsidizes any religion or act of worship'. Some people, examples of whom are cited below, judged that the wearing of the *hijab* in school was a request for such recognition, an unacceptable demand that Islam be made an exception to the principle of *laïcité* in the educational institutions of the Republic. The lawmakers of 1882 considered the school to be the starting point for a laicization of the whole state. So it is felt that any delaicization of the school will lead to a delaicization of the Republic, a new obscurantism, and an Islamic invasion of the French body politic.

Anglophone readers of this chapter may be more familiar with the Salman Rushdie affair, the reaction to the publication of his novel *The Satanic Verses*. This can be compared with the *affaire du foulard*, not solely because the two affairs have been perceived as the most important flashpoints in tension between Muslims and British or French societies. Jørgen Nielsen (1995: 158) points out that the education of children is an important field affecting relations between Muslims in the West and the wider society:

> The 'affairs' exposed tensions between ideological secularists in the political and cultural establishments of Europe, the bearers of the culture of the nation state, and those who saw religion as having an active and critical role to play in public life. Above all, issues of the education of children were central: were they to be educated into a national culture, or did parents have the right to determine the nature of their children's education?

One person who I spoke to while doing ethnographic research in France told me, memorably, that '*le foulard, c'est pas un vêtement*' (the headscarf is not an item of clothing). On one level, of course, the *hijab* is an item of clothing, but we can already see that there are several other levels which affect some of the ultimate questions of modernity and citizenship, inter alia questions of religion and secularization, the essence of the nation state, and the autonomy of the family. Readers of this book will not be surprised to discover that an item of dress can possess a remarkable social and political significance.[2] But why the *hijab*? A headscarf can be mainly functional, a means of protecting its wearer from the elements, or it can be a fashion item (or both). In neither case does it serve as a tool in any struggle between religion and secularization, nor does it even possess any religious significance. Other items of religious dress possess some social significance, but they are not usually connected with ultimate questions of modernity and citizenship. There are rarely problems with school pupils in France wearing a crucifix or a yarmulke, for example, and even when there are, these tend to be perceived and addressed as private troubles rather than public issues. In order to understand why the *hijab* is so different, we must consider the history of relations between Islam and the West, and the meaning of the *hijab* in Islam. Then we will be able to understand the French debate.

The Context of Orientalism

The history of relations between Islam and the West has been analyzed in terms of Orientalism since the publication of Edward Said's (1995; first published 1978) book of that name. By Orientalism, it is understood that Islam has been perceived as essentially different from the West, inferior to the West, and homogeneous. Such perceptions have been central to three distinctive types of Orientalism: the academic discipline of Oriental studies; a comprehensive Western discourse, popular and literary; and a system of colonial institutions. I have addressed this issue in more depth elsewhere (Brown 1999, 2000), but there are two points which are particularly germane to the question of why the *hijab* provoked such an intensity of debate in France.

Firstly, Orientalism *was* premised on a stereotype of the Orient as exotic and sensual, exemplified by the European imagination of the Arabian nights, snake charmers, harems and so on. This was particularly the case in French Orientalism, which saw an almost Freudian domination of sexual symbols over Oriental society, in which the Oriental woman was seen as the sensual object par excellence. According to Said, Gérard de Nerval, a French writer and traveller, saw the Orient as a kind of dreamworld, '"*le pays des rêves et de l'illusion*", which, like the veils he sees everywhere in Cairo, conceal a deep, rich fund of feminine sexuality'. Said also notes that this discovery brought out complex responses, even frightening self-discoveries, in the Orientalists (Said 1995: 182, 188).

So there was already something frightening about the 'veil' in the nineteenth century, and that has still not disappeared. However, the sensual stereotype of the Orient and of Muslim society is scarcely recognizable in contemporary discourse. In the late twentieth century, the Orient and the West are closer together, so to speak, so this exoticism is no longer convincing. It has been largely replaced with a discourse about the alleged fanaticism of so-called Muslim 'extremists' and 'fundamentalists'. Thus, the Western stereotype of the Muslim woman shifts from the sensual object to the victim of misogyny. In my research, Muslim interviewees often cited the role of women in this connection, that is, as an example of Western stereotypes of Islam, and only rarely as an illustration of what was perceived to be Western decadence. One interviewee, Ismael,[3] did believe that women were beginning to dominate men – politically, culturally and demographically – and that this was a sign of the end of the world. He argued that men were always tempted in the presence of women due to the work of the *shaitan* (devil) and the seductive power of women themselves. The divine norm, on the other hand, was that men should protect their *own* women.

Others argued that Muslims had given an impression of misogyny, even though it was contrary to Islam. Fatima,[4] like others in France, saw this in terms of the *hijab*, and pointed out that it varied from culture to culture. For example, she argued that women would not usually wear the *hijab* in Senegal, but would in the Maghreb. In France, many women were wearing the *hijab* by choice, not as an act of submission, but as an attempt to escape from Western materialism through a *'retour aux sources'*. Another interviewee, Saïd, was particularly critical:[5]

Muslims give a very bad image of Islam. So, when a French person sees . . . a Muslim, he sees in a mirror, so he doesn't see the image of Islam. When he sees in a mirror, of course, he sees this defiled image, so Islam is sad, this Islam corrupts, this Islam which kills people . . ., this Islam which leaves the woman in a little corner. No, that's not it.

The second point which is particularly relevant to the question of why the *hijab* has provoked such an intensity of debate in France, is that the geographical focus of Orientalist discourse has lost its significance. In other words, the Orient is no longer a geographical area, to the south and east of Europe, because people have migrated from these areas to Western Europe, and have come to form a part of Western society. Colonial control over the Orient is no longer defined geographically, but as control over a group of people, a society, a culture, and a system of values. Muslims in the West have a number of options in responding to this 'internal Orientalism', which have been summarized in three ideal types: assimilation; withdrawal from Western society; and a combined Muslim-Western identity (Brown 1999: 188ff). But these options all reinforce Orientalist stereotypes, because a decision to assimilate can be understood as accepting the superiority of Western culture and values, a decision to withdraw can reinforce a perception of Islam as radically incompatible with Western, 'civilized' values, and a combined identity will be seen as either contradictory and irrational, or a barrier against the West, or an attempt to infiltrate the West. Thus, in some ways, the interaction between Islam and the West pushes the two further apart, creating a negative rather than positive dialectic.

Furthermore, when the decision is taken to assimilate, and the perception that Western culture and values are superior to their 'Muslim' or 'Oriental' equivalents is reinforced, those Muslims who are valued by the West come to be valued according to a perception of what they have in common with the West. Examples range from Muslim academics who have apparently signed up to the Western scientific world view (even though this world view has its roots in Arab Muslim thought), to Muslim traders who sell 'Western' products. Significantly in this context, Muslim women who refuse to wear the *hijab*, or who resist arranged marriages, also fall into this category. What is valued is that they are perceived as being Western. By extension, when women do choose to wear the *hijab*, either as a token of withdrawal or of a combined Muslim-Western identity, this is perceived as a rejection of the West, or even an attack on its values and essence.

The Qur'an and the *Hijab*

When Muslims respond to internal Orientalism by withdrawal from Western society, this entails accepting an exclusion from Western society, forming a world-rejecting *Gemeinschaft*, and carving out a distinctive identity in the West. The *Tablighi Jama'at* has some characteristics which come close to this ideal type: as a movement, it 'addresses itself entirely to Muslims, and makes no attempt to preach to the unconverted', and some members 'who live within the movement rather than in society tend to wear specific dress' (King 1994: 14, 18). The principles as set down by the founder, Muhammad Ilyas, in 1934, seem to fit the withdrawal ideal type quite well, and the integration of dress and the role of women with more obviously religious beliefs and practices is noticeable:

> Article of faith;
> prayer;
> acquisition and dissemination of knowledge;
> adoption of Islamic appearance *and dress*;
> adoption of Islamic ceremonies and rejection of non-Islamic ones;
> *seclusion of women*;
> performance of *nikah* or marriage ceremony in the Islamic manner;
> *adherence to Muslim dress by women*;

non-deviation from Islamic beliefs and non-acceptance of any other
    religion;
protection and preservation of mutual rights;
participation of responsible persons in every meeting and convention;
pledge not to impart secular instruction to children before they have had
    religious learning;
pledge to strive and endeavour for the preaching of religion;
observance of cleanliness;
pledge to protect the dignity and respect of one another (Haq 1972:
    110–11).

Yet there are differences of opinion among Muslims on the obligation, or
otherwise, of Muslim women to wear the *hijab*. The following verses from
the Qur'an may, on the face of it, seem clear:

And say to the believing women that they should lower their gaze and guard their
modesty; that they should not display their beauty and ornaments except what
(must ordinarily) appear thereof; that they should draw their veils over their bosoms
and not display their beauty except to their husbands their fathers their husbands'
fathers their sons their husbands' sons their brothers or their brothers' sons or their
sisters' sons or their women or the slaves whom their right hands possess or male
servants free of physical needs or small children who have no sense of the shame
of sex. (Surah 24: 31)

O Prophet! Tell thy wives and daughters, and the believing women, that they should
cast their outer garments over their persons (when abroad): that is most convenient,
that they should be known (as such) and not molested. (Surah 33: 59)[6]

Yet these verses are interpreted in different ways. Muslims in France, and
indeed worldwide, have different views regarding the *hijab*. It is undoubtedly
true that some have taken a literalist interpretation of these texts, and it
may be true, as Camille Lacoste-Dujardin (1995), an important French writer
on ceremonies, festivals and gender roles in Arab-Muslim societies, and others
have argued, that this interpretation is the one most favoured by Islamist
ideologues. However, there are other interpretations of the texts, which situate
them in the context of broader principles, such as the importance of education.
Following this interpretation, which has been propounded by some Sufi thinkers,
parents would not be justified in allowing their children to be deprived of
education in order to make a point about the *hijab*.[7] Another interpretation,
similar in effect, is that of Soheib Ben Cheikh, the Grand Mufti of Marseilles
(cited in Aziz 1996: 233):

Today, we need to ask ourselves: why did God want to veil women? When we carry out a textual exegesis, I think it necessary to avoid ridiculing God. When He imposed the veil on women, it was with the sole purpose of preserving their dignity and personality according to the means of the time. Today, the way to preserve the dignity and personality of women is no longer the veil, but education.

Interpretations of the Qur'an, as with any sacred text, are based on an assumption about its purpose. Where the Qur'an is seen as a rule book, revealing a number of propositions, a literalist interpretation is logical. Where it is seen in more contextual or even existential terms, God revealing *Himself*, literalist interpretations frequently become untenable.

Arguments Against the *Hijab*

When it comes to the debate in French society about the *hijab*, it is instructive to consider the *affaire du foulard* as an example of *laïcité* in practice, and being contested. It enables us to see why *laïcité* is important to relations between Muslims in France and the rest of French society. While the ban on the *hijab* may appear to verge on racism, and this charge has indeed been made, it has been strongly resented by opponents of the *hijab*, particularly those who see themselves as the defenders of *laïcité*. One of these people, the academic Emmanuel Todd (1995: 32), was asked to comment on the reported opposition of 80 per cent of French people to the *hijab*, and replied:

> It shows, paradoxically and in an unfortunately repressive fashion, what France has always opposed: the lower status of women and endogamy. There's a call there, inept but real, to *mixité* [mixture, integration, co-education]. Looking at it from that angle, opposition to the headscarf is the very opposite of racism.

It is true that opposition to the *hijab* has been widespread, and has sometimes been based on an understanding of the Revolutionary principle of equality. When the *affaire du foulard* returned to media prominence in the autumn of 1994, it was instructive to note that press coverage on the political left and right wings was generally hostile to the *hijab*. Put simply, the right were opposed to what they saw as an attack on French culture and institutions, while the left saw themselves as defending the progressive principle of *laïcité* and, in some cases, equal rights for women. The Catholic press, such as *La Croix*, seemed to be the only prominent dissenters from this view, arguing that the ban on the *hijab* was a denial of religious liberty.

Indeed, some of the self-appointed defenders of *laïcité* have displayed an Islamophobia which has bordered on paranoia, though they are not unique in this respect. Guy Coq (1996: 6), an editor of the French journal *Esprit*, wrote a polemical article in *Libération* in which he referred frequently to the *hijab* as the *voile islamiste* (Islamist veil). In doing so, he confused the *hijab* with the full veil, and *islamique* (Islamic) with *islamiste*, which often has overtones of so-called 'Islamic fundamentalism'. At the stroke of a pen, schoolgirls who wore the *hijab* were aligned with religious extremism, terrorism, and the subjugation of women. Jean-François Monnet (1990: 54) expressed this amalgam more explicitly, stating that 'behind the young girls in headscarves hides the strategy of the Islamists'.

On Coq's use of the term 'veil', this often implies a garment which covers the face, whereas *hijab* usually refers to a garment which covers the top and sides of the head, and the shoulders. While the Arabic word *hijab* does mean curtain, or covering, so 'veil' is a legitimate translation, the connotations are misleading. Having said that, Lacoste-Dujardin (1995) has lent some credibility to Coq's polemic by distinguishing between the Arabic terms for different kinds of veil or headscarf – such as *khimar*, *jilbab* and *hijab* – charging that the latter has been invented and prescribed quite recently by Islamist ideologues. We shall return to this point shortly.

Coq's argument was that the *hijab* was fundamentally anti-republican and inimical to the rights of women, and that the French constitutional court, in upholding the rights of schoolgirls to wear it, were upholding religious liberty at the expense of equality. His polemic ended with a call to legislate against the *hijab* in schools:

The Islamist headscarf is disturbing the educational community deeply . . . If the jurist-ideologues cannot see that it is calling the Republican order into question, they must be shown. When all the classes, where the veil has been imposed by bureaucrats ignorant of pedagogic problems, are unable to function, the Republican state will have to make a clear choice to assert itself. (Coq 1996: 6)

Coq's argument did not go unchallenged, and a letter in *Libération* argued that the attempt to change the law was playing games with xenophobia. However, more expulsions were reported, and the minister for education, François Bayrou, also called for a law against the *hijab*. Debates in the press seemed to turn around the question of whether or not the *hijab* should be illegal, while it was assumed that it was indeed harmful and '*antilaïque*'.[8] One school in the Lille area attempted to define the principle that children should be educated into a national culture (to use Nielsen's distinction which is cited above), and that this formed an important part of democratic, republican principles. The school circulated a paper among its staff, as they had decided not to expel pupils for wearing the *hijab*, but to use persuasion. I was able to obtain a copy of this paper, which is quoted in full in the appendix at the end of this chapter. There are a number of important points which can be made with reference to this document, as they encapsulate the arguments and contradictions in the position taken by opponents of the *hijab*.

Firstly, the document seeks to provide a negation of criticisms made by those in favour of allowing the *hijab* to be worn in state schools, by insisting that opposition to the *hijab* is not a racist or Lepenist act, it does not imply exclusion (unless this is a self-exclusion on the part of the pupils concerned), it does not call any religious beliefs or practices into question, it is not a Qur'anic obligation (on the basis that 'it was not seen in our schools ten years ago'), the education system is not Catholic, and it does not marginalize Islam.

Secondly, the document reflects a particular conception of the Republic, the nation, and *intégration* (which has a similar place in French political discourse as 'race relations' in the United Kingdom), which are common to left-wing opponents of the *hijab*. The Republic means *laïcité*, equality, and respect for the law, which is the same for everyone. The nation means unity and openness to others, and therefore cannot permit fragmentation or the establishment, in any way, of communities which are autonomous or closed. Such communities would cause intolerance, exclusion, ghettoization and confrontation, and it is only the nation which can prevent this. Integration means accepting these principles, believing oneself to be welcomed and equally treated, whatever the reality might seem to be.

Thirdly, it is alleged that there is a stark choice between *laïcité* on the one hand, and exclusion, racism and persecution on the other. The document states: '*Laïcité* even ensures *protection* for religious beliefs, it is a bulwark against exclusion, racism . . . and persecution: in questioning it, one exposes oneself to these dangers.' It should be noted that one does not have to oppose *laïcité* in order to become exposed to these dangers. Even questioning *laïcité* has this effect, and can be identified with a rejection of freedom, though the document does not say whether questioning *laïcité* means questioning the principle, the ideal, or the way in which it has been interpreted in French legal doctrine, and put into practice in French political and civil society, including the state education system.

Fourthly, the document betrays certain perceptions, or misperceptions, of Islam which are common to Orientalist discourse, and which tend to support Said's rather harsh view that the West is only capable of understanding Islam in a demeaning way (see Said 1995: 162–73). I have already mentioned the contention that the 'veil' is not a Qur'anic obligation, on the basis that it was not worn in French state schools ten years before, even though the one-time non-appearance of the 'veil' in French schools does not affect the obligations laid down in the Qur'an, whatever diversity of interpretations exists regarding the relevant verses. In addition, the *hijab* is alleged to be a symbol of sex discrimination, inferiorization, manipulation and imposition by men, the negation of citizenship, and a symbol of religious discrimination against schoolgirls (Muslim or non-Muslim) who do not wear it. The allegation of sex discrimination is unsurprising, given the context of the Orientalist shift to a fanatical stereotype of Islam, but it is interesting that the *hijab* is held to discriminate simultaneously against those who do wear it, and against those who do not.

Arguments For the *Hijab*

It is not surprising that such popular discourses (even though this is a popularization of an important strand in French academic thought) should be problematic, but even Lacoste-Dujardin's argument lacks force, due to her insistence on identifying *the meaning* (singular) of the *hijab*. Thus, she neglects what is demonstrated clearly by Gaspard and Khosrokhavar (1995), that the *hijab* has different meanings for different people. To some it means oppression; to others it means religious devotion, or even liberty. To some it implies sexism; to others it valorizes women. Even where the Arabic distinctions are followed, we find that many Muslim women, whether they wear it or not, regard the *hijab* as more liberal than, for example, the *chador. Chador* is an Iranian term for a black garment which is longer than the *hijab*: it completely hides the hair, face, and even hands. Among French Muslims, the term is sometimes used pejoratively (see Altschull 1995: 46–7).

It may seem that opposition to the *hijab* came from all sections of (secular) French society. However, some have taken a different position, whether for academic, political or legal reasons. The charge of racism has been lent credibility by academic analyses such as that of Bernard Defrance (1996: 78), who cited a legal maxim at the heart of *laïcité* and the Republic: 'No-one can be implicated in an act for which he or she is not responsible, of which he or she is not personally the author.' To punish someone for belonging to a community, or for abiding by the norms of that community, is tantamount to racism. Similarly, Michel Wieviorka's (1995: 126–7) analysis associates opposition to the *hijab* with racism and xenophobia, though he avoids the mistake of conflating these categories, that is, charging that opposition to the *hijab is* racist and xenophobic. He also suggests that the focus on the *hijab* has served to deflect attention from shortcomings and inequalities in the education system. In other words, the whole debate has become a tool of legitimation:

> The more the problem of schooling is experienced ... as one of immigration or Islam, the more one sees, on the one hand, individual behaviours which establish

a de facto segregation and, on the other, resentment on the part of those French people 'born and bred' who do not have the means to take their children out of schools with a high proportion of immigrants. And the more one also sees media and politico-ideological explosions like the 'Islamic headscarf' affair, which betray the presence of fear and anxiety, and sometimes also more or less overt racism or xenophobia. Would it not be desirable for the interest here to be shifted more clearly towards debates on the goals of education, towards conflict and protest around what the schools produce, around teaching methods, academic under-achievement, the aims of training or the autonomy of educational establishments?

Some have argued against the banning of the *hijab* on political grounds. Danielle Mitterrand remonstrated: 'If, today, two hundred years after the Revolution, *laïcité* cannot welcome all religions and forms of expression in France, then there has been a step backwards ... If the veil expresses a religion, we must accept all traditions, whatever they are.' At the time of the first *affaire du foulard* in 1989, Lionel Jospin was Education Minister in the national government. When he was asked in the National Assembly what the head teachers should do, he replied: 'The school cannot exclude because it is made for welcoming.' However, he was strongly opposed within the National Assembly, by the teaching unions, and the silence of his own Prime Minister was interpreted negatively (Gaspard and Khosrokhavar 1995: 21–2).

Nevertheless, the legal position has been settled, in the absence of a change in the law, in favour of the right to wear the *hijab* in state schools. The *Conseil d'Etat* (French constitutional court) ruled, on 10 July 1995, that the wearing of the *hijab* was not in itself an attack on *laïcité*, and therefore did not constitute a sufficient reason to exclude pupils. Exclusion could only be justified in case of an 'ostentatious wearing of religious signs', implying proselytism, or in case of a disordering effect on the school curriculum, such as a refusal to participate in physical education (Durand-Prinborgne 1996: 79-80). However, this is unlikely to please anybody. The ruling of the *Conseil d'Etat* can easily be circumvented by claiming that the *hijab* is being worn in an 'ostentatious' or 'disordering' way, and expulsions have been reported since 1995. In addition, some defenders of *laïcité* have attempted to raise a cry of 'judges against the Republic' (Coq 1995), and to have this decision overturned by the introduction of a law against the *hijab*.

Multiple Meanings of the *Hijab*

This chapter has undoubtedly been more critical of the arguments employed by opponents of the *hijab* than the arguments employed by its supporters. However, I hope there is some balance in this respect, for two reasons. Firstly,

I have argued that the *hijab* is not necessarily a Qur'anic obligation for all Muslims, though it becomes a Qur'anic obligation for some Muslims, in the context of a particular understanding of the purpose of the Qur'an. Secondly, I insist that opposition to the *hijab* is not in itself to be identified with racism – indeed, some people have opposed it in good faith in order to oppose racism and other forms of discrimination – but it is associated with racism in the public sphere. The *hijab* means different things to different people, whether they wear it or not, or, indeed, whether they are Muslims or not.

In making this point, I am expanding on an earlier point, that, to some people, the *hijab* means oppression, while to others, it means religious devotion or liberty; to some it implies sexism, while to others it valorizes women. One Catholic priest in the Lille area told me an anecdote about having arranged a visit to a mosque for some school pupils. One girl asked the Imam why Muslim women had to wear the *hijab*, and he replied that it was to protect women from the male gaze, and to protect men from sexual temptation. The girl replied that she also found some boys attractive, and asked why they did not wear a veil to protect her from temptation. Of course, the Imam had not really been replying to her question, but had given her an already established pat answer, and so he was unable to cope with a challenge to it.

Having said that, the same point is argued by some Muslim women, who find that they are protected by the *hijab*, or that it gives them a certain dignity within the Muslim sub-culture and within the wider French society. *A forteriori*, the *hijab* can thus be seen as a feminist symbol of liberation, providing a secure social space for women which, at least symbolically, is free from male invasion. However, Muslim women who wear the *hijab* rarely express explicit support for feminism, although this is not a universal rule. Any reader who wishes to know more about Muslim feminism would be well referred to the work of Fatima Mernissi (e.g. 1987, 1991), as well as Farid Esack (1997: especially 239–51), whose writing has strongly influenced my own perspective on the study of Islam and its diversity.

For others, the *hijab* is more of an identity statement, and this complicates the debate still further. In Paris, I saw a photograph of a woman on a public beach dressed in a bikini and *hijab*. In this case, it is unlikely that the *hijab* was being worn for religious reasons, otherwise the rest of the body would have also been covered. One interviewee, Naïm,[9] told me that he had seen girls leaving school, wearing the *hijab* and smoking a cigarette. To him, smoking contradicted the Islamic ethos more strongly than failure to wear the *hijab*, though he regarded himself as a 'non-practising' Muslim. When the *hijab* is worn as an identity statement in this way, or perceived as such, opponents have claimed that, since it is not being worn as a religious obligation, it should not be worn at all. However, defenders of the *hijab* have been able to reply that it is not being worn as a religious garment, and therefore in no way contradicts the principle of *laïcité*. On this subject, complexity breeds complexity.

Conclusion

My own view on the subject of the *hijab* in state schools it that it should be permitted, because a ban would have the effect of fulfilling, in part, the agenda of the extreme right in France. On the other hand, Muslim organizations should consider the Qur'anic data and context in more depth, and emphasize that Muslim women and girls should not be forced to wear the *hijab*, nor should they feel obliged to wear it. Freedom of conscience should be recognized, whether the import of this, in individual cases, is the wearing of the *hijab* in state schools or not. However, this view has the limitation that it encapsulates an individualistic view of freedom, with may ultimately be an ethnocentric Western view. Because of this, the issue of Muslim identities in the West is important, as is the observation that the *hijab* is a symbolic or even material affirmation of such identities.

As Muslim identities have often been constructed in opposition, or at least in contrast, to Western identities and values, it must be recognized that an attempt to denigrate Muslim identities, or to suppress the symbols and materials of these identities, has the opposite effect. It strengthens these identities, which in turn has the effect of exacerbating the polarization which already exists between Islam and the West, causing further conflict and misunderstanding. In the end, it becomes impossible for Westerners to appreciate the real value of Islam, and, in a vicious circle, Islam by necessity becomes more authoritarian, and the *hijab* is more likely to be seen as an obligation which must be imposed if necessary, rather than a valid choice which expresses religious devotion or identity. My hope is that Islam and the West can demonstrate that they are capable of mutual dialogue and enrichment, and that this vicious circle can be avoided. But my fear is that we have already entered this vicious circle, and it can no longer be avoided. Instead, we must try to break out, and this will be demanding and painful.

So, a local dispute over a small square of cloth, an apparently unimportant item of clothing, is connected with the macro-social challenges of the present age. There is more to the political sociological significance of dress than meets the eye. This constitutes a challenge for political sociology, and other branches of 'traditional' sociology, who may have preferred to ignore the significance of dress. Not only that, it also constitutes a challenge to the branches of cultural studies which approach the study of dress from a postmodern or semiotic angle. Neither can they ignore the realities of political sociology.

Appendix: School Document Against the *Hijab*

Sketched outline of argument suggested by the study group set up in response to the meeting of Friday 27 September at 5.30 p.m. (on the subject of the Islamic veil or *hijab*).

(This contribution aims to respect the clarity of the principles of the Republic on the one hand, and the effort of openness and persuasion on the other.

It is not unaware of the difficulty which some pupils will have in understanding it; e.g. the notion of *laïcité*.)

The request for the withdrawal of the *hijab* is not, as rumour has it, a racist and Lepenist act. That interpretation (with respect, notably, to our colleague J.T.) completely contradicts its meaning.

It does not express a desire to exclude (apparent paradox to be refuted).

On the contrary, it shows a desire for integration in the national (or civic) community, without distinction on the grounds of sex, religion . . .

Requesting that the *hijab* be removed within the establishment *does not mean demanding that religious convictions be renounced*: the pupils concerned keep their faith, which is not called into question, but respected; they put the veil back on as they leave school, if they so wish; the public sector (and the principle of *laïcité*) preserves freedom of conscience.

The veil is not a Qur'anic obligation, contrary to what may have been said. Remember that it was not seen in our schools ten years ago.

The importance of gestures at the school entrance (leaving inappropriate ostentatious signs behind): *the educational establishment is not a place like any other*; one does not enter it as one enters a shopping mall or a public place, it is important to respect the place and its function, just as one does not enter a mosque or a church or other special places without respect.

(Besides, once again we can deplore the behaviour of certain pupils in the school corridors or playground! to repeat once more . . .)

The Republic (and the public sector) facilitates the equality of all citizens; to that end it makes common laws: the law is the same for everyone; but equality does not entail the absence of diversity: *therefore, co-existence is made possible by respecting the rules. Laïcité* avoids the law of one dominant group or religion, and therefore enables others to exist.

French schools do not come under the aegis of Catholicism, even if their calendar is linked to certain religious festivals. *Laïcité* even ensures *protection* for religious beliefs, it is a bulwark against exclusion, racism (cf. current affairs) and persecution: in questioning it, one exposes oneself to these dangers.

The veil as sex *discrimination* (even though it gives some girls a feeling of value): inferiorization and manipulation by men, negation of their prerogatives as citizens.

(The veil as religious discrimination: with respect to girls who are not veiled, with respect to non-Muslims. Yet the religious field remains on the edge of our prerogatives). => the veil as a tool *of self-exclusion.*

The Republic cannot allow the Nation to break up into communities subject to their own laws, whether they are religious, regionalist or even nationalist or otherwise; such a process leads logically to intolerance, exclusion, ghettoization, confrontation . . .

The pupils concerned must avoid seeing the school as hostile to their confession. *They also are a part of the public sector.* They can and must enter on the same terms as the others and contribute to its success.

Our education system is not indifferent to Muslim civilization: it teaches it (for example, in the second year [for pupils aged approximately 16] history syllabus); it is aware of having inherited the spirit of tolerance displayed by the Muslim world when it was more tolerant and more 'civilized' than the Christian West; equally, it benefits from the classical cultural heritage transmitted and enriched by the same Arab world during the same period of history: scientific knowledge (mathematics, anatomy . . .), philosophy etc . . . : it is because of this that certain Greek and Roman works have been saved from disappearance.

The cultural heritage of the Nation has thus developed through an openness to others.[10]

Notes

1. My thanks go to Professor Robert Miles and Dr Nicole Bourque for their supervision of this project.

2. Another item of 'Muslim' dress which has taken on political significance is the Palestinian *kefiyyeh* (see Seng and Wass 1995: 243).

3. Ismael (pseudonym), male, tea room proprietor, born in Morocco, lives in Fives district of Lille (untaped interview).

4. Fatima (pseudonym), female, nurse, born in France, of Algerian origin, lives in Moulins district of Lille, regards herself as 'non-practising' (two untaped interviews).

5. Saïd (pseudonym), male, imam, also studying *sciences religieuses* at university in Lille, born in Algeria (taped interview).

6. All quotations from the Qur'an are taken from the revised edition of Yusuf Ali's translation, published by the Amana Corporation, Brentwood, Maryland, 1989.

7. I am grateful to Dr Nabil Salem for this information.

8. *Libération*, 12.12.96, p.13; 4.12.96, p.12; 5.12.96, p.6; *La Voix du Nord*, 28.11.96, pp.1, 4, 12.

9. Naïm (pseudonym), male, social worker, born in France, of Algerian origin, lives in Roubaix, 'non-practising' Muslim (untaped interview).

10. Names and locations have been removed from the document to preserve confidentiality.

References

Altschull, E. (1995), *Le voile contre l'école*, Paris: Editions du Seuil.

Aziz, P. (1996), *Le paradoxe de Roubaix*, Paris: Plon.

Brown, M.D. (1999), 'Orientalism and Resistance to Orientalism: Muslim Identities in Contemporary Western Europe', in S. Roseneil and J. Seymour (eds), *Practising Identities: Power and Resistance*, pp. 180–98, London: Macmillan.

—— (2000) 'Conceptualising Racism and Islamophobia', in J. ter Wal and M. Verkuyten (eds), *Comparative Perspectives on Racism*, pp. 73–90, Aldershot: Ashgate.

Coq, G. (1995), 'Des juges contre la République', *Libération*, 11.10.95.

—— (1996), 'Foulard islamique: pour un retour à la loi républicaine', *Libération*, 6.10.96.

Defrance, B. (1996), 'L'apprentissage de la citoyenneté à l'école', *Migrations société*, 8 (46–7): 59–79.

Durand-Prinborgne, C. (1996), *La laïcité*, Paris: Dalloz.

Eicher, J.B. (1995) 'Introduction: Dress as an Expression of Ethnic Identity', in J.B. Eicher (ed.), *Dress and Ethnicity*, pp. 1–5, Oxford: Berg.

El Guindi, F. (1999), *Veil: Modesty, Privacy and Resistance*, Oxford: Berg.

Esack, F. (1997), *Qur'an, liberation and pluralism: an Islamic Perspective on Interreligious Solidarity Against Oppression*, Oxford: Oneworld Publications.

Gaspard, F., and Khosrokhavar, F. (1995), *Le foulard et la République*, Paris: La Découverte.

Godechot, J. (ed.) (1995), *Les constitutions de la France depuis 1789*, Paris: Garnier Flammarion.

Haq, M.A. (1972), *The Faith Movement of Mawlana Muhammad Ilyas*, London: George Allen and Unwin.

King, J. (1994), *Three Asian Associations in Britain*, Monograph in Ethnic Relations No. 8, Coventry: CRER, University of Warwick.

Lacoste-Dujardin, C. (1995), 'Le *hidjâb* en France: un emblème politique', *Hérodote*, 77: 103-18.

Mernissi, F. (1987), *Beyond the Veil: Male-Female Dynamics in Modern Muslim Society*, Bloomington: Indiana University Press.

—— (1991), *Women and Islam: an Historical and Theological Enquiry*, Oxford: Blackwell.

Monnet, J.-F. (1990), 'A Creil, l'origine de «l'affaire des foulards»', *Hérodote*, 56: 45-54.

Nielsen, J.S. (1995), *Muslims in Western Europe*, Edinburgh: Edinburgh University Press.

Said, E.W. (1995), *Orientalism: Western Conceptions of the Orient*, London: Penguin.

Seng, Y.J. and Wass, B. (1995), 'Traditional Palestinian Wedding Dress as a Symbol of Nationalism', in J.B. Eicher (ed.), *Dress and Ethnicity*, pp. 227–54, Oxford: Berg.

Todd, E. (1995), 'Les maghrébins s'intègrent trop vite!', *La Vie*, 19.01.95.

Wieviorka, M. (1995), *The Arena of Racism*, London: Sage Publications.

6

'Gestus' Manifests 'Habitus':
Dress and the Mormon

Douglas J. Davies

Dress is as far from being a neutral phenomenon for members of the Church of Jesus Christ of Latter-day Saints as is life itself. In their publicly visible clothing, in the unseen sacred undergarment of daily life, in the ritual clothes of temple ceremonies and in the dressing of their dead, Mormons express their involvement in what they call 'the plan of salvation'.

To describe Latter-day Saint dress is, inevitably, to engage in at least a double level of analysis where an account of officially explicit Mormon dress codes needs to be complemented by appropriate social scientific analysis. Here we will furnish an account both of what Latter-day Saints wear, and of their own reasons for adopting their clothing, before moving from this descriptive to a more interpretative level of analysis. The theoretical perspective adopted is drawn, primarily, from social anthropology and its understanding of human embodiment. In particular we will employ Pierre Bourdieu's notion of *habitus* as a central feature of our analysis. For him this notion is directly related to the idea of a 'generative principle' (1977: 78). In this way of talking about society it is the generative principle of a culture that influences, directs, and informs the way people behave and the things they do. The generative principle of Mormonism identified for use in this chapter will be expressed in the phrase, commitment and control. Accordingly we may speak of the generative principle of commitment and control underlying diverse aspects of Mormon cultural practice being disclosed in the habitus of dress and the habitus of ritual. Although our account will be limited to selected aspects of dress and to only one example of religious behaviour, that of giving a testimony, this generative principle of control and commitment could be traced very extensively in family life, in organizational behaviour and in details of temple ritual. For brevity's sake no general comment on Mormon history, life and cultural development will be provided (cf. O'Dea 1957; Mauss 1994: 181ff.).

In parenthesis we might add that commitment and control could be criticised as a description of Mormon cultural life precisely because it could also be a description of many religious, political, economic or kinship groups; and that criticism would be valid. Despite that caution, we will contend that this idea of control and commitment cannot be ignored in any descriptive and interpretative account of Mormon life, for, once it is invested with the distinctive doctrinal and philosophical content of Mormonism, it proves to be invaluable in increasing our understanding of the significance of Mormon dress and ritual.

Any realistic account of the nature and function of Mormon dress must also embrace the profounder ideas of embodiment both implicit and explicit within Mormonism, since clothes do not simply hang upon a body in some sort of arbitrary display. One important reason for pressing the point of the interaction of clothing and behaviour lies in the fact that each derives significance from the other, as also from the context within which they relate to each other.

While, for many non-Mormons, there already exists a popular image of Mormon dress, in the form of neatly turned-out pairs of evangelists in suits, it comprises only one facet of Mormon society. The fuller picture involves dimensions that form no part of this popular image. In fact, the most significant aspects of Mormon dress are invisible to the population at large, hidden either by the walls of temples, or else by everyday clothing. To explore these levels we will consider the three broad realms of daily life, of missionary life, and of temple activity as well as the basic fact of the body itself with which we begin.

Embodiment as Dress

The essential base of the Mormon approach to dress begins in what might appear strange to some non-Mormons, in that the body, itself, is a form of dress. According to LDS ideology there existed, eternally, what is called intelligence. This intelligence came to take a form through a birth, brought about by the Heavenly Father in the context of eternity, and resulting in a spirit-child with a spirit-body. This is set within an underlying scheme called the plan of salvation. It involves spirit-children being born to human parents who, thus, afford an opportunity for life in the flesh (McConkie 1966: 748, 750). This state of embodied life is one in which, it is believed, a high degree of opportunity for obedience to God is afforded. Such obedience to God during one's earthly life is paramount, for it echoes the belief in the obedience to God in a pre-existent world. In that world not all were obedient, indeed some fell from divine favour because their lack of it. Being born into a fleshly body is now believed to be an opportunity – itself a distinctive Mormon noun – to prove one's prior obedience even more through one's need to be dressed, cared for, and used in this earthly arena of obedience. In terms of the analytical view of this chapter such obedience is closely linked to commitment. This also reinforces that part of the rationale of Mormon spirituality which argues that one should, in the body, endeavour to 'gain a testimony' of the reality of God, of the Latter-day Saint movement and its prophetic leaders (Davies 1987: 131ff). So it is that the body, itself, is not a neutral entity. Its spirit base comes from eternity and, after this life, it will proceed through a resurrection to become a spirit-body of a higher order.

The Daily World

Daily life within the ideal Mormon institution of the family provides primary care for the body, a care that is deeply rooted in the Mormon institution of what is called 'The Word of Wisdom'. This phrase names section 89 of the LDS sacred text, *The Doctrine and Covenants (D&C)*, which proscribes wine and strong drink, tobacco, and hot drinks, and advocates meat in moderation and then only 'in times of winter, or of cold, or famine' (D&C 89: 1–13). This dietary code has not been uniformly applied within the Church and it was largely only after the demise of plural marriage between 1890-1910 that the Word of Wisdom came more to the fore as a marker of Mormon identity and status. Today it is of considerable significance as a personal sign of identity of the Saint, as well as serving as a more public boundary marker in contexts of contact with non-Mormons (Davies 1996: 35–45).

There is, too, an interplay between the control of diet and the control of dress, for both speak of that ultimate obedience to God, as the Saint would see it, or of that commitment and control of the individual by the group as it might be interpreted more sociologically. Mormons have been self-consciously concerned about dress from the beginning of their Church. Part of the inevitability of this lies in the fact that the Protestant world out of which Mormonism emerged was, itself, much concerned about the style and fashion of clothes that ought or, rather, ought not to preoccupy Christian minds. When the text of the *Doctrine and Covenants* (42: 40) gives to the Saints the command of the Lord, 'let all thy garments be plain, and their beauty the beauty of the work of thine own hands' we can also hear the echo of other early twentieth-century Puritan movements. But, as Grant Underwood suggests, when Brigham Young, the second prophet and leader of the Church, declared that 'every flounce, every gewgaw that is purchased for my family needlessly robs the Church of God' he gave the Saints 'a degree of breathing room in the matter of fashion' by employing the word, 'needlessly' (1993: 100–1). While the Mormon tendency in the later nineteenth-century was not towards any extreme simplicity the Church always possessed a variety of texts that called it away from styles of showy display. Early in the Mormon sacred text, *The Book of Mormon*, there is an account of 'the church of the devil' in which 'gold, and silver, and silks and scarlets, and the fine-twined linen, and the precious clothing' bedeck the wicked (1 Nephi 13: 7–8). These are, obviously, tendencies to be avoided by Latter-day Saints.

So it is that the key feature of quotidian dress involves relative simplicity, cleanliness and propriety of clothing. Not least in styles that clearly mark those male and female differences that frame Mormon ideology in which the man-woman relationship is of crucial import as far as the eternal dimensions of existence and of salvation are concerned. It is the husband and wife pair that furnishes the basis for a family that will exist after death in an ever-increasing family kingdom of eternally progressing individuals bonded together for the purpose of attaining 'exaltation' a state that represents the real LDS category of salvation. A temple ritual of 'sealing' effects this bond between husband and wife and between them and their children. The sex difference is also marked in ordinary clothes. Women attending church or relatively formal gatherings will, for example, hardly ever wear trousers though, where the normal culture does so, some will do so for leisure, home or work-wear. At church meetings the male-female distinction is clear as the men, very largely, wear darker coloured suits, shirts and relatively sober ties, while the women wear rather longer than shorter skirts. Individuals do not wear anything that definitely differentiates them from other same-sex congregation members. There are also separate meetings for the two sexes at specific times during the Sunday morning fixed period of religious services.

For weddings the standard dress tends to follow a fuller-styled white dress for women and a formal suit for men. When weddings take place in the temple, as ideally they should, the men wear white tuxedo-style formal suits. White is the colour of other temple wear, too, hence the preference for white wedding clothes, whether for women or men. Irrespective of that, the gender difference between bride and groom is firmly established. In temples special 'brides' rooms' are set aside for the dressing of the bride prior to the ceremony.

In any context the notion of modesty remains important and low-cut dresses or blouses will be avoided. So, too, with overly tight clothing, whether for men or women. A good example of this can be found in the Church-managed flagship educational institution, Brigham Young University at Provo in Utah, whose honour code includes explicit rules of dress for male and for female students. This is related to the underlying Latter-day Saint ideal of sexual activity being restricted to the marriage bond. Dress should reflect this sense of physical control as it does, typically, in the figure of the missionary.

But it is the family that stands as the focal arena of Mormon embodiment. Not only is the family the prime context for the proper practice of sexuality and of the Word of Wisdom but its role in caring for family members also extends into care for the dead. Beginning with genealogical research to establish the family lineage it leads into that distinctive pattern of Mormon behaviour of vicarious baptism. Once details of dead ancestors are obtained, a living relative may undergo a physical rite on their behalf. It is as though the body of the living replaces the body of the dead in the crucial rites of the temple without which the ultimate salvation of the dead cannot be achieved. As to the physical bodies of the dead they, too, at death remain within a scheme of Mormon bodily control in that they are prepared for their funeral by other Latter-day Saints and are dressed in part of their temple clothing.

The Missionary

As already mentioned, the figure of the Mormon missionary has, for decades, presented a readily identifiable representative of the Church of Jesus Christ of Latter-day Saints. Descriptions such as 'clean-cut' describe the two young men, and it is more often young men, who serve as official missionaries of their Church for a two-year period during their late teens and early twenties. Their short and well-groomed hair complements a white shirt with dark tie, suit and shoes. This, then, completes the public image of the Mormon missionary.

In terms of dress the missionary is not out of place at ordinary Mormon Church meetings. In Great Britain and many North American contexts many men are likely to wear dark suits, shirt and tie and dark shoes. Active socialization into dress for men begins at approximately the age of twelve when boys are ordained into the first grade of the Aaronic, or lower, Priesthood. Already they are acquiring an implicit symbolic understanding of commitment and control through the dress code of congregational life. By the time they attain their very late teens or early twenties they are, normally, ordained into the Melchizedek, or higher, Priesthood. Young men are always ordained into the Melchizedek Priesthood prior to serving their mission when they become official and idealized representatives of the Church of Jesus Christ of Latter-day Saints. Melchizedek priests hold the title of Elder. At the church meeting, then, the missionary is part of the well-ordered group within which no individuals stand out from the others because of their distinctive dress.

In the streets of many towns and cities, however, this is not the case. In the cross-section of a public world the missionary is a relatively highly visible person because of his dress. One important element of this dark-suited pair, or in sunnier climates of short-sleeved and white shirted individuals, is the fact of the plastic label giving their surname preceded by the formal title 'Elder'. It also carries the full and official name of the Church. So it is that we encounter, for example, Elder Smith or Elder Sorenson of the Church of Jesus Christ of Latter-day Saints. It is as such that they visit homes in door-to-door visiting or meet people in the street as part of their general evangelistic approach to non-members of their church.

Neither the title of 'Elder', nor the name of the Church on the name badge should be ignored as constituent elements of dress and identity. Within the Church at large, very few are formally addressed by the title of 'Elder'. In fact, apart from missionaries, the term tends to be restricted to the most senior of the central leadership figures. Men are often designated as 'The Brethren'. The visible use of this title in the labelled figures of missionaries reflects the fact that these are men who, for a period, carry a distinctive responsibility within the Church. Just as 'The Brethren' stand as Elders at the centre of Church organization so the missionary Elders stand at the evangelistic cutting edge of the Church. Indeed, missionaries are viewed as distinctive and significant people within Mormonism; they are respected and helped by members of the congregation even though their inexperience may, occasionally, be noted with genial judgement. Symbolically speaking they stand as one ideal type of Latter-day Saint believer, one who is seeking to spread the message to outsiders whilst demonstrating his own obedience and developing his own testimony. Both the notions of obedience and testimony are significantly Mormon as we saw above.

And this is where the name of the Church on the name badges of the missionaries becomes important. The name of The Church of Jesus Christ of Latter-day Saints is far from an arbitrary and random name. Originally, from 1830, the Church was known to members as The Church of the Latter-day Saints, or the Church of Christ. From 1838 the current title of The Church of Jesus Christ of Latter-day Saints became its prime designation (Porter 1992: 276ff.) The significant fact, however, is that this Church was believed, from its inception, to be the one true vehicle of divine revelation and salvation upon earth. For the young founding prophet, Joseph Smith, the single great religious issue concerned which church was true? From his doubts and confusion over the competing claims of many churches this group was the prophetic outcome. Its name designates its singularity as a means of salvation. From this perspective the name enshrines the history of the Church's birth. Each Latter-day Saint local meeting house, church, chapel or Stake House, as they are often called, bears the name proudly on its outer, public, wall. It is this name, as a written symbol, rather than a cross or any other iconic representation, that marks the Mormon meeting place. And it is that same name that publicly marks the missionary name label and completes his dress. It is, of course, quite unlikely that a passer-by will be familiar with this historical state of affairs, indeed, it may be only partially apparent to the missionary himself, but the fact of the name as a mark of identity will be deeply significant to the missionary.

Temples and Dress

Mormonism established the body as the key ritual focus of life in a much more accentuated way than other Western forms of Christianity. Joseph Smith, the founding Prophet, officially launched Mormonism as a religious denomination in 1830, the same year as the publication of the Book of Mormon. Up to and including this point the body, as such, is of little concern to Mormons. Primacy of place is given to doctrines and belief about Church order and the forthcoming Advent of Christ. It was only from the mid-1830s that direct ritual addressed itself to the body as a ritual medium of and for ideology. So it was that foot-washing and the anointing of the body with scented oils began in 1836, during the Kirtland period of the group. It was a period of intense religious experience involving visions and glossolalia and early rites of endowment, as they came to be called. These were very much developed after Joseph Smith was initiated as a Freemason in 1842, a fact that influenced the form taken by newly developed rites and by some of the clothing associated with them (Buerger 1994: 87ff). In 1843 Smith also advocated plural marriage as part of the belief that persons not only gain a guaranteed eternal life through the rites but that the rite of sealing woman to man ensures that marriage is also an eternal phenomenon. Not only so, but additional rites of anointing men and women were also to make them become kings and queens, gods and goddesses in the afterlife.

The Mormon body was now the focus of ritual activity of eternal consequence, and temples gained an increasing status as the sacred spaces within which the majority of these rites took place. So much so that from the close of the nineteenth century it is impossible to analyse Mormon bodies without analysing Mormon temples. Though it cannot be fully pursued here, the Mormon architecture of temples is an integral part of Mormon embodiment. What must be portrayed, however, is the link between body and temple that is forged, in a physical way, by the temple garment worn by committed Saints under their ordinary social dress.

The temple garment, a single item combining vest and underpants with abbreviated sleeves and legs is, both literally and symbolically, the Mormon foundation garment. In symbolic terms it is multivocal. It links contemporary

Mormon life with Mormon history as the garment, which came to distinguish the rise of newly revealed rites. In wearing it, Saints are reminded of the key temple ritual through which they are taught the more esoteric aspects of the religion, those which distinguish Mormonism from other forms of Christianity. In these rites the clothing of the ordinary life-world is abandoned for special temple clothing, basic to which is the temple garment. It is, initially bestowed upon the individual in the ritual associated with washing and anointing, of making covenants with God, and of receiving promises from God concerning the ultimate destiny of salvation. That ritual is, itself, only accessible after gaining a special recommendation from a local church leader who validates the good standing of the individual Saint. An interview that ensures that the individual assents to church doctrine and leaders, follows a morally acceptable life, and pays a tithed sum of money to the church. At the end of the temple rite, the other temple clothing is left within the temple, but the temple undergarment continues to be worn under the ordinary clothing of the life-world, a garment that is now saturated with these religious meanings.

To wear the garment is to announce to the self, and to family members, the personal commitment of the individual to the Mormon Church while, concurrently, it contributes to the personal sense of self-identity. It marks the wearer as a temple-Mormon. From an analytical perspective, it also links the wearer to the past in two ways, one historical and one mythical. Historical in that it reflects the divine restoration of truth through ritual as given to the Church by Joseph Smith its founding prophet; mythological in that the garment is said to be the same as that worn by Adam and Eve in the garden of Eden. Symbolic marks placed upon the garment include a strong echo of the compass and dividers that display the close link of early Mormonism and Freemasonry, though this interpretation will not be apparent to most ordinary Latter-day Saints.

The history of the garment itself involves a depth of folk-tradition reflecting its significance as an identity marker for, at various times, it has been thought to protect from danger, whether the perils of war or the hazards of childbirth. Another Mormon garment, a robe worn in temple rites of endowment has also been seen by some as borrowed by those late nineteenth-century native American groups that engaged in Ghost Dance millenarian movements. These ghost-shirts were also invested with much symbolic power, even to the point of being viewed as bulletproof (Turner 1982: 214). The various temple garments have, themselves, undergone a series of design changes in their evolution into and through the twentieth century that cannot be detailed here (cf. Alexander 1986: 301ff.).

Dressing for Eternity

Although Mormons categorize reality into the pre-existence, current existence, and post-mortem existence, these periods are set within the broader category of time and eternity. These divisions of time and eternity are of fundamental importance to Mormonism as a framework of the body and its identity. As already indicated, the Mormon belief in the pre-existence of the human spirit continues with the belief that the body furnishes a home for that spirit until death, when the spirit leaves until such time as it is reunited with the resurrection body at the day when Mormons are resurrected to be with Christ. In theological terms the Mormon body is a temple, not primarily of the Holy Spirit, but of the human spirit of that particular individual. But, both because that body possesses an eternal future and because earthly life is a kind of testing of obedience, it merits care through strong control of the body.

At death the body is dressed in appropriate temple clothing, including a ritual apron before being buried, and burial is the strongly preferred form of funeral, in a grave that is specially dedicated for the task. The garments placed on the dead are associated with the ritual of endowment at the temple which is heavy with symbolism of the conquest of death (Davies 1987: 101ff.). In the endowment rites vows and covenants are established between human beings and God. Truths are learned through verbal statement and physical activity that will enable the individual to pass through death and through future realms of eternal life. In areas of high Mormon population there will be LDS funeral directors able to carry out this formal dressing of the corpse. In other parts of the world, Church members will undertake this work as an act of good-will towards the deceased and also because non-members of the Church should not, normally, be allowed to see the funeral clothing.

The sacredness of all temple garments, as of the rites themselves, is a crucial feature for the Saints. They do not like critics talking about the secret nature of rites or clothing; Mormons prefer to affirm their sacredness. This is a significant issue for theoretical analysis since the adjective 'secret' refers to institutions and actions, which are precisely what the critic often wishes to disclose to the world at large. For the Saint, by contrast, the 'sacred' nature of these phenomena refers more to their personal significance, to the part played by rite and dress in the framing of personal and corporate identity.

The temple is a world of its own. In classical terms of the history of religions it is an *axis mundi,* the place where heaven and earth meet or, in Mormon terminology, where time and eternity intersect. This is symbolized through dress. On coming to the temple, after due examination by the local church leader who tests the strength of institutional affiliation and moral standing of the applicant, members undress and put aside the clothing of daily life. They dress in special, white, temple clothing, and this can be from shoes through skirts and trousers to blouses and shirts, to gloves and hats, as well as with special temple robes. The participants thus become, in a sense, different people for a while. Attention has already been drawn to the white of the temple clothes compared with the dark colours of clothes worn to ordinary Church meetings. This distinction matches the deep symbolic difference in Mormonism between heaven and earth, eternity and time, the otherworld and this world.

In a similar symbolic vein the body of the everyday world is ritually prepared for its involvement with the sacred domain. During the initial endowment ritual parts of the body are washed and anointed with oil as a form of consecrating them for their respective functions. The special temple garment is given, and this will be worn at all times, and will leave the temple as an undergarment, once normal dress is reassumed. Other temple robes and the apron are not worn outside the temple. Temples possess extensive changing rooms for privacy, as well as rooms for washing and anointing the body and, in more utilitarian mode, extensive facilities for washing the clothing used in the temple rites. A laundry area is a necessary complement for ritual activity involving many items of clothing.

It is these temple rites that include baptism for the dead, the sealing of man and wife and children for all eternity, and the conferring of endowments, that establish Mormonism as the distinctive religious tradition that it is. It is a religion in which all ordinary members are expected to participate in temple rites and, thus, to wear distinctive dress. To be an active temple Mormon is to wear elaborate symbolic dress in the temple, in rites that seek to prepare human beings for their transformation into a divine identity, especially after death, and also to wear the undergarment in all daily activities. Mormons who have not undertaken to obtain their endowments and, accordingly, to participate in the fuller range of temple rites that foster their own and facilitate the salvation of other family members, do not share in the full symbolic dress of their Church. Of all Christian traditions, whether Catholic, Orthodox, Protestant or Anglican in origin, Mormonism is the only tradition to have salvation directly related to dress.

Interpreting Dress

These various ritual activities based on dress need some form of theoretical interpretation that goes beyond that of simple description. Here we adopt a two-fold approach, both elements of which focus on identity with one, already outlined above, emphasizing styles of embodiment of the individual within the group and drawing on the notions of *habitus* and *gestus,* and the other stressing forms of social control of the individual.

Marcel Mauss's essay on 'Body Techniques' of 1934 afforded one firm starting point for that concern with the body and its socialisation that has multiplied in studies focused upon embodiment. Mauss specifically, and pragmatically, isolated the Latin word *habitus* to describe socially learned patterns of bodily activity reflected in, for example, eating, walking, swimming and the like (Mauss 1979: 101). Mauss was, very obviously, engaged in the most preliminary of sketches of human deportment and of the differing cultural styles of many sorts of cultural activity, for example, the way French and British soldiers differed in the way they used spades. Indeed, he was only engaged in a note-form approach to the great variety of human acts that could be subjected to systematic description and classification. Here we draw on him only as one who drew attention to the idea of *habitus* as a means of studying human activity

When Pierre Bourdieu took up the notion of *habitus* some forty or so years later it was in an expanded form that described a 'generative principle', a source that could 'regulate improvisations' of cultural practice in appropriate ways (1977: 78). This and other work has done a great deal to explore embodiment as a process of behavioural and dispositional acquisition of value, mood and affect, as a means of social control and in terms of identity formation.

Another valuable contribution to embodiment in the sociology of religion lies in Tyson, Peacock and Patterson's (1988) analysis of the notion of *gesture* in their significant theoretical and descriptive volume *Diversities of Gifts,* a collection of ethnographic studies focused on various independent Protestant churches located in North Carolina. They emphasize gesture as a theoretical notion precisely because it had 'no standing in the conventions' of basic social scientific disciplines (1988: 14). They describe gestures within speech, singing, bodily movements and dancing as a means by which beliefs and rituals unfold both for the participation of devotees and for scholarly analysis. Also in 1988, though independently as far as I can see, Talal Asad's seminal essay on the 'The Concept of Ritual' (1988) also adopted the notion of gesture in its Latin form of *gestus.* Classically, in Latin, *gestus* referred both to the carriage of the body, its posture and motion, and also to the more artificial posture of actors. It also employed *habitus* to describe forms of attire. This similarity of meaning between *gestus* and *habitus* is reflected in these anthropological authors and their approach to the significance of bodily activity.

Asad utilised *gestus* in a more directly social sense to describe 'the disposition of an entire structure of thought, feeling and behaviour which must be properly learnt and controlled' (1988: 84). Here then, from Mauss to Assad, via Tyson and Bourdieu, with others left unconsidered, there emerge interpretative concepts that focus attention more on cultured bodily action and its motive source than on formal belief systems or structure of institutions for use in the social scientific study of religion. One major qualification, however, needs to be made to these interpretative concepts as far as this chapter is concerned, viz. that dress can be, and often is, an integral part of physical movement. In other words the body is not utilised simply as a bare, physical, system but is dressed, and in its dressed form it acts. Very often this vested feature of the body is entirely taken for granted but, as the descriptive part of this chapter has made very clear, the clothing can be a determinative feature of the actual body and the way it behaves. The temple-garment is not simply a sign of the need for bodily control but is a symbol of control, in the sense that a symbol partici-pates in that which it represents. The temple-garment is part of the bodily sense of control in the ethical domain of daily life just as the temple robes contribute to the Saint undertaking his endowments. There is, of course, a full literature on the phenomenology and hermeneutics of bodily-felt knowledge (Levin 1985: 53) as there is for the anthropology of sensation (Howes 1991: 167ff.), fields that lie beyond the scope of this chapter but which could be extensively explored for Mormon ritual.

Here we will, however, include one Mormon body-technique, one gesture that expresses and constitutes a Latter-day Saint *habitus* within the domain of the life-world. It is that of the testimony, a verbal affirmation of the individual's commitment to God and Jesus Christ and to Mormonism, its founding prophet and current leaders. In an earlier study I approached this topic from a more phenomenological viewpoint within the history of religions tradition to speak of the ideal-typical Mormon *Homo religiosus* (1987: 131ff.) and that, too, is a worthwhile emphasis. In relocating the emphasis, here, on the importance of the gesture we affirm, with Bourdieu that, 'each technique of the body is a sort of *pars totalis*', by which each element may 'evoke the whole system of which it is a part' (1977: 94). This is the case for Mormonism in which body behaviour bespeaks Mormon ideology and practice in a variety of intersecting ways. We have already alluded to this in terms of temple ritual and, now, by including the rite of testimony-giving we can also draw on a significant ritual of the local, chapel level, of Latter-day Saint religious life.

Habitus Through *Gestus* of Testimony

To possess a testimony of the truthfulness of Mormonism is a prime goal of the Latter-day Saint religious life. It implies a shift in emotional experience towards commitment to Mormon teaching and marks assent to the historic

Restoration of truth and to the prophet-president leader of the one true Church upon earth.

Although the testimony consists in words it is, essentially, a verbal performance. In a more technical sense it can be viewed, to a degree, as a performative utterance in that to give one's testimony is not only to foster and strengthen one's testimony but is to 'make oneself' a believing Saint in the hearing and seeing of the community of Saints. For the testimony is as much seen as it is heard and, as such, the gesture of testimony is complex but identifiable. It does not lie in one single act or in one medium; the sight of the fellow member complements what is heard. It involves the individual Saint getting up out of their seat to become the only person standing while all the others sit. They 'take the stand' and become the central focus of the meeting. Unlike someone speaking in tongues in a Charismatic Church group, where many may be standing, swaying, holding up their arms and, communally, engaging in ecstatic speech, the Latter-day Saint stands alone and faces the congregation, while others pay attention to what they say. It is the discrete individual who is giving voice to their personal experience. The tone of voice is relatively quiet and not loud, and as such marks the LDS ideal of sincerity and of being Spirit-influenced, the person's overall demeanour is restrained and, in a sense, passive. The very carriage of the body expresses a degree of humility which reflects the verbal message that the person is grateful for having received a certain kindness or encouragement. The arms are never raised but remain down or are clasped in front of the speaker or may be placed on the lectern in front of the speaker. The person may look at particular individuals if they are specifically mentioned within the testimony.

The verbal part of the testimony refers to other members of the local LDS community as well as family and friends and often includes some recent or earlier aspect of autobiography. It usually ends by a dual expression of gratitude to people and to God for the privilege of church membership along with an affirmation of the Church of Jesus Christ of Latter-day Saints as the true Church, with Joseph Smith and the current prophet as true prophets of God.

The voice may falter at some part of the testimony, often towards the close, as a mild wave of emotion chokes the free flow of expression. In some cases the person may even shed a tear of thanks, joy and gratitude. Such a testimony is viewed as authentic and coming from the heart. It is a visual statement to the other members of the group that genuine faith lies in that one individual. For the person bearing their testimony it is a moment of entering into a fullness of identity as a Latter-day Saint. From a more analytical position we can see this testimony as bearing a family resemblance with the historic witnesses to the reception of the Book of Mormon and to the early pioneers who testified to Joseph Smith as a prophet. For the one bearing testimony it is a moment of assonance with the religion. Here personal faith and the cumulative tradition of the group intersect.

But not all testimonies are the same. Not all are equally authentic. Some may appear rather formulaic and routine; they may lack the authenticity of deeply held feelings. On this one occasion an individual may, simply, not feel or express himself or herself in the way they have done on previous occasions and will do on subsequent occasions. A child or young person may give a testimony, which sounds like a pre-written set of words. Still, they may be encouraged as young people who are learning the format of bearing a testimony. The very fact they have stood up to bear a testimony reflects part of the gesture, even if the words and their ethos do not fully echo the ideal format. Still, the very fact that some testimonies fall short of the ideal enhances the fully authentic version when it emerges. At the close of a testimony the person receives supportive glances and even touches from other members of the congregation as he or she returns to their seat and rejoins their family or friends. The members of the congregation then await to see who will rise next to tell of the benefit they have received from the Lord and from fellow Saints.

Analytically we may compare this rite of testimony giving as a ritual of the chapel level of Mormon organization that reflects the formal rite of endowments at the temple-level of Mormonism. In the temple the Church member is fully clothed in temple garments, distinctive and separate from ordinary life, and makes covenants with God. In the chapel the same person will be wearing the temple garment as an undergarment with ordinary clothes on top, and will appear to be normally dressed. In this form of ordinary dress believers now affirm their personal conviction of the truth of this religion. Both endowments and testimony are typical Mormon gestures expressing a principle of control and community bonding under the influence of a divine Spirit and grounded in a belief in a divinely restored religious institution is reflected in each. Here we have the 'generative principle' of commitment and control underlying diverse aspects of cultural practice (ibid.: 78) and can see how *gestus* manifests *habitus*.

Controlling Dress

Another established anthropological approach to behaviour follows Mary Douglas's analysis of what she called grid and group factors of social life (1970). Both are concerned with forms of social control and individual behaviour. Grid refers to the control of ideas and systems of thought while group deals with control of behaviour, including forms of dress and of grooming the body and managing bodily movements. Accordingly any community, and its constituent individuals can be analysed in terms of being strong or weak on grid or group elements. Many fundamentalist religious movements exert strong control over what their members believe (high grid element) and over what they do (high group element), other groups such as the Anglican Church tend to be relatively low both on the grid and group factors. Some ethnic communities, as with some Jewish communities are relatively strong in control over behaviour, especially dietary rules, but very low as far as ideological control is concerned.

As far as contemporary Mormons are concerned the Church exerts a high control over behaviour (high group factor) but with a slightly less tight control over what people actually believe (moderately high grid factor). A Mormon could be a very well accepted member of the Church as long as his or her moral life exhibited strong sexual control, an integrated family life, payment of tithes and an active participation in chapel and temple activity. It would not matter so much if they held slightly unusual beliefs or interpretations of Mormon ideology. If, by contrast, they reckoned to be absolutely orthodox in belief but did not practise these various acts, then they would not be deemed truly authentic Saints.

Mary Douglas argued that a degree of uniformity of dress codes and bodily grooming would be found in groups with a strong control of behaviour (high group factor), and this we do find to be the case with Latter-day Saints. So too with the grooming of the body and the hair. Douglas postulated the rather oddly named notion of what she called 'the purity rule', to describe such forms of bodily control. The idea being that if a society was strongly in control of individuals then those individuals would exert strong control over their own bodies. This, too, is true of Mormons, most especially of those in positions of authority, those serving as missionaries and those performing rites in the temple. The well-kept clothing and hair of the missionary are but one expression of bodily control, others involve early rising for bible-study and prayer. An even stronger practical control lies in sexual behaviour. The Church, itself, uses the word 'purity' to refer to the moral control of the sexual life. Adultery and pre-marital sex are forbidden and masturbation strongly discouraged on the moral basis that sexuality itself is highly valued and ritually dedicated as an intra-marital expression of love and commitment of the eternal partners. Homosexuality is also strongly opposed (Schow et al. 1991). The young are encouraged to marry early so as to develop their sexuality within wedlock (Corcoran 1994).

Finally it must be said that the theoretical link between social control and personal control of behaviour is difficult to establish, not least because of the unfortunately traditional antipathy between much anthropological and psychological material (cf. Moscovici 1993: 12ff.). That there is a strong link cannot be doubted, and some have sought explanations within the psychological causations of Freudian and other analytical traditions, pursuing the relation between public and private forms of symbolism. Obeyesekere did this, for example, in his analysis of hair in some Sri Lankan ascetic behaviour (1981), as did Leach's anthropological re-analysis of Berg's psycho-analytical link between shaved heads and castration (1958). Here we can simply affirm the fact that those persons who are, from a sociological perspective, in situations of strong social control as with Latter-day Saints, do display a strong control over their own dress and hair grooming.

So, while the language of *gestus* and *habitus* affords no psychological explanation of how these correlations function it does allow a deeper level of sociological description. Accordingly, the temple garment, the grooming of missionaries and the testimony, all display the 'generative principle' of control and commitment, underlying diverse aspects of cultural practice (Bourdieu 1977: 78), in this we can see how *gestus* manifests *habitus* in Mormon social life.

References

Alexander, T.G. (1986), *Mormonism in Transition, A History of Latter-day Saints 1890–1930*, Urbana and Chicago: University of Illinois Press.

Asad, T. (1988), 'Towards a Genealogy of the Concept of Ritual,' in W. James and D.H. Johnson (eds), *Vernacular Christianity*, Oxford: JASO.

Bourdieu, P. (1977), *Outline of a Theory of Practice*, Cambridge: Cambridge University Press.

Buerger, D.J. (1994), *The Mysteries of Godliness, A History of Mormon Temple Worship*, San Francisco: Smith Research Associates.

Corcoran, B. (ed.) (1994), *Multiply and Replenish, Mormon Essays on Sex and Family*, Salt Lake City: Signature Books.

Davies, C. (1996), 'Coffee, tea and the ultra-Protestant and Jewish nature of the Boundaries of Mormonism', in D.J. Davies (ed.) *Mormon Identities in Transition*, London: Cassell.

Davies, D.J. (1987), *Mormon Spirituality*, Nottingham: University of Nottingham Series in Theology.

Douglas, M. (1970), *Natural Symbols*, London: Pelican.

Howes, D. (ed.) (1991), *The Varieties of Sensory Experience*, Toronto: University of Toronto Press.

Leach, E. (1958), 'Magical Hair', *The Journal of the Royal Anthropological Institute*, 88 (2): 147–64.

Levin, D.M. (1985), *The Body's Recollection of Being*, London: Routledge and Kegan Paul.

Mauss, A.L. (1994), *The Angel and The Beehive*, Urbana and Chicago: University of Illinois Press.

Mauss, M. (1979), *Sociology and Psychology*, London: Routledge and Kegan Paul.

McConkie, B.R. (1966), *Mormon Doctrine*, Salt Lake City: Bookcraft.

Moscovici, S. (1993), *The Invention of Society*, Cambridge: Polity Press.

Obeyesekere, G. (1981), *Medusa's Hair: An Essay on Personal Symbols and Religious Experience,* Chicago and London: University of Chicago Press.

O'Dea, T. (1957), *The Mormons*, Chicago: University of Chicago Press.

Porter, B.D. (1992), 'Church of Jesus Christ of Latter-Day Saints', in D.H. Ludlow (ed.), *Encyclopedia of Mormonism*, New York: Macmillan Publishing Company.

Schow, R. Schow, W. & Raynes, M. (1991), *Peculiar People, Mormons and Same-Sex Orientation*, Salt Lake City: Signature Books.

Turner, V. (1982), *Celebration, Studies in Festivity and Ritual*, Washington, DC: Smithsonian Institution Press.

Tyson, R.W., Peacock, J.L. & Patterson, D.W. (1988), *Diversities of Gifts: Studies in Southern Religion*, Urbana, Ill: University of Illinois Press.

Underwood, G. (1993), *The Millenarian World of Early Mormonism*, Urbana and Chicago: University of Illinois Press.

7

Vampires and Goths: Fandom, Gender and Cult Dress

Milly Williamson

Introduction

To many commentators the vampire is said to symbolize Western fear of the female body. Bram Dijkstra for example, suggests that the vampire demonstrates the way that Western culture simultaneously hates, fears and fetishizes the female body. He argues that even when the vampire is nominally a male figure, it translates into a male-generated fear of '*woman* (sic) as vampire' (Dijkstra 1996: 7). Dijkstra argues that we should begin the 'daunting task of exorcising the vampires of misogyny from our imagination'. Linda Williams (1984: 87) also proposes a link between the monster and the female body. She argues that both are seen as a 'biological freak with impossible and threatening appetites'. For Williams (ibid.: 88) the monster is 'a particularly insidious form of the many mirrors patriarchal structures of seeing hold up to the woman'.

Creed (1993: 71), from a different perspective, suggests that vampirism depicts a version of the 'monstrous feminine' and argues that with its repeated emphasis on opening up a wound, 'the vampire narrative points continually to the imper-fection of the body and the particularly abject nature of the maternal body'. However, while Dijkstra (1996: 443) argues that we should reject the 'mass media's lure of "evil sister" stereotyping', Creed and Williams point to the potential for empathy between monster and woman. Yet this empathy ultimately offers a 'distorted reflection of their own image' (Williams 1984: 88) and a recognition of shared freakishness. But what of those women who dress the part of the vampire? These theoretical accounts of the vampire offer rich interpretations of the figure's possible symbolic articulation of femininity generally in Western culture, but can only speculate on what the figure says to women who identify themselves as vampire fans and indeed ignores what these women are saying about themselves in their construction of vampiric sartorial identities.

Rather than suggesting that women who identify with the image of the vampire are internalising patriarchal conceptions of the feminine as monstrous, this chapter will offer an alternative account of the vampire's meaning by grounding it in the sartorial inspiration that women vampire fans themselves derive from the image. This chapter will not propose that these fan accounts can elucidate the vampire's significance to women per se (not least because most women are not vampire fans), as many feminists have argued, the experience of femininity is not homogenous (hooks 1984; Wallace 1990; Young 1996). Instead this chapter will address the common attitudes of these fans towards the vampire and how this informs their sartorial choices. This is not to argue that the fictional vampire does not speak of broader cultural concerns. Numerous theorists of the vampire have provided outstanding accounts of the relationship between textual transformations of the figure and historically specific social concerns (Auerbach 1995; Gordon and Hollinger 1997; Gelder 1994; Carroll 1990; Tudor 1989; Jancovich 1992; Roth 1984; Zimmerman 1984). Indeed, this chapter will argue that the sartorial choices of the women vampire fans have to do with their cultural experience. Part of the pleasure of appropriating vampiric symbols is that they provide women with means of handling ambivalent cultural categories such as femininity and self. The women fans' self-presentation as vampiric, it will be argued, are specific responses to the broader context of gender that women face, but experience and deal with differently.

The analysis presented in this chapter is based on twelve in-depth interviews with British women vampire fans conducted between 1996 and 1997. The intention of grounding this analysis in the accounts offered by women vampire fans is to allow the categories and frameworks of interpretation to emerge from the types of things *the fans* say about what they do. This has pointed me in the direction of two theoretical areas not generally associated with theories of the vampire. The first is the relationship between the paradoxical experience of femininity and sartorial behaviour of women as detailed in the empirical studies of women and dress provided by Tseëlon (1995). The second comes from the literature on fashion, particularly the discussions offered by Wilson and Hollander on the role of black in oppositional dress. These approaches offer valuable conceptual means of analysing the women fans' self-declared motivations for appropriating symbols of outsiderdom. This chapter will therefore consider what these alternative approaches can offer to an understanding of women vampire fans and their attitudes towards dress and identity.

This chapter will begin with a discussion of the category of femininity and the potential experiences that may be generated by its paradoxical status. It will then examine how the women vampire fans articulate their experience of femininity and their motivations for adopting vampiric sartorial schemes.

The relationship between these will be examined through three interrelated themes: the first is the women's experience of 'not fitting in' to ideas about feminine norms. Connected to this is the appropriation of vampiric imagery in their dress as a way of producing identities that stand out as different. Thirdly is the role of a particular Gothic use of black apparel (drawing on the colour's anti-fashion or oppositional symbolism) in the construction of these identities.

Femininity as Ambivalence: Experiencing a Paradox

For Tseëlon femininity is a paradoxical category which frames women's experiences of 'self' in the West. Tseëlon (1995: 2) agues that woman is an 'impossible creature who is given a space and no space at all, who is offered a position while being denied that position, who embodies a thing and its opposite at the same time'. Furthermore, Tseëlon argues that this ambivalence is centred on the notion that femininity is constructed as artifice and then derided for lacking authenticity. This leads to a further paradox that woman signifies beauty, but that women do not embody beauty because of the threatening nature of the female body. Tseëlon (p. 79) argues that, 'woman is placed in a no-win situation. She is expected to embody a "timeless" cultural phantasy, but is not naturally more attractive than a man. Her special beauty is at best a temporary state, and it takes hard work and concerted effort to maintain.'

Tseëlon (ibid.: 3) considers that as a result of this ambivalence, 'personal appearance' comes to frame women's social positions and influences 'the way she comes to think of herself'. Analysing the way that women handle this contradictory category in an empirical study of women and dress, Tseëlon (p. 54) suggests that women are highly conscious of their 'visible self' when dressing. Women, claims Tseëlon, make subtle distinctions not only about the situation, but also about the audience and their own state of mind. They distinguish between significant audiences, whose opinions matter and those that do not; between comfortable and uncomfortable situations taking greater effort, care and consciousness of what they wear in the latter. Women worry about being dressed inappropriately because they are made conscious of their appearance. Tseëlon (p. 54) argues therefore, that feeling 'visible, exposed, observed or on show appear to be internalised into the self-conception'.

The Experience of Not Fitting In

The context of femininity which Tseëlon suggests is the realm of impossible contradictions, also frames the experiences of the women vampire fans, for they face the same ambivalent category of 'femininity' that other women face. But their experience of femininity, and the sartorial identities they construct as a result are *specific* responses to these more general conditions. The women vampire fans, rather than struggling to internalize the impossible, instead experience themselves as not fitting in. They have a notion of normal femininity which is symbolized in the colour pink and is to do with competently following fashion trends, which many of the fans have never felt able to manage. Many of the fans comment that pink frilly dresses and little pumps were not for them. The notion of 'not fitting in', of being different, is evidenced in the following comments from different fans:

Fan A: at school I found it difficult to make friends and wear trendy clothes. I didn't fit in so you're looking for something else to be instead . . . I don't know, perhaps that's why you identify with vampires because you feel a bit of a misfit.

Fan F: I went Goth at the age of 16 when I was training as a hair dresser . . . [because] I just didn't fit in and I didn't like the way I looked . . . I guess I have always been a little bit different.

Fan C: I didn't fit in with the trends and things . . . And besides I look terrible in pink.

This sense of not fitting in could be interpreted along psychoanalytic lines (as suggested by Williams above) that the fans are experiencing themselves through the distorting mirrors that patriarchy holds up to women. Feminist psychoanalysis has suggested that the woman is fixed by the male gaze which objectifies and/or distorts her image through the processes of fetishism and voyeurism. This in turn robs her of the power of self-definition. This view was inaugurated by Mulvey's ground-breaking article on the cinema and visual pleasure (Mulvey 1985). Mulvey (p. 804) argues that the cinema's structures of looking reproduce the patriarchal unconscious in which 'woman stands as the signifier of the male "other"'. The woman, then, can only experience herself as the object of the male gaze, or in the case of the cinema by either adopting the (dominant) masculine point of view, or oscillating between passive femininity and active masculinity (cf. Mulvey 1990).

However, many feminists have criticized this perspective as monolithic both in terms of the processes of spectatorship (Gledhill 1987; Byars 1991; Pribram 1988) and in terms of women's experiences of self (Tseëlon 1995). As Tseëlon (1995: 68) argues, this ignores the 'plurality, contradiction or resistance that exists' in the realm of feminine identification. Tseëlon suggests that the effect of the general framework of femininity on women's sense of self is also influenced by local environment, on the people and situations and whether one feels secure or insecure. The comments from the women vampire fans demonstrates that they do not feel secure with trends and normal femininity and they experience this as not fitting in. But this in turn has lead to a more potent self-definition as different. This is not to argue that the women's sense of self is cut off from, or resides outside of, the framework of femininity; the women's comments illustrate an unhappiness not simply with the norm, but also with themselves (as misfit) in that context.

While rejecting a monolithic view, Tseëlon does maintain that the sense of self is always produced in relation to others and this is the case for the women fans whose sense of not fitting in comes from how they feel they are perceived by others. Tseëlon argues that the self is a social process, residing not in the individual but as an 'outcome of human interaction' (ibid.: 40). This is paradoxical for women because women are expected to be authentically feminine and yet femininity is a construct, not a given. Tseëlon (p. 38) draws on Sartre to pull out this 'twofold paradox'. The very attempt to be authentic (i.e. feminine) for Sartre suggests that originally 'one is being what one is not' (ibid.: 38). That is, women can only become 'authentically feminine' with considerable effort, it is not an a priori condition. Furthermore, Tseëlon (p. 38) suggests that being authentic for woman is not 'being' for herself. Because 'authentic' femininity is constructed, it 'implies objectifying oneself, of seeing oneself through the eyes of the Other'. Women therefore, face cultural expectations to do with the 'gender meaning assigned to appearance' (ibid.: 39). Women experience a relationship between appearance – how they are seen by others – and a sense of self and so come to experience the self through appearance and the eyes of others. Furthermore, woman's essence and appearance are intertwined and therefore her essence is ultimately conceived of as, in essence, artifice, vanity, insincerity and display. The women in Tseëlon's study manage these cultural expectations and the fragile sense of self that can result by having many sartorial faces for different situations and wearing their clothes like armour. Tseëlon emphasizes that women are not being insincere or deceptive about self. Rather that confidence is bound up with feeling good about one's appearance. The women vampire fans, too, experience themselves through the eyes of others and are adopting sartorial identities which make them feel good about themselves. But for the vampire women feeling good does not translate into looking good for others. Instead, looking 'good' means looking different to others by rejecting pink, frilly femininity. The women vampire fans' sense of self is thus contextualized, but not immobilized by the paradox of femininity and results in an active construction of their appearance and self-presentation.

The women vampire fans sartorial identities are no more nor less artificial or authentic than other outfits that other women armour themselves in. That the women stand out as a result of their sartorial choices and feel themselves to be different in the eyes of others is a reminder of how taken for granted are the standards of dress for women in each epoch, but also how women can and have challenged norms to create innovative styles through which to express self. Entwistle (1997), who has also offered an empirical analysis of women and dress, argues that the process of self-presentation takes place both within broad cultural discourses and specific practices. She argues that dressing is a 'situated practice'. Dress, being the interface between the individual and the social world, is both structured by social forces and 'is produced through the actions of individuals directed towards their bodies in particular ways' (Entwistle 1997: 10). For the women vampire fans, then, the experience of not fitting in to the perceived expectations of others has not lead to an increased attempt to internalize ideal femininity. Instead it has lead to a rejection of those norms and the construction of an alternative sartorial identity. The women fans dress the part of the vampire with long capes in velvets and satins, silky dresses with flared sleeves and lace gloves, converting 'not fitting in' to 'standing out' as different. The following section will discuss the women's use of black to 'stand out' in the context of Western ideas about this colour in sartorial schemes. It will then examine what the women are telling others about themselves through their vampiric sartorial identities.

Dressing in Black and Standing Out

Combined with a rejection of pink femininity, the women vampire fans' alternative dress is intended to ensure that they stand out as different. Their sense of not fitting in has not lead to a self-effacing sartorial identity, but one that calls attention to their difference. The following two exchanges from the women, when asked why they dress in black, demonstrate this impulse:

Fan D: Perhaps we're just trying to make a point . . . that you are different and not the same, you're not just following everybody else.

Fan E: I go to work conventional, but come home and rip it off and put something on different straight away. I can't stand it.

Fan D: Just walk in the door and take it all off, I hate it.

The second pair comment:

Fan J: It's difficult to explain it really. Part of it is that you don't want to feel like normal people.

Fan K: Yeah, not conforming.

Fan J: It's a lot of things . . . the style of dress, it's different. People look at you if you dress like this.

The women fold together their dislike for fashion trends, wanting to feel different and wanting to be seen to be different by cladding themselves in black. Black is the central colour in these women's wardrobes and is central to their sartorial identities. That the women choose black as the symbolic polar opposite of pink is not only to do with their perceptions of the norms of femininity.

Black has long provided its wearers with the mark of difference. Hollander (1993: 377) argues that there is a tradition of wearing black 'which seeks to isolate and distinguish the wearer'. For Hollander (p. 365) black can offer power and distinction drawing on its 'ancient flavour of antifashion'. Furthermore, leading up to and following the Romantic era, black accrued connotations of the sinister and satanic. As Hollander (p. 376) argues: 'Black appears as the colour suitable to delicious forbidden practice and belief – the courting of death, not the mourning of it – in a great deal of Romantic literature.' The powerful symbolism invoked by black attire, its ability to isolate and draw attention to its wearer as well as its ability to conjure 'fear of the blind darkness of night and the eternal darkness of death' (Hollander 1993: 365), makes it a particularly appealing colour to the women fans who are drawing on this symbolism. As one fan puts it:

Fashion trends, fine you can keep them. Because that is not me. I am always in black. It's a strong colour, people look at it as a very negative colour, but it isn't, black will stop negativity. Anything light or bright will attract negativity 'cause it is bright. It is a welcoming colour, . . . [but] Black keeps people at a distance, it gives people the image of you know, 'don't approach me, back off, leave me alone. I'm not the sort of quite little mouse that sits in a corner. I will not tolerate any one trying to invade or to put me down.'

This fan is drawing positively on black's ominous symbolism and it is clear that a link is being made between self-perception (black 'is me'), the perception of others ('black keeps people at a distance from me') and sartorial behaviour. It is interesting that all of the women comment that black is 'the real me' and yet talk about their dress in terms of the effect it will have on other people. This seems to support Tseëlon's argument that woman's sense of self is bound up with how she appears to others. This woman is using black to say to *others* 'I am different', 'I am unapproachable' and 'I am strong'.

While the women's self-presentation is intended to stand out as different, it is a particular kind of standing out. By appropriating vampiric images they are presenting themselves specifically as outsiders and expect others to recognise the symbolism. As Hollander notes, there are different ways of wearing black. Black has expressed bourgeois respectability, a professional demeanour, and mourning. It can also mock these connotations through exaggerated display. In the latter half of the nineteenth century it was considered the suitable colour for those of 'straightened means' (Hollander 1993: 379) such as the shop girl, clerk and domestic servant. But simultaneously, Hollander (p. 379) argues, 'rich and idle men were considered properly dressed in black in the evening, and rich and idle women properly dressed in black for ostentatious mourning or, suitably décolleté, for occasional dramatic evenings'. In the twentieth century, black has taken on a variety of symbolic connotations. Indeed, Hollander (p. 388) considers that in the late twentieth century black has lost its symbolic significance, 'through the fragmentation and multiplicity of styles in dress' and 'chiefly through the self-consciousness of fashion'. For Hollander (p. 388), to wear black today is to 'refer to a variety of earlier manifestations of black clothes – earlier styles, former meanings, obsolete conventions'.

The women vampire fans adorn themselves in a black that harks back to the 'former meanings' of the Romantic era. They emphasize the sinister drama of black through the use of antique and out-of-fashion clothing styles, worn in silks and velvets which many combine with dyed black hair, yellow contact lenses and sometimes the donning of dental caps fashioned as vampire fangs. The intention is to stand out, to adopt an aloof stance. But the vampiric symbolism is also intended to startle and shock in its difference. As one fan comments about wearing fangs:

> So, you walk into a pub, you sit down, you order a drink and you sort of look around and you smile at someone and its just a look of shock, of disbelief as if to say 'I know what I'm seeing doesn't exist', but it still doesn't stop them from backing away, so I feel better with them in, well I'm quite a confident person anyway, but again it gives me the upper hand.

This sense of being remote and startlingly different echoes the connotations of black attire worn by the Romantic man. As Hollander argues, the Romantic man wore black to establish his remoteness. It was a style with strong literary connections which marked him out as a 'fatal man' (ibid.: 375). For Hollander (p. 375), the fatal man was 'specifically connected with spiritual unrest and personal solitude . . . [in league with] . . . a dark power that exempted him from the responsibilities of common feeling and experience'. The vampire fans too want to display their outsiderdom and draw sartorial inspiration from the vampire as Romantic outsider. Yet the women do not view the vampire as the wicked villain depicted in numerous adaptations of *Dracula*. Instead they look unanimously to the vampires in Anne Rice's *Vampire Chronicles* (1976, 1985, 1988, 1992, 1995) which offer a contemporary reinterpretation of the vampire as a sympathetic eighteenth- and nineteenth-century Romantic hero; one who suffers his isolation from humanity with the pathos more appropriate to the heroine of the Gothic novel than its black-clad villain. Black keeps its demonic edge in the women's sartorial schemes, but it signifies the pathos of outsiderdom as well as its force, evidenced in the women's comments about not fitting in and feeling a misfit.

Black as Revolt

Added to the Romantic implications of black as difference are those of black as revolt. Elizabeth Wilson (1985: 189) in her analysis of fashion has suggested that black has long been the appropriate colour of revolt: the 'colour of bourgeois sobriety, but subverted, perverted, gone kinky'. For Wilson (p. 189), 'Black is dramatic and plays to the gallery, as the costuming of revolt must always do.'

But more specifically, Wilson proposes that it was the Romantics and Dandies, influenced by the revolutionary upheavals in the latter half of the eighteenth-century, that actually inaugurated the notion of dress as revolt. For Wilson (p. 186) it was the 'combined influence of the dandies and the Romantics that made of black a resonant statement of dissent'. While Hollander suggests that black has long signified 'antifashion', Wilson (p. 183) argues that it was actually the style invented by the dandies that lead to conventional menswear, 'and thus to antifashion'. Furthermore, Wilson (p. 184) argues that style of the dandy lead in another direction, it 'contained the germs of something utterly different, of oppositional style'. Wilson (p. 184) suggests that oppositional style aims to express 'views hostile to the conformist majority'. For Wilson (p. 183), then, the society that gave birth to the dandy and oppositional style ensured that oppositional dress was always 'above all *anti-bourgeois*'.

This notion of black-as-revolt chimes with the women's accounts of their sartorial identities as non-conformist. Black not only affords the women fans the means to stand out as different, they are also drawing on its oppositional connotations of sartorial revolt. As one fan puts it:

It just makes people think. They see me in black, they see the fangs, they see the contact lenses[...]They say you can't fight the system or buck the system, well yeah you can, but in your own way, and you do it in such a [...]way that people don't realise that you're actually being a little revolutionary in your own way.

The attitudes expressed by the women in their choice of black as declaring their difference could be interpreted as a sign of the women producing elitist distinctions between themselves and 'normal' people (cf. Thornton 1995). Alternatively, we could interpret their accounts as the proto-political act of subverting mainstream society (cf. Jenkins 1992). However, Wilson offers an alternative explanation. Wilson (1985: 186) argues that while black has been a sign of 'anti-bourgeois revolt', it has also been a deeply contradictory sign, 'as contradictory as the society that gave it birth' (ibid.: 183). Just as this 'transitory epoch of capitalism' (ibid.: 183) was an era poised between the extension of democracy and the politics of reaction, so too did the style of revolt appeal equally to the 'republican radical' and 'the reactionary, the dis-affected aristocrat' (ibid.: 182). It was thus of both past and future. Baudelaire, for example, wore black in protest against the 'sartorial vulgarity of French bohemian circles' (ibid.: 183). In fact, Baudelaire seems to express the con-tradictory impulses of the dandy. For Baudelaire, the dandy was a disenchanted rebel who celebrated decadence, but he was also one who 'attempts to create a new aristocracy of genius, or at least of talent' (ibid.: 183). Nevertheless for Wilson (ibid.: 183), this oppositional dress, whether looking to past or future was always 'anti-bourgeois' and she reminds us that capitalism is *'permanently transitory'* (ibid.: 183). Condemned to perpetual change, it repeatedly throws up 'ambiguous rebels whose rebellion is never a revolution, but instead a re-affirmation of Self' (ibid.: 183).

The women vampire fans can be seen as latter day versions of Wilson's 'ambiguous rebels'. For the women, the appropriation of black attire is to do with a non-conformity which is centrally about the construction and affirmation of self. It is also significant that the women look to the past for sartorial inspiration and look precisely to the (Romantic) period in history that Wilson defines as producing the contradictory germs of oppositional style. The women vampire fans are drawing on the idea of black as a rebellious colour but conceive of the styles of the past contradictorily as both 'more feminine than today as well as offering them nonconformity with femininity. So one fan who comments that 'pink' (as the standard colour of femininity) is 'not for her' and wants her sartorial identity to say 'look, I'm different' also comments: 'I don't think women look feminine now-a-days. I think the velvets and the satins and the laces of the past look so feminine. It emphasises you as a woman, I think, more.'

There is a simultaneous sense of not fitting in to the norms of femininity (expressed in a rejection of pink and preference for black) which nevertheless continues to embrace notions of femininity by looking to the past for sartorial inspiration. This seems explicable in terms of Wilson's formulation of the con-tradictory character of oppositional dress. Wilson emphasizes the notion that the conditions that give rise to oppositional style are ambiguous, and that as a response to those conditions oppositional style is itself filled with contradictions. The experience of the paradox of femininity that frame the women's choice of black can lead to ambiguities in their sense of what being different means. Wilson has highlighted how sartorial revolt is simultaneously a mode of past and future; that the impulses for nonconformity in dress can appeal to those looking to the past while also drawing those who desire the potential of the future. The following section will propose that for the women vampire fans, the past/future impulses of oppositional dress are combined. Rather than looking to past or future, the women vampire fans are looking in both directions at once.

The Dialectics of Past and Future

The implication of a preferable and emphasized femininity in historical dress may be conceived of as a form of regressive nostalgia for the past. But this is complicated by the ambiguity of the vampire figure with whom the women travel. The Romantic connotations of the vampiric that the women draw on are those of otherness in past as well as present, which problematizes any simple notion of their looking to the past for a better way of life. The vampire simultaneously symbolizes the pathos and power of outsiderdom. It is a figure which expresses, as Richard Dyer (1988: 11) comments 'the despicable as well as the defiant, the shameful as well as the unashamed, the loathing of oddness as well as pride in it'. It is through vampiric modes of the past that the women express ambivalence about femininity and self. This is further revealed in the way that thinking about the vampire produces the means of articulating contradictory attitudes towards gendered sexuality. For while the vampire offers a way for the women to conceive of their identities as both not feminine and more feminine, it further leads to the women questioning the very boundaries of gender and the associated sexualities. All of the fans favour the vampires of Anne Rice's *Vampire Chronicles* (1976, 1985, 1988, 1992, 1995), particularly 'Louis' and 'Lestat'. The homo-eroticism which infuses the relationship of these two male vampires is widely recognized (cf. Auerbach 1995; Dyer 1988; Gelder 1994; Hodges and Doane 1991) and does not go unnoticed by these women fans. For instance, one fan comments about Louis and Lestat: 'I don't think they're so male or female looking. I think they sort of cross both lines don't they . . . aren't vampires bisexual anyway? So it doesn't matter that I'd be a skinny little vampire with no bosoms.'

This comment articulates the many issues of self, gender and sexuality raised by the vampire, for the women. The idea that having 'no bosoms' as her vampire self 'doesn't matter' echoes the notion of not-fitting in to femininity and expresses the duality raised by Dyer above, an uneasy recognition of difference which converts to pride. But this conversion is at least partly possible through engagement with the vampire's bisexuality – its crossing both lines. All of the women comment positively on the love between the (same sex) vampires and approve of their androgenous looks.

Some post-Freudian theorists have suggested that the vampire signals an end to gender distinctions. For Craft (1990) and Case (1991), the vampire is a subversive borderline figure which problematizes representation and destabilises the boundaries of gender. For Case (1991: 4), the vampire disrupts because it exists between the boundaries through which we conceive of being; the bi-polarities that enclose the heterosexist notion of being are punctured and 'new forms of being, or beings, are imagined through desire'. For Craft it is the vampire's mouth that poses the vampire as a multi-gendered being by displacing sexuality onto this ungendered space. Craft's vampire exposes the insubstantiality of gender barriers; it 'exists to dissolve opposites' (Craft 1990: 109). Both Case and Craft, then, pose the vampire as symbolic of ways of 'being' beyond what they consider to be unstable gender distinctions. From this perspective the women's identification with the vampire and their articulation of the vampire's bisexuality would suggest that through sartorial means, the women are producing subversive identities beyond the constructs of gender. However, this position cannot take into account the women's looking to the past in their ambivalent not feminine/more feminine constructions of self.

There are other theorists who warn against analyses of the vampire that prematurely pose the end of stable gender categories. Hodges and Doane (1991: 158), for example, argue that recent post-Freudian psychoanalysis is lured into a trap 'that seems to promise a solution to oppressive constructions of sexual difference'. For these theorists celebrating the end of gender too soon has had a conservative influence on the narratives of mass culture. They argue that Anne Rice typifies this post-feminist posturing. In Rice's androgynous world of polymorphous sexuality 'imbalances of power are effaced' (Hodges and Doane 1991: 168) only to reassert the monstrosity of the non-maternal mother through the figure of Akasha, the original vampire mother who returns to the world in the third *Vampire Chronicle* (1988) with plans to kill all her sons. According to Hodges and Doane, the polymorphous sexuality of the male vampires is undercut by regressive notions of nurturing femininity and Akasha (who tries to rule in the symbolic rather than the pre-symbolic) is punished by death for her transgression. Readers thus 'greedily ingest' (ibid.: 158) these conservative fantasies, taking pleasure in the early disavowal of 'disturbing differences' (ibid.: 168) which nonetheless continue to assert the values associated with that difference. Analysing the women's comments from this perspective would suggest that the fans' identification with the line crossing of the vampire is a deeply conservative fantasy to mask their deeper acceptance of the precarious place of the feminine in the symbolic order. However, neither the celebrations of the vampire as subversive of gender representations nor the claims to the contrary capture its duality and equivocal status in culture, nor the ambivalence in women fans' articulation of their appropriation of this symbol in their construction of self.

The women read the vampire as crossing the lines of gender and blurring the boundaries of heterosexuality. They draw sartorial inspiration from what is (at least nominally) a male figure of the past to express their own desire for the future acceptability of androgeny. Yet the past to which they are looking is one in which women are conceived of as more feminine in dress and so by implication are they by drawing on those fabrics and cuts. However, alongside of these attitudes are the women's repeated emphasis on not fitting into present feminine norms and *wanting* not to, suggesting that they consider the unwanted boundaries of gender to be in place. This complex blend of attitudes, expressed in dress, cannot be accounted for by the either/or explanations discussed above. Walter Benjamin offers an alternative way of understanding these contra-dictions, ambivalences and ambiguities.

Benjamin contributes the concept of 'wish image' to the discussion of the modern consciousness noting the tendency to 'thirst for the past' (Benjamin in Buck-Morss 1989: 110) to symbolize a reality that has not yet come into being. According to Benjamin, the 'not-yet' of the new is expressed in archaic symbols rather than in the new forms 'commensurate with it' (ibid.: 114). Wish images, then, express the desire for the not-yet by 'intermingling the old with the new in fantastic ways' (Benjamin in ibid.: 115). The imagination looks to the past to express the new because of the fetters of the present; the potential of the new is constrained by still-existing social relations and so wish images 'reach back to a more distant past in order to *break from* conventional forms' (ibid.: 116). For Benjamin 'every epoch dreams the one that follows it' (Benjamin in ibid.: 114), but because a dream is not yet knowledge of a new reality, dream wishes take on the symbols of the past. Buck-Morss comments that Benjamin's evocation of the wish image is not utopian. She (p. 114) comments that 'Benjamin was reluctant to rest revolutionary hope directly on imagination's capacity to anticipate the not-yet-existing' because a wish image is interpreted through the 'material objects in which it found expression' (p. 115). The material through which the women fans' identity construction finds expression are the garments of self-presentation. It is therefore relevant to note that Benjamin applies this concept to dress and writes that 'fashion [. . .]stands in the darkness of the lived moment' (Benjamin in ibid.: 114). The wish image cannot dream the future; rather, it dreams desire for the not-yet. The women fans' 'not-yet' is one of personal emancipation from the paradoxical parameters of femininity and the potential for a more androgynous, less rigidly gendered way of being. This finds expression in past modes of dress inspired by their interpretation of the (male) Romantic vampire. But it has been argued throughout this chapter that women experience themselves in the context of femininity, and while they are not immobilized by this context, neither can they step outside of it. Thus their desire for the potential of a new way of being is contained in the inescapable present; they desire something different but (like any member of society) cannot anticipate it.

If it is the case as Benjamin proposes, that the wish image must look to the past to dream the future because the imagination is limited by the present, this may explain why the women look to the Romantic past for their modes of sartorial rebellion and why they simultaneously continue to hold to a feminine self-definition while raising the desire for a potential beyond this. If none can transcend the horizons of the present in imagining things not as they are, then as Buck-Morss (1991: 124) asks: 'where else *but* to the dead past can imagination turn in order to conceptualise a world that is not-yet?' The vampire women are aware, despite their construction of self as vampiric, that the vampire raises desires and potentials rather than realities. None of these women believe that they 'are' vampires and this recognition is evidenced in comments which illustrate their rueful distance from the vampire rather than identity with it. The women have not achieved the desired state:

Fan D: it would be just the perfect life style, it really would, . . . you could live a life that you had always wanted to.

Fan C: I'd love it [to be a vampire] yeah, I'd love it. You could do what you wanted to do, nobody could oppose you, you'd be very dextrous . . . you'd work under the shadow of darkness, you know. Who'd miss the sunlight, who'd miss the day?

Fan E: We could have lived that life quite happily . . . And back in where they live, that would suit us to a tee. We could live there.

Fan F: They don't have to bother with the rigmarole and the palaver that us humans have to go through sometimes. I'd love to dispense with it all and just have none of it. It would be ideal wouldn't it.

The vampire offers a way of imagining the past for the women which poses potential, not realization; a desire for a different way of being, not its fulfilment. The women clearly feel that the vampire offers an alternative possibility to the way things are which casts a particular light on their passion for the past. The past is a mode of casting present desires about self and trying out alternative possibilities of self by the creation of vampiric sartorial identities through which they can stand out as different to current normative definitions of self for women. The vampire is an appropriate symbol for these women who want to be different both because of the experience of not fitting in and the desire for alternative ways of being in the world. The vampire's duality captures these impulses; the pathos of not fitting in, of being an outsider, a desire for alternatives tinged with a recognition of non-fulfilment.

Conclusion

This chapter has attempted to demonstrate that dressing the part of the vampire for the women fans is a complex means of self-expression. By drawing on the dualistic connotations of the vampire as Romantic rebel and pathos-steeped outsider, the women are 'rebelling' and they are testing out possibilities of self in a manner which recognises non-fulfilment. The women's desire for alternative ways of being takes expression in their appropriation of black and vampiric attire as a means of producing nonconformist identities though oppositional dress. It has been suggested that this manner of rebellion is as contradictory as the context that produced its impulse: both rejecting and re-taining ideas of femininity, looking to the past to imagine the future, expressing the pain of outsiderdom and the strength of non-conformity. These contradictions stem from the inability of the self to transcend the constraints of the present while still being able to imagine things not-as-they-are. The women vampire fans are not fixed by the framework of femininity but neither can they simply step outside of social context and thus their desire for potential identities out-side of this context are akin to the vampire with whom they identify; they are desires that do not die but neither do they live.

References

Ang, I. (1982), *Watching Dallas: Soap Opera and the Melodramatic Imagination*, London: Routledge.

Auerbach, N. (1995), *Our Vampires, Ourselves*, Chicago: The University of Chicago Press.

Bobo, J. (1988), 'The Color Purple: Black Women as Cultural Readers' in E.D. Pribram (ed.), *Female Spectators: Looking at Film and Television*, London: Verso.

Brooks, P. (1976), *The Melodramatic Imagination: Balzac, Henry James, Melodrama and the Mode of Excess*, York: York University Press.

Buck-Morss, S. (1989), *The Dialectics of Seeing: Walter Benjamin and the Arcades Project*, Cambridge, Massachusettes: The MIT Press.

Byars, J. (1991), *All That Hollywood Allows: Re-reading Gender in 1950's Melodrama*, London: Routledge.

Carroll, N. (1990), *The Philosophy of Horror: or Paradoxes of the Heart*, New York: Routledge.

Case, S.E. (1991), 'Tracking the Vampire', *Differences: A Journal of Feminist Cultural Studies*, 2 (3).

Craft, C. (1990), '"Kiss Me with Those Red Lips": Gender and Inversion in Bram Stoker's *Dracula*' in E. Showalter (ed.), *Speaking of Gender*, London: Routledge.

Creed, B. (1993), *The Monstrous-Feminine: Film, Feminism, Psychoanalysis*, London: Routledge.

Dijkstra, B. (1996), *Evil Sisters: The Threat of Female Sexuality and the Cult of Manhood*, New York, Alfred A Knopf, Inc.

Dyer, R. (1985) 'Entertainment and Utopia' in B. Nichols (ed.), *Movies and Methods*, Volume II, Berkeley: University of California Press.

—— (1988), 'Children of the Night: Vampirism as Homosexuality, Homosexuality as Vampirism' in S. Radstone (ed.), *Sweet Dreams: Sexuality, Gender and Popular Fiction*, London: Lawrence and Wishart.

Entwistle, J. (1997), 'Fashioning The Self: Women, Dress, Power and Situated Bodily Practice in the Workplace'. Unpublished PhD Thesis.

Freud, S (1919), 'The Uncanny', from *Freud No. 14, Art and Literature*, London: Pelican.

Gelder, K. (1994), *Reading The Vampire*, London: Routledge.

Gledhill, C. (1985) 'Recent Developments in Feminist Criticism' in G. Mast and M. Cohen (eds), *Film Theory and Criticism: Introductory Readings*, 3rd Edition, New York: Oxford University Press.

—— (ed.) (1987), *Home is Where the Heart is: Studies in Melodrama and the Woman's Film*, London: BFI Books.

Goldmann, L. (1980), *Method in the Sociology of Literature*, translated and edited by William Q. Boelhower, London.

—— (1972), *Towards a Sociology of the Novel*, translated by A. Sheridan, London.

Gordon, J. and Hollinger V. (1997), *Blood Read: The Vampire as Metaphor in Contemporary Culture*, Philadelphia: The University of Pennsylvania Press.

Hall, S. (1973), 'Encoding/decoding in television discourse' in S. Hall, D. Hobson, A. Lowe, and P. Willis (eds), *Culture, Media, Language*, London: Hutchinson.

Hebdidge, D. (1979), *Subculture: The Meaning of Style*, London: Methuen.

Hobson, D. (1990), 'Women Audiences and the Workplace' in M.E. Brown (ed.), *Television and Women's Culture: The Politics of the Popular*, London: Sage.

Hodges, D and Doane, J.L. (1991), 'Undoing Feminism in Anne Rice's Vampire Chronicles' in J. Naremore and P. Brantlinger (eds), *Modernity and Mass Culture*, Bloomington: Indiana University Press.

Hollander, A. (1993), *Seeing Through Clothes*, Berkeley: University of California Press.

hooks, b. (1984), *Feminist Theory: From Margins to Center*, Boston: South End Press.

Jancovich, M. (1992), *Horror*, London: B.T. Batsford Ltd.

Jenkins, H. (1992). *Textual Poachers: Television Fans and Participatory Culture*, New York: Routledge.

Jenson, J. (1992), 'Fandom as Pathology: The Consequences of Characterization' in L.A. Lewis (ed.), *The Adoring Audiences: Fan Culture and Popular Media*, London: Routledge.

Morley, D. (1992), *Television Audiences and Cultural Studies*, London: Routledge.

Mulvey, L. (1985), 'Visual Pleasure and Narrative Cinema' in G. Mast and M. Cohen (eds), *Film Theory and Criticism*, 3rd Edition, Oxford: Oxford University Press.

—— (1990), 'Afterthoughts on "Visual Pleasure and Narrative Cinema" inspired by Duel in the Sun' in E.A. Kaplan (ed.), *Psychoanalysis and Cinema*, London: Routledge.

Pribram, E.D. (ed.) (1988), *Female Spectators: Looking at Film and Television*, London: Verso.

Rice, A. (1976), *Interview With The Vampire*, New York: Ballantine Books.

—— (1985), *The Vampire Lestat*, New York: Ballantine Books.

—— (1988), *The Queen of the Damned: The Third Book in the Vampire Chronicles*, New York: Alfred A. Knopf.

—— (1992), *The Tale of the Body Thief: The Vampire Chronicles*, New York: Ballantine Books.

—— (1995), *Memnoch the Devil: The Vampire Chronicles*, New York: Alfred A. Knopf.

Roth, L. (1984), 'Film, Society and Ideas: Nosferatu and Horror of Dracula' in B.K. Grant (ed.), *Planks of Reason: Essays on the Horror Film*, Metuchen: The Scarecrow Press, Inc.

Skal, D. (1993), *The Monster Show: A Cultural History of Horror*, London: Plexus.

Thornton, S. (1995), *Club Cultures: Music, Media and Subcultural Capital*, Cambridge: Polity.

Tseëlon, E. (1995), *The Masque of Femininity*, London: Sage.

Tudor, A. (1989), *Monsters and Mad Scientists: A Cultural History of the Horror Movie*, Oxford: Blackwell.

Wallace, M. (1990), *Invisibility Blues*, London: Verso.

Williams, L (1984), 'When the Woman Looks', in P. Mellencampe et al. (eds), *Revisions*, Los Angeles: University Publications of America. The American Film Institute Monograph Series.

Wilson, E. (1985), *Adorned in Dreams: Fashion and Modernity*, London: Virago Press.

Young, L. (1996), *Fear of the Dark: 'Race', Gender and Sexuality in the Cinema*, London: Routledge.

Zimmerman, B. (1984), 'Daughters of Darkness: Lesbian Vampires on Film' in B.K. Grant (ed.), *Planks of Reason: Essays on the Horror Film*, Metuchen: The Scarecrow Press.

8

The Fall and Rise of Erotic Lingerie

Dana Wilson-Kovacs

Introduction

The ways in which the body is packaged and visually exhibited are an essential part of consumerism. With a tradition that can be traced back to the eve of modern times, consumerism cannot fully account for the unprecedented attention surrounding the clothing of the body, and the multitude of codes, readings and interpretations accompanying its display. The cultural practices that define the body influence its representations and contemporary ideas of femininity and masculinity. These ideas are reflected, in turn, by bodily display and conveyed through our choice of dress. Furthermore, while metaphors of masculinity abound in images conveying movement and action, those of femininity relate to ornamentation and echo overtly the cultural practices that they circumscribe.

Drawing attention to the ways in which dress and body display emphasize the dichotomy between masculinity and femininity, commentators have discussed how cultural materials have provided a basis for disciplining the body (Betterton 1987). Furthermore, feminist theory has focused on the constitutive role of such materials in the cultural construction of sexual representations (Brownmiller 1984), and examined their ideological role as 'technologies of gender' (de Laurentis 1987). As such, not only do models of femininity circumscribe the configuration of material bodies as desirable; but equating traditional ideas of femininity to submission, this view depicts women as passive recipients of men's needs (Jackson & Scott 1997). Such approaches denounce ornamentation and the display of the body as co-ordinates of a disembodied sexuality (cf. Holland et al. 1994).

Though the cultural implications of this dichotomy have captivated feminists and non-feminists alike, few exegetes have concerned themselves with its reflection into everyday practices. Furthermore, as adornment is primarily feminine in the Western world and configured by its consumerist potential, the little amount of interest given by social theorists to this field of material culture is surprising. While the analysis of codes and ideologies surrounding the female ornamentation has benefited from detailed investigations into the ways in which these reflect gender and power relations and circumscribe social practices (Brownmiller 1984; Betterton 1987), research has seldom focused on how the artefacts involved in these practices have been materially and symbolically developed. This is even more poignant in the case of female erotic lingerie: fervent ideological wars are fought over sexual meanings, codes and roles but few studies have examined the ways in which these items of clothing have outlined current perceptions of eroticism and sexual attractiveness. These artefacts are in themselves metaphors of modern femininity, and understanding their development and gradual infiltration into the consumerist psyche will enlighten not only some of the debates surrounding female sexuality, but also the modern cultural construction, production, and marketing of the female body.

This chapter focuses on the cultural history of such an item – the suspender-belt (UK) (or, its Northern American equivalent, garter belt) – and examines its material rise and semiotics in relation to the general development of the underclothes industry. While historians of fashion have covered marginally the emergence and impact of the suspender-belt, the sociological interest in the handling, packaging and presentation of the female body has been focused primarily on the laced corset (Kunzle 1982; Steele 1985). The cultural approach advanced in this chapter attempts to explain the ways in which the suspender-belt have articulated distinct modes of consumption and more elusive ideas of femininity which have shaped the construction of consumerist needs. Moreover, such an approach enlightens the connections between ideology, cultural practices and the production of commodities, and offers a broader interpretative framework to the relationship between the material and symbolic value of this artefact.

Being an essential part of the cultural construction of femininity, the contemporary iconography of erotic lingerie is indicative of the ways in which the factors circumscribing femininity (for example, body, attitude and artefacts) have been configured over the last hundred years. Divided into two sections this chapter suggests that both the development of ideas concerning the cleanliness of the body and its sexuality, and a corresponding rise in technical innovation, industrial processing, and advertising techniques are an essential part of the iconographic production of erotic lingerie. While the first section presents the main historical co-ordinates in the emergence of the suspender-belt, the second section dissects its ideological, economic and social influences, and, in relation to those, discusses the symbolism of this artefact and its relevance for erotic iconography.

The Suspender-Belt: A Brief History

Initially designed to keep up the stockings and as an alternative to the garter, the suspender-belt developed in the mid-nineteenth-century in combination with the corset. Its emergence can be explained by the obsession with health and hygiene which took hold in the latter half of the nineteenth century and gave rise to a growing anxiety over constricting garments. While various attempts were made to suspend the stocking by various contrivances, only with the invention of vulcanized rubber was a feasible replacement for the garter produced. By the 1880s the National Health Society championed the suspender as a better alternative to the constrictions of the garter (Farrell 1992: 68). Consequently, garters started to be replaced by suspenders. They were manufactured as either part of the corset or as a separate item. Added to the corset, this last arrangement had four attachments for stockings and two buttons to fasten at the waist.

At the beginning of the 1890s suspenders were increasingly popular and different types were available to the public. Because stockings were fairly short in the leg, the suspenders were exceedingly long. They were 'usually gathered satin-covered elastic, terminating in hefty, workmanlike clips' which made them unpleasant to wear (Hawthorne 1993: 81). Despite claims to the contrary, there is no evidence that the suspender-belt enjoyed the erotic frisson of corsets in the first fifty years of its existence. The popular image of the suspender as an accessory of the French can-can dancer is a Hollywood fiction; for such erotic displays of the period the garter was not only preferred but also considered indispensable.

Furthermore, while already established articles of lingerie were promoted with suggestions of eroticism, in the case of the suspender-belt the emphasis was upon its utilitarian virtues. Compare for instance these two advertisements from the 1890s: 'SMART FRENCH SEWN CORSET (made in Paris). With the New Straight Front, very daintily trimmed with Lace and Ribbon, and fitted with stocking Suspenders and Rich Black Lace. Can be had in White, Black, Maize, sky, Pink, and Mauve-coloured Brocade, with coloured Silk Floral design, to contrast. Exceptional value, 21/9. Same Corset in Rich Satin Brocade, 42/9' (Pearsall 1981: 10), and 'by the aid of these ingenious and comfortable contrivances, garters are entirely dispensed with, and ladies fond of athletic and outdoor exercises have found them a boon. This daintily got up suspender is made in different forms, and of a variety of suitable materials, and is fitted with the HOVEN CLIP, whose grip is bull-dog in tenacity' (Hawthorne 1993: 74).

With the beginning of the twentieth century '(e)very sort of cunning arrangement is advertised, from the sublime to the ridiculously complicated. Such marvels as the Portia Combined Stocking Suspender and Shoulder Harness, which in 1900 is described as "very useful for little boys". There is the Hookon Hose Supporter, manufactured by Kleinerts (. . .) and the Velver Grip Hose Supporter with "patented rubber cushion button" – both from 1906' (ibid.: 79). Before the First World War the United States started to manufacture suspenders separately as a belt, and in 1912 the modern combined suspender and belt was patented and advertised as 'needing "NO CLASP TO GRIP AND HOSE TO RIP"'(ibid.: 85).

After 1918 changes in fashion dictated a lighter appearance and technological improvements, together with a variety of materials used, created a more comfortable suspender-belt. While the choice of suspender-belt was decidedly prompted by financial considerations – the belt retailing for half the cost of the corset – changes in fashion and a boom in the stocking industry also contributed to the successful acceptance of the suspender belt as an everyday accessory. This is the period when the brassiere started to be manufactured, and the new ensemble created by the suspender-belt, bra and camiknickers replaced the constricting corset and accompanying petticoats. The start of the fashion for short skirts encouraged the unprecedented development of the stocking industry and advances in technologies improved their quality and appearance. Suspender belts gained increasing popularity, and together with glamorous nylon stockings and the brassiere were recognised as an essential foundation garment after the Second World War. By then, they were perceived as functional, erotic and indispensable to every woman or girl, justifying their 1960s advertising craze. They were promoted, for instance, by such improbable artifices as the Kayser Bondor Teenage Advice Bureau, which aspired 'to help schoolgirls "sort out their underwear problems"' and Teenform, an American range of brassieres and suspender belts marketed in Britain and designed for girls between ten and twelve years old (ibid.: 108).

This manufacturing euphoria was soon tempered down with the introduction of tights, a garment initially promoted as children wear. The 1960s' and 1970s' tendency towards diminutive underwear made stockings drop 'from holding 72 per cent of the (. . .) in 1964 to holding a mere 5 per cent of tights and stockings in 1971' (Ewing 1978: 169). By 1978 a fashion writer could state that 'today [the stocking] only just survives, having to be sought out by the dwindling tiny minority of older women faithful to tradition' (ibid.). Yet, by the end of the 1980s the stocking/suspender belt combination was back in fashion, being estimated that women under the age of twenty-five purchased one pair of stockings to every three pairs of tights (Farrell 1992). While the revival of this ensemble can be partially explained by the last decade's concern with health, stockings and suspender belts have been mainly marketed with reference to their supposed eroticism. Having now limited practical value, suspender-belts have come to symbolize the sexualized woman and to reflect a nostalgic feeling for glamorous fashion. How can we explain the fall and rise of the suspender-belt and of erotic lingerie in general?

Moreover, how and why did the suspender-belt become the archetypal symbol of knowledgeable sexuality? The perceived sensuality of underclothes is culturally constructed and inspired by ideological shifts and historical changes in the economic and social milieus. The following analysis identifies the social and material factors that influenced the emergence of underclothes, and examines the rise of the elusive erotic value attributed to lingerie.

Preamble: Underclothes Before the Nineteenth Century

Though underclothes (in the form of corsets, stockings and garters) existed before the nineteenth century, it was only at the beginning of the last century that they achieved momentum and developed from artefacts belonging to a cottage industry to fully recognised items of male and female dress. Thus, female underclothes did not really exist before the mid-1800s: until the previous century stockings had been barely sexually differentiated, and underskirts were simply duplications of overskirts added for warmth. Additionally, corsets were perceived as ruthlessly functional, and though they had been used as early as the sixteenth century, they were neither worn next to the skin, nor recorded as eliciting any erotic interest until the last hundred years.

The scarcity and sheer practicality of underclothes before the nineteenth century justifies the lack of documentary evidence portraying lingerie as sexually stimulating. Occasionally however, underclothes had been looked upon as gratifying sexual pleasure before the 1800s. The garter was virtually the only item of lingerie to achieve a powerful erotic status prior to this time. Although stockings reached only a little above the knee, the allure of a device that demarcated a clothed body from a naked one was strong. Famously in 1348 while retrieving one of the Countess of Salisbury's garters which had fallen to the ground, Edward III admonished his court with the words, 'Honi soit qui mal y pense' (Hawthorne 1993: 37).[1]

While garters figured erotically in the discourses of the time, stockings achieved sexual recognition only in the eighteenth century when their gender differentiation took place. Stockings developed from virtually unisex items before this time, to separate male and female accessories, the latter being attributed an increasing erotic value. The sexual innuendo elicited by this gender differentiation is captured by Dr Johnson's confession to David Garrick, the actor, in 1750: 'I'll come no more behind your scenes, David, for the white silk stockings and white bosoms of your actresses excite my amorous propensities' (ibid.: 36). This frank association of exposed underclothes, revealing contours and erotic reveries, has dominated the last hundred years and produced some of the most powerful images of sexual desirability.

Last century's shift to mass production was accompanied by novel ideas of presenting the body, the product and its wearer, and the growing market of undergarments was directed especially to women. Nineteenth-century consumerism culture offered for the first time products designed for a specific buyer and provided a set of ideologies and values circumscribing body presentation and appearance. Parallel to the rise of the underclothes industry in the last hundred years, a subtler process of redefining eroticism and reinventing the boundaries between licit and illicit sexuality took place. While these issues are touched upon at a further point in my analysis, an insight into the emergence of undergarments market and the ideological premises behind this process will enlighten their understanding.

Perhaps the first important element in a conceptual analysis concerning the development of lingerie is that the gender differentiation of underclothes brought with it an erotic sense of the undergarment in question when designed for, and used by, women. The next section looks at the ways in which the perceived eroticism of underclothes was accompanied by a different attitude to the body and its functions. Not only was this ideology backed up by a growing consumerist structure, industrial developments and technological innovations also aided it.

Understanding the Shame Frontier

One crucial, yet underestimated, factor in the evolution of underclothes has been the emergence of the 'shame frontier'. Elias argues that the development of civil society in Europe was predicated upon codes of etiquette that formed the basis of social intercourse. Enlightening the attitudinal shift towards a restrictive exposure of the human body in modern societies, the shame frontier was one component of this new etiquette: an increased awareness to naked exposure and bodily functions. Until the sixteenth century 'the sight of total nakedness was the everyday rule' for bathing and for sleeping (Elias 1978: 164). Not only were both activities communal, also 'people ran naked through the streets to the bathhouse while visitors shared the family bed' (ibid.: 168). The next three centuries witnessed the gradual disappearance of these attitudes at first in the upper classes and then in the middle and lower classes. In this process the female body and sexuality were sensitive issues: the former for its complex clean/unclean dichotomy, the latter for its powerful association with the loss of rationality over senses. The visual and textual representations of female body and sexuality followed the restrictions imposed by the shame frontier, and the new physical awareness brought with it a tight regime of representational conventions, which was reflected in the art and medical science of the time. The rise of the shame frontier was paralleled by a surge into rationality, Puritanism and temperance that was to affect sexual attitudes. As sexuality became confined to reproduction, the female body was subjected to a stricter observation and regulation. This closer reign of interpretation viewed reproduction as the sole possible permutation and circumscribed sexual pleasure to an illicit medium, and this shift in sexual attitudes was reflected in pornographic writings. Thus while 'in the seventeenth century (. . .) normal women were thought to be at least as libidinous as men, (. . .) after about 1740 the only situation in which women were represented as enthusiastic about sex was in pornographic fiction' (Harvey 1994: 43)

Reflecting on the fundamental change in interpersonal relationships and behaviour brought about by the shame frontier and expressed in our manner of living, Elias draws attention to the covert way in which the bed and the body have become 'psychological danger zones' in modernity (1978: 168). If the development of underclothes reflected successfully the need of containment and concealment, a resistance to the imposition of the new code of behaviour documented an adverse reaction. Thus, casting his mind back to the middle of the eighteenth century, an old voyeur commented that:

> [U]nder the Empire, women did not wear drawers (. . .), our imagination climbed the length of their stockings and seduced us into ecstasies toward those regions as intimate as they are delicious. We did not see, but we knew we could see, should the occasion arise. (. . .) But today (. . .) we know that our view would be irremediably arrested by an obstacle, that our suggestive voyage would end at a hollow of batiste and we come to a stop at the base of the wall. (in Steele 1985: 199).

This hostility towards female drawers was also shared by the anonymous author of *My Secret Life*, who complained that: 'More and more this fashion of wearing drawers seems to be spreading, (. . .), formerly no woman wore them, but now whether lady, servant, or whore, they all wear them. I find they hinder those comfortable chance feels of bum and cunt, of which I have had so many' (in Marcus 1974: 98). Women's underpants – the first item of underclothes to be introduced on a mass scale – were only slowly accepted in the course of the nineteenth century, in the face of a long and powerful resistance. Similar to the introduction of tights more than a century later, the drawers were initially presented as children fashion and worn by little girls. Later we find them referred as a 'demi-masculine' article of dress and used by courtesans, actresses, and dancers (Steele 1985: 198). What seemed to trigger their extensive everyday use was a mixture of cold weather and persistent medical advice that recommended them to all mature British women. The reluctance to use drawers instead of flannel petticoats is documented by *Cassell's Magazine* as late as the 1880s. A similar attitude is found on the Continent. The French fashion for underpants, for instance:

> was gradually adopted by women for sporting pursuits, such as horseback riding, and for more active dances, such as the polka and the waltz. But in 1873, Le Sport argued that while it might be necessary for certain pursuits, 'it is never gracious (. . .) and because of that, women who have the true intuition of elegance of their sex will always abstain from it'. (ibid.).

There is a similarity here between the late nineteenth-century advertising of suspender-belts and the reaction to drawers, the emphasis being put in both cases on the functional aspects of these two items. Their proximity to genitalia appears to diminish erotic connotations such as those given to corsets and garters, and to hinder their successful acceptance. By the end of the century, however, a different pattern of presenting underwear emerged.

In the case of drawers, the focus of resistance changed from the whole item to a detail of that item – i.e. the closed drawers (Carter 1992). Generally, the emphasis seemed to be put less on the hygienic and practical qualities of underclothes and more on their texture, quality and sophistication. The period of the Belle Époque (from 1890 to 1913) witnessed an increase in the choice and quality of undergarments, which were now included with nightwear under the appellation 'lingerie': 'typical day lingerie sets comprised, in the 1890s, a fancy chemise and drawers or combinations, a corset with suspenders, black stockings, camisole and one or two petticoats' (ibid.: 83).

By then the restrictions imposed by the shame frontier were not only accepted but had successfully contributed to the emergence of a sophisticated market. So far, we have observed the ways in which these restrictions influenced the introduction of female underwear, and how by being included in a more general presentational package which contained items with recognised sexual connotations, drawers and suspender-belts could also be marketed with erotic appeal. While the gender differentiation of undergarments brought with it a discernible eroticism, this developed in parallel with the shame frontier, and the gradual acceptance of female underclothes. Once the functionality of these items became recognized, their marketing turned towards fully emphasizing their eroticism and sensuality, either as a package or, especially after the First World War, as separate items. The rise of modern consumerism and the emergence of middle-class values made this development possible.

Consumerism and the Development of Underwear Industry

Although the shame frontier can explain ideologically the development of under-clothes, it cannot account for the unprecedented rise of the underwear industry in the nineteenth century. The entrepreneurial variety generated by the gradual acceptance of underwear items had its roots in the beginning of the modern period. Commenting on Weber's concept of ascetic rationality, Mukerji observes that the culture of early Europe was essentially one divided between the hedonism of the consumers and the asceticism of the entrepreneurs. Not only did this hedonism provide the 'cultural rationale for increased interest and participation in economic activity' (1983: 2), it also shared (together with the asceticism of the producers) a similar interest in material accumulation. With the beginning of the sixteenth century, the existent patterns of consumption became focused on choice and, in turn, they facilitated the emergence of models intended for guiding the accumulation. 'Consumerism,' comments Mukerji (1983: 22), 'made sense out of increased production and trade, by tying patterns of consumption to new systems of self presentation, new ways to make claims about social station.'

In this process, the middle class had the political and economic powers to configure changes in fashion and to inspire the desire for technical innovation and novelty in fabric, design and form. Early methods of mass production and the development of a cottage industry based on the sewing machine led to a substantial increase in the manufacture of underclothes and a fall in retail prices. In turn, technological advances facilitated the general development of underclothes and initiated shifts in fashion. As the nineteenth century pro-gressed underclothes were gradually differentiated into a range of separate garments: petticoats, camisoles, corsets, drawers, knickers, suspender-belts, basques, and brassieres.

Little was achieved before the nineteenth century, but in the 1840s vul-canized rubber was introduced. It marked the beginning of technical innovations that made possible the development of the underwear industry. Chemical dyes, which improved greatly elasticity and the choice of colour in underclothes (and especially stockings), were introduced forty years later. The invention of artificial silk (later known as Rayon) in the 1890s contributed to the creation of an even wider range of underwear: 'underclothing is now made of soft silk,' *Sylvia's Home Journal* observed in 1880, 'and is as much trimmed with lace as our dresses, with hand embroidery most beautifully done' (in Ewing 1978: 85).

The North American manufacture of artificial yarn in 1912 made possible the production of glamorous lookalike silk stockings at affordable prices (Hawthorne 1993: 87). The proliferation of elastic materials, the introduction of nylon in the 1940s (a new artificial fibre superior to rayon in its weight, versatility and strength) and its mass production since the 1950s, have further enhanced the texture of underwear (and in particular stockings and suspender-belts), and presented the consumer with luxurious hosiery at reasonable prices.

Alongside technical innovations, the evolution of advertising has contributed to the overall development of underwear. The development of print technology meant that within a quarter of a century simple line drawings had given way to explicit illustrated spreads of luxury underwear with distinct erotic appeal. Though corsets, drawers and suspenders were still worn by both sexes at the turn of this century, they were markedly differentiated by their elaboration. Not only underclothes had become lighter in appearance and feel by then; also, they were more luxurious in conception and more delicate in their execution.[2] Commenting on this development at the end of the nineteenth century, the French fashion historian Octave Uzanne identified the elaboration of under-garments as 'the most special characteristic of contemporary dress' (Steele 1985: 192). The evolution of advertising techniques played an important role in this recognition.

After advertising duty was abolished in the UK in 1853, there was a huge increase in press advertisements. The methods of advertising underclothes were also rapidly changing. From 1877 illustrated display advertisements were introduced into English magazines and it was found that 'selling messages, (. . .) could be put across by means of visual symbols as well as by words' (Nevett 1982: 86); additionally, lithography enabled the production of illustrated posters in colour. The late 1870s, for instance, had corsets as being attractively packaged in decorative boxes that often had coloured labels. While early advertisements in newspapers and fashion magazines appeared as line drawings or the occasional hand-coloured fashion plate, their ostensible message pointed to the erotic connotations of the advertised garment: drawers, for instance 'were rather shyly drawn – folded with just parts of the embroidery or lace showing. As the quality of lingerie improved and the choice broadened in the late 1880s, advertisements became more and more explicit to match the luxury and erotic appeal of the garments' (Carter 1992: 64).

As well as supporting a growing underwear industry, nineteenth century advertising fuelled its consumers' desires and shaped conspicuously their perception of a beautiful and desirable female body. Though the corset and garter were already sensual reference points in the marketing representations of the fashionable female body, the overall development of the underwear industry inspired more persuasive advertising techniques that took into consideration the erotic possibilities of every item of lingerie. Parallel to the creation of an aesthetic geography of female form, advertising introduced and elaborated the artefacts of this transformation: corsets, stockings, suspender-belts and brassieres. As previously discussed, this introduction was based in the beginning on ideas of functionality and containment. The spirit of fashionable change, together with technological advances and refined advertising techniques gave way to a more leisurely discourse on the luxurious, sensual and ultimately sexual possibilities opened by the purchase of underclothes.

While some of the artefacts themselves created controversy when presented to the public (for example, the voluminous correspondence of *The Englishwoman's Domestic Magazine* on corsets and stays which 'like that of the domestic whipping of girls, (. . .) was republished separately' (Hyde 1964: 149); the manner in which their customers were introduced to these items points to the modern birth of the fetishist (as both an excessive consumer and sexual deviant). The incitement raised by the advertisement of underclothes, and especially those referring to corsets, stimulated new ways of introducing underwear: undergarments being presented, for instance, as floating in space but filled out by an imaginary torso. According to Finch (1991) this technique exhibited 'the space occupied or, rather, not occupied by the female body as strangely empty and fraught (though ambiguously) with meaning' (in Craik 1994: 121); in its skilful manner, this advertising display further fetishized the female body and its sexuality. The development of underclothes has not created the fetishist; but in a complex process – paralleled by the rise of scientific explanation surrounding sexual behaviour – has given this persona weight and prominence. In the case of female drawers, for instance, the opportunity to catch a glimpse of women's sexual organs was replaced by a voyeurism directed toward the sight of the underpants themselves. In turn, the corset attracted attention to the shape of the body and was the first item of underclothes to present female form in an erotically constructed fashion and to become an object of fetishist enthusiasm.[3] While the corset created a prototype for an everyday pleasurable body that reflected the aesthetic ideal and also contained and disciplined the female body, the suspender-belt took over this prototype and enhanced its erotic qualities by focusing overtly on the lower part of the female body.

The advent of the illustrated mail order catalogue and the development of department stores further fuelled fetishism. Other publications aimed at those interested in the fetishist aspects of female underwear appeared. Alongside the above correspondence in the *Englishwoman's Domestic Magazine*, *London Life* and the French *La Vie Parisienne* catered to enthusiasts while masquerading as fashion magazines. As these publications provided the uninitiated with valuable information on both underwear and female anatomy, the department stores increased the mystery surrounding female underclothes by confining lingerie sections to the back portion of an upper floor, and discreetly camouflaging them against the unexpected appearance of men (Hawthorne 1993). The 1920s enhanced this sense of secrecy: 'department stores began to model "foundation" garments and to consciously design ladies' underwear departments as "intimate" and "refined" spaces to which women were, purportedly, "particularly susceptible" (Hirst & Reekie 1977: 294). While this décor underlined the association of lingerie with romance and helped to fix the meaning of underclothes as an ultimately feminine realm, it simultaneously reinforced more dangerously seductive connotations.

The rise of consumerism, advances in technology and advertising techniques, the emergence of women's periodicals and specialized publications, and the growth of the department store contributed all to the successful acceptance of underwear by increasingly underlying its eroticism. Nevertheless, what helped lingerie most in becoming a permanent feature of erotic iconography was the advent of the cinema: the medium that has created most contemporary sexual stereotypes. To understand its contribution to sexual semiotics we also have to take into consideration the position of women in Victorian society, and late nineteenth-century sexual attitudes.

Ideology, the Semiotics of the Suspender-Belt and the Media

As the middle classes achieved growing political and economic influence in the nineteenth century, their cultural values became paramount to the construction of body ideologies, and reshaped the boundaries of the shame frontier for a more comfortable fit. The novelty of urban and industrial experiences brought with it a tighter regulation of social interaction and required the separation of the public sphere from the private one (Mulvey 1989). Following this separation, gender roles became polarized. While men were identified with activity, production and the public domain, women were confined to consumption and the intimacy of the domestic sphere. The fashions of the day echoed this polarization and, as menswear became generally more functional, women's attire was oriented towards conspicuous consumption and artifice to such an extent that 'the image of restrained and respectable womanhood contrasted with the elaborate and highly decorative underclothes worn by women' (Craik 1994: 121).

Consumerism reflected these ideologies in its discourses. As it was previously discussed, the dressing of the female body was regulated by fashionable change and its representation in the media was simultaneously a celebration of the new form and an image that could be purchased as any other commodity. Not only did the mid-nineteenth-century explosion of discourse on women operate on different levels, but was, as Boardman argues, constructed in reference to 'contrary polarities: display and excess and regulation and constraint' (1998: 96). These polarities have been captured most prominently in the polemics raised by the corset, which was simultaneously 'an affirmation of female form and beauty, and a denial of female sexuality and desire' (Turner 1984: 197). The corset captured the dichotomy between artifice and restraint and reflected the highly ornamental status given to the female body throughout this period. Although the popularity of the corset with women across the social and moral spectrum associated this item with scandal, it did not hinder the emergence of fashionable concepts of beauty. The corset attracted attention to the shape of body and promoted an essentially aesthetic female form. With the decline of the corset and changes in fashion, its architectural role was transferred to the suspender-belt, which, by bridging the gap between the stocking and the mysterious recesses of the female anatomy, has changed the erotic focus of the female body from the waist emphasized by the corset, to genitalia.

This overt emphasis on the impure and ambiguous area of the female lower body has also reflected the problematic of a body that had to be both the sites of sexual conduct and contact. Perhaps more than men's sexuality, that of women became of special concern, as the body had to be protected as well as disciplined in order to control its sexual impulses (Craik 1994: 115). Restricted to reproduction and subjected to irrational drives, female sexuality was for Victorians focused in her womb. Accordingly, a woman's sex drive was 'powdered by the uterus and its appendage' (Mason 1994: 221). In comparison with the drawers that, by protecting the female genitalia, were in direct contact with it, the suspender-belt shaped, very much like the corset, the female form. Unlike the corset, however, the suspender-belt has concentrated on the lower part of female anatomy and presented the whole body in reference to it. This item of lingerie is, in essence, inherently erotic as a surgical appliance. It does not follow or enhance the contours of the female body, but segments the area around the loins horizontally and vertically; and this brutality is emphasized when the stereotypical ensemble of black suspender-belt and stockings is worn against a white skin, the loins and curves of the bottom being jarringly framed by stark rectangles. Its suggestive power has been fully developed by the cinema, which through its skilful metaphors has equated the suspender-belt, and underwear in general, to eroticism.

The advent of the cinema reinforced novel norms of behaviour and promoted images that associated everyday retail goods with youth, luxury and beauty. Appealing to hitherto suppressed desires, the cinema fuelled the credo of a new consumerist culture that has been one of continuous improvement in the quality of life and personal appearance (especially female). It also gave women the opportunity to imitate in both behaviour and appearance their female screen idols. 'Film industry,' comments Featherstone, 'offered the quickest route to high street interpretation when women were filled with the simple desire to emulate the glamour of a favourite female star' (in Featherstone et al. 1991: 172). In addition, in the late 1920s 'moviemakers acknowledged that the men in the audience liked watching their favourites in silken hose or other undergarments' (Shipman 1985: 20). Consequently, movie stars were often presented in underwear – apart from its financially successful titillation, this display helped in the creation of presentational codes and the perpetuation of sexual stereotypes. Clara Bow's producers, for instance, advised her scriptwriters and directors 'to get her into as many situations as possible that required her to appear in bathing suits and lingerie and other stages of undress. The lingerie industry had her to thank for a boost in sales of clingy nightgowns, slips and "scanties"' (Lottie 1990: 47).

If before the 1920s the interest in underwear could be maintained through intense advertising techniques and compelling illustrations of stockings and suspenders in the cabaret programmes of the time (Hawthorne 1993: 92), by the 1930s the associations between erotic scenery, underwear and suspenders were enriched with the help of the film industry. Hollywood provided a mass source of material that broadened out women's images into popular mythology and collective fantasy (Mulvey 1989). Now marketing, advertising and film backed fashion and the underclothes industry. Films, as Laver points out, influenced taste: 'undressing scenes were frequently shown and had the curious effect of immensely improving women's underwear in real life: the abandonment of linen and the substitution of real or artificial silk' (in Wilson 1985: 103). The 1950s established the erotic ensemble of suspender-belt and stockings in the consumerist psyche. Advertising laws were also more relaxed in this period and it was possible to advertise underwear on television for the first time. A whole new art form develop around the portrayal of underwear in film and on television, in advertising, in photography and magazine illustrations and in slogans (Carter 1992).

While all these factors contributed to the success of the underclothes industry, the 1960s 'sexual revolution' – when it seemed that one way of achieving sexual freedom was to renounce constricting underclothes – the introduction of minimalist underwear and the success of tights eclipsed the use of suspender-belts and stockings, and diminished the erotic impact of other items of lingerie. The final part of this chapter examines the survival and revival of erotic connotations given to underwear and, in the light of my previous analysis, discusses the patterns within which these emerged and developed.

Conclusion

So far, we have discussed the shift from a functional discourse to an essentially erotic one accompanying the presentation of the fashionable female body, and the ways in which middle-class ideologies influenced this display. The study of advertising techniques, visual displays and cinema influences is also particularly useful for an understanding of how consumerism has shaped sexual desire. As women's underclothes were gradually given sexual overtones, their variety and elaboration also reflected the concerns raised by the shame frontier. Though lingerie was justified as being functional – emphasizing health, comfort and practicality – it also drew attention to the body by modelling it and creating new forms and codes of desire.

The symbolism of seduction and eroticism given to underclothes functioned in parallel with that developed in the 1920s by advertising techniques and department stores, which gave lingerie a more feminine and romantic meaning. The sexual association of the suspender-belt, however, developed long before this image of femininity took hold. Female sexuality was for the nineteenth-century medical practitioner located in her womb. Furthermore, this fascination with the lower part of the female anatomy was reflected in the Victorian obsession with buttocks, which were considered a displacement of the genitalia. Their size elicited particular interest in the case of the Hottentot woman. Gilman (1985) establishes a clear link between the Victorian concept of black African sexuality (which was perceived as primitive and deviant) and the nineteenth-century prostitute, who was regarded as the archetype of the sexualized woman. In this context it is not surprising that, as well as being popular for its concealment of dirt, the colour black was used to suggest wantonness and availability, and that the symbolism of the black suspender-belt and black lingerie has been for most of this century associated with cheapness and prostitution. Thus, we can understand the suspender-belt's derogatory status and the successful fascination it has elicited as an artefact which packages female sexuality – a primitive, deviant and irrational element – for presentation and consumption.

The erotic connotations given to lingerie reflected its association with prostitutes and showgirls, which explains the reluctance of the 1920s models 'to "do lingerie jobs". This attitude persisted long after underwear was transformed into luxury lingerie' (Craik 1994: 127). So infamous was the association between sex for sale and erotic lingerie, that *Penthouse Magazine* created a stir by promoting female underwear (especially black garments) in its 1960s' illustrations (Gabor 1973). The black colour amplifies the erotic potency of lingerie and reinforces the sexual iconography of the suspender-belt. As I have discussed previously, the suspender-belt frames the female body in a way in which her pudenda has been dissociated from the rest of her anatomy, and concentrates the viewer's gaze on her genitalia. In combination with the soft and frilly underwear accompanying it and the silkiness of stockings, the suspender-belt packages the whole body and suggests that the female loins constitute the totality of a woman's sexual attraction.

Harvey (1994: 34) observes that an essential feature in the process of freeing the female body from restrictive clothing since the seventeenth century has been 'the restoration to visibility of the outline of the bottom' and suggests that those changes in fashion have involved a re-evaluation of female sexuality. Following from this argument, the decline of the corset and the fashion for short skirts 'liberated' the female derrière, only to give way to the discipline imposed by the suspender-belt. The powerful connotations of the suspender-belt are a mixture of aestheticism and meticulous focus on an object of clinical observation. By according its wearer an aura of sexual sophistication and presenting her as a sexually active agent, the suspender-belt or garter belt has emerged as a symbol of 'knowledgeable' female sexuality that implies pleasure, desire and willingness.

Fuelled by the 1970s minimalist underwear, the revival of the suspender-belt and underclothes in general can be explained by the nostalgic feeling of bygone eroticism. This is reflected in successful enterprises such as the lingerie sets of speciality shops or department stores, the *Ann Summers* range and, in the USA, *Victoria's Secret* (which markets its products with suggestion to an elusively erotic golden age) (Workman 1996; Juffer 1998). Far from being restricted to underground meanings and negative connotations, the revival of erotic lingerie indicates a consumerist need for a sensual package rich in sexual symbolism, nostalgic reveries, and striking visual clues. Moreover, the iconography of the suspender-belt owes its symbolism to the complex cultural processes surrounding the production and advertising of female underwear and the parallel development in attitudes and ideas about sexuality.

In conclusion, though articles of underclothing had sometimes been worn previously, it was only in the nineteenth century that they became sufficiently defined and ubiquitous for erotic stereotypes to develop. Barthes (1977: 89) maintains that 'a narrative is never made up of anything other than functions: in different degrees, everything in it signifies'. These narratives derive from tradition, and, as they provide a repertoire of sense-making devices, their impact is both social and individual. The most visible narratives and codes related to underwear are evident in advertising: they modify the self and the body by initiating and reinforcing social norms. Underwear advertising has been influential in creating, maintaining, and modifying feminine stereotypes by prescribing patterns of social presentability that include personal habits as well as appearance. Its narratives, however, have been supported by subtler scientific discourses and media representations that indicate the more complex processes in the development of underclothes.

Lingerie fashion has also been partly dictated by considerations of health and comfort, and partly by concepts of sexual enhancement. Though many innovations were originally considered 'unfeminine', as production and consumption persisted, new ideas were formulated as to what was sexually attractive in a woman. The initial perceived unfemininity of some articles of underwear was offset by arguments recommending them for their comfort and hygiene. Once the articles became established, variations were manufactured. The culmination was provided by the luxurious items that concerned themselves with charm and eroticism rather than with comfort and hygiene. While the emergence of plastic sexuality (Giddens 1992) and the freedom from reproductive needs can also account for this development, the media and advertising techniques have influenced most the choice of the consumer, and configured the symbolism of erotic lingerie.

Simultaneously, a subtler process of redefining femininity and eroticism has taken place. Through its consumerist culture, modern capitalism has advocated the manufacture, extension and detail of desires, rather than their suppression (Turner 1984: 25). The commodification of fantasies has gradually gained erotic lingerie its place in the contemporary sexual iconography. In this process discourses on erotic lingerie have become constitutive of the social reality they portray; in turn, novel conceptual tools are required to understand the practices surrounding the everyday use of these artefacts. The idea of consumer 'love maps' (Gould 1991), for instance, opens new insights into the ways in which underclothes configure the intimate universe of their users. It also acknowledges the role of these artefacts in current cultural practices, and reveals their importance and impact in packaging the female body for the most elusive encounter.

Notes

1. 'Shame on him who thinks evil.'
2. 'The Rational Dress Society, founded in 1881, promoted bifurcated undergarments such as combinations at the International Health Exhibition of 1884, held in London. In April 1888, in the first issue of its magazine *Gazette*, Lady Harberton recommended that the maximum weight for under-clothes should be 3.2 kg (7lb)' (Carter 1992: 50).
3. Finch in Craik (1994: 121).

References

Barthes, R. (1977), 'Introduction to the Structural Analysis of the Narrative', in R. Barthes, *Image-Music-Text*, London: Fontana.
Bell, Q. (1976), *Of Human Finery*, New York: Schocken.
Berger, J. (1973), *Ways of Seeing*, New York: Viking.
Betterton, R. (ed.) (1987), *Looking On: Images of Femininity in the Visual Arts and Media*, London: Pandora.

Boardman, K. (1998), 'A Material Girl in a Material World': The Fashionable Female Body in Victorian Women's Magazines, *Journal of Victorian Culture*, 3 (1): 93–110.

Brownmiller, S. (1984), *Femininity*, London: Hamish Hamilton.

Carter, A. (1992), *Underwear. The Fashion History*, London: B.T. Batsford Ltd.

Craik, J. (1994), *The Face of Fashion. Cultural Studies in Fashion*, London: Routledge.

de Laurentis, T., (1987), *Technologies Of Gender: Essays On Theory, Film And Fiction*, Bloomington: Indiana University Press.

Elias, N. (1978), *The Civilising Process*, Oxford: Basil Blackwell.

Ewing, E. (1978), *Dress and Undress*, London: B.T. Batsford Ltd.

Farrell, J. (1992), *Socks and Stockings*, London: Butler and Tanner.

Featherstone, M., Hepworth, M, and Turner, B.(eds) (1991), *The Body: Social Processes and Cultural Theory*, London: Sage Publications.

Finch, C. (1991), 'Hooked and Buttoned Together. Victorian Underwear and Representation', *Victorian Studies*, 34 (3): 337-63.

Gabor, M. (1973), *The Pin-up. A Modest History*, London: Pan Books.

Giddens, A. (1992), *The Transformation of Intimacy. Sexuality, Love and Eroticism in Modern Societies*, London: Polity Press.

Gilman, S. (1985), 'Black Bodies, White Bodies: Towards an Iconography of Female Sexuality, in the Late 19th Century Art, Medicine and Literature', *Critical Inquiry*, 12 (1): 204–44.

Gould, S. (1991), 'Towards a Theory of Sexuality and Consumption: The Consumer Love Maps', *Advances in Consumer Research*, 18: 381–3.

Harvey, A. (1994), *Sex in Georgian England. Attitudes and Prejudices from the 1720s to the 1820s*, London: Duckworth.

Hawthorne, R. (1993), *Stockings and Suspenders*, London: Souvenir Press.

Hirst, I.R.C & Reekie, W.D. (1977), *The Consumer Society*, London: Tavistock Publications.

Holland, H. (1994), 'Power and Desire: The Embodiment of Female Sexuality', *Feminist Review* (46): 21–38.

Hyde, M. (1964), *A History of Pornography*, London: Heinemann.

Jackson, S. & Scott, S. (1997), 'Gut Reactions to Matters of the Heart: Reflections on Rationality, Irrationality and Sexuality', *Sociological Review*, 45(4): 551–76.

Juffer, J. (1998), *At Home with Pornography: Women, Sex and Everyday Life*, New York: New York University Press.

Kunzle, D. (1982), *Fashion and Fetishism*, Ottowa and New Jersey: Rowman and Littlefield.

Levitt, S. (1986), *Victorians Unbuttoned. Registered Designs for Clothing, Their Makers and Wearers, 1839-1900*, London: George Allen & Unwin.

Lottie, D. (1990), *Bad Girls of the Silver Screen*, London: Pandora Press.

Marcus, S. (1974), *The Other Victorians*, New York: Basic Books.

Mason, M. (1994), *The Making of Victorian Sexuality*, Oxford: Oxford University Press.

Mukerji, C. (1983), *From Graven Images: Patterns of Modern Materialism*, New York: Columbia University Press.

Mulvey, L. (1989), *Visual and Other Pleasures*, London: Macmillan.

Nevett, T. (1982), *Advertising in Britain. A History,* London: Heinemann.

Pearsall, R. (1981), *Tell Me Pretty Maiden,* Exeter: Web & Bower.

Saint-Laurent, C. (1968), *A History of Ladies Underwear,* London: Michael Joseph.
Shipman, D. (1985), *Caught in the Act. Sex and Eroticism in the Movies,* London: Hamilton.

Steele, V. (1985), *Fashion and Eroticism,* Oxford: Oxford University Press.

Turner, B. (1984), *The Body and Society: Explorations in Social Theory,* Oxford: Basil Blackwell.

Wilson, E. (1985), *Adorned in Dreams*, London: Virago Press.

Workman, N. (1996), 'From Victorian to Victoria's Secret: The Foundation of Modern Erotic Wear', *Journal of Popular Culture,* 30 (2): 61–73.

9

Dress Freedom: The Personal and the Political

William J.F. Keenan

[I]t is utterly unmeet to be too rigorous in urging a Uniformity of Gesture, or for any to be censorious of other men for a Gesture.

Richard Baxter, *Practical Works (1707: 676)*

A Precarious Freedom

Wherever and whenever we have regard to dress, questions of freedom and unfreedom are unlikely to be very far away from our reflections on why this person or that group dress the way they do. Dress freedom is easy to take for granted and we habitually employ the language of personal choice and individual decision with regard to our clothing options. However, in many contexts and circumstances, the language of constraint, control and compliance is more appropriate to describe the enormous range of petty and gross restrictions on dress experienced by many people throughout history and in the present age. This concluding chapter explores different dimensions of dress liberty, construing our dress freedoms as precious, fragile and, sadly, all too often, unduly, even harshly, limited, and sometimes denied outright. It can be usurped as much by the dictates of the fashion market and peer pressure to conform as by tyrannical sumptuary laws.

Dress liberty is precariously poised in any society at any time. While governance of the body politic through dress controls is as old as government itself (Langer 1959) – and, arguably, has its legitimation, at least in the context of Western society, in the story in the Book of Genesis of the divine imposition of the fig-leaf on Adam and Eve prior to their expulsion from the Garden of Eden – the experience of dress code controls extends far beyond the tentacles of formal government and is underpinned by a rich variety of rationales. It is in the everyday, quotidian settings of life – family, school, work and leisure – that we experience the limits of dress freedom most often and, usually, most painfully.

Children and young people, particularly teenagers who, typically, like to stretch the limits of sartorial tolerance, know this in their bones; so, too, do candidates for job interviews, recruits to the uniformed services, inmates of carceral institutions, and denizens and habitués of the 'classier' sorts of drinking, dining and dancing establishments (complete with burly dress code enforcers at their portals). In the midst of the most self-confident modern, democratic society, universal de facto dress freedom is rarely assured for long. It is not only a mistake of etiquette and proper decorum to presume unlimited dress freedom; it can be politically naïve to do so and can, indeed, prove dangerous to life and limb. The sports fan proclaiming tribal loyalties through his team shirt and scarf of choice who wanders off safe limits into 'enemy' territory, risks harassment and attack; so, too, does the religious devotee whose 'regulation' sacred garb serves as a trigger to otherwise unprovoked violence and abuse.

For such reasons, then, we should value that most individual and personalized of freedoms, dress freedom, and seek to nurture and safeguard it when we can in the wider interest of individual liberty within the open society. It requires eternal vigilance, no less so than other rights and freedoms with which dress liberty is intimately connected, such as are associated with freedom of conscience, freedom of expression, and the free exercise of personal beliefs. In this connection, John Stuart Mill's uncompromising principle of liberty in *On Liberty* (1859) provides the guiding maxim: '[T]he sole end of which mankind are warranted, individually or collectively, in interfering with the action of any of their number, is self-protection. That the only purpose for which power can be rightfully exercised over any member of a civilized community, against his will, is harm to others.' If we are to respect the 'bold, free expansion in all directions,' that Mill considered integral to the nurturing of individuality and well-being (Mill, ibid.: ch.3), a high tolerance of diversity of dress expression is a measure of our practical commitment to a democratic, open society, to which Mill's advocacy of the 'no harm' criterion was so elegantly tailored (Collini (ed.) 1989).

The chapters in this volume have addressed numerous facets of the social life of dress across a wide range of historical and cultural circumstances. In every setting, there are to be found bodies conforming to their local dress codes, whether these be adopted voluntarily in compliance with the 'dictates of fashion' (cf. Kellner 1992: 174), self-imposed as a signal of group, cult or movement membership, or formally decreed by governing bodies and regulatory officials. Always and everywhere bodies are impressing themselves on society through dress. And society reciprocates with a vengeance. In this dialectical interaction between dress-in-society and society-in-dress, we negotiate our precarious freedom of dressed self-expression, with greater or lesser success, as Thomas Carlyle recognized in his seminal study, *Sartor Resartus* (Carlyle 1869).

A Carlylean Tack

A singular virtue of the Carlylean approach to dress, body, culture and society, is that it holds that each of us, whatever our station in life, makes a mark upon society, whether in the small or in the large, the local or the cosmopolitan context, just as, assuredly, society stamps us with its own virtually ineradicable brands. All that is meant by the term 'impress' in the context of the Carlylean perspective adopted here and accentuated in the title of this book, is that a major part of the very texture, contouring and colouring of the social fabric and the cultural identities that give it life, is the marking made upon them by the layers of dressways that signal the traces, be they extant or extinct, of human culture and society. This does not mean to say that individual or corporate dressed bodies necessarily make a favourable or formidable impression. To the Carlylean eye, indifferent to the 'cut' of commoner or king, 'all is vanity'. This sceptical gaze on human finery has much to recommend itself to the dress scholar of any generation and cast of mind.

Each of the preceding substantive chapters demonstrates a basic Carlylean truth: though we remain, lifelong, as fundamentally naked as the day we were born, clothes (re-)present us to ourselves and to the world. Dress, 'the summarizing symbol' (Joseph 1986: 120), comes to stand for us and our standing in society. Body-selves are made up to 'look the part': the religious or political 'affiliate' or 'joiner' deploys the requisite 'look' of his/her adopted ideological reference group (Barker, Chapter 2); the ballet dancer adjusts to professional trends in limb exposure (Gabriel, Chapter 3); the well-turned-out 'gentleman/woman' fashions a 'classic' persona through iconic Burberry attire (Goodrum, Chapter 4); the Muslim female adapts the prescribed headdress of her world-faith community to local national circumstances (Brown, Chapter 5); the Mormon devotee honours the body and embraces the tradition through the sacred dress ritual prescriptions of the community of believers (Davies, Chapter 6); the fan in garments of 'outsiderdom' better secures incorporation within the subcultural community (Williamson, Chapter 7); and the private self, even as fantasist, secures a temporary seductive aura via lingerie designs evolved well beyond practical functionality (Wilson-Kovacs, Chapter 8).

Dress is clearly neither culturally nor politically neutral. It is loaded with significance. Clothes are stuff that 'speaks volumes'. But what they say is never entirely clear. We must interpret the language of dress in any given situation. As far as clothes are concerned, we are all inveterate hermeneuticians engaged in a never-ending round of conjecture and refutation as to what this or that 'look' is 'saying'. We can guess right or wrong. It does not do to mistake a party-going pope, prostitute or police officer for the real thing (or vice versa, one suspects)! Below the surface of material appearances, then, lie deeper layers of social, cultural and political implication. Dress studies provide openings to these embedded and embodied worlds within worlds.

A major challenge facing the future of dress studies – and it is a challenge that promises students and scholars considerable excitement, adventure and fulfilment – is that of building-up a knowledge-map piece by piece of the wondrous mosaic of dressways that have made their mark on human life. All clothes are grist to the dress scholar's mill: those tucked away in out-of-the-way recesses of society and those that have fossilized; those that have blazed momentarily across the firmaments of fashion as much as those that have endured to become the conventional and humdrum attire of the period. There is much foraging to do and many surprises still in store in the wardrobe of human dressways.

Dress Studies: An Open Field

At the same time as the piecemeal empiricist labour in the great catwalk of human society, to coin a phrase, proceeds afoot, the capacity to theorize the subject must be cultivated, so that the larger picture can be glimpsed, and its connecting threads woven into logico-meaningful patterns whose different herme-neutical and explanatory merits and limitations can be openly and critically appraised. Interpolated in each of the preceding chapters is the desired theoretical engagement, whether it spins off the ideas of an Elias or a Bourdieu or a Goffman or a Douglas – or, indeed, a Carlyle. Throughout the volume, this essential quest for theoretical connections, patterns, linkages and associations has been worked into every piece, bringing the substantive material to life and hooking it – and, hopefully, the reader – into the infinitely variable and always transforming world of dress, body and culture with its all intricacies and loose ends.

A pressing task in this connection is the need to encourage newcomers to dress studies to exercise their own imaginations in pursuit of interesting new lines of investigation, both empirical-historical and conceptual-theoretical. Established, emerging and entirely new students of dress bring what they have to the subject, be that a professional career of deep immersion in historical archives and anthropological arcana; or a lifetime, however long, of making daily and nightly decisions about what to wear, how to wear it and where it might 'fit in'. As a relatively new field and, certainly, one that is taking-off in the present-day with considerable vim and vigour, there is a pioneering spirit abroad within the subject field, an ethos that is typically welcoming, supportive, energetic, experimental, expansive and inclusive. Hopefully, the present collection has helped to awaken future students' interest in the subject as a worthwhile academic enterprise full of many interesting tucks and alert them to familiar and unfamiliar folds whose exploration can bring much intellectual refinement and enlargement and not a little good Carlylean fun (Dale 1981; Haney 1978).

Important to the achievement of this goal of stimulating undergraduate and postgraduate enthusiasm for the subject field of dress studies, is the active participation of established scholars from many diverse academic specialisms bringing their own special talents, insights and learning to investigations of dress, body and culture. Examples from the present collaborative collection are good cases in point. Professor Eileen Barker and Professor Douglas Davies have formidable international reputations in their specialist areas of the soci-ology and anthropology of religion and have provided here, in their respective chapters, exemplary proof texts that dress studies benefits enormously from the borrowed robes of scholars of this stature. Their particular angles of vision serve to expand and deepen the sense of what dress is, how it works, why it operates in the ways it does, and, by implication, perhaps, most vitally, how our understanding of it is dependent on openness to the contributions of the boundary-less 'invisible college' of dress studies.

Many academic sub-fields and areas of academic expertise have a hidden dress dimension: for example, the 'going native' practices of anthropologists and sociologists; the 'dress for success' manoeuvres of aspirants to join the academic executive class; laboratory coat fashions; academic subject area dress codes; academic dress tradition and innovation; institution-specific dress cultures; cross-national variations in departmental formality and informality; local norms of interview dress; image management and the academic feminist, new man, black activist, culture wars conservative, postmodern intellectual; and so forth. The possibilities for 'community self-surveys' (Stein 1972: 332-3) among participant observer 'insiders' of the dress code behaviours and beliefs of professional academics are endless. Likewise, a comparable 'in-house' dress culture research programme could be constructed for any other corporate organization in the contemporary 'society of the sign' (Harris 1996; Lash and Urry 1994), from public relations, law and accountancy firms; to welfare and healthcare institutions; to chain stores, and sports, media and entertainment outfits.

We live in 'high modern' times when not only is the tradition of dress studies growing and becoming more self-reflexive (Giddens 1991), but, in addition, the membership of the dress studies 'academic tribe' (Becher 1989) is becoming less 'invisible' and more known to itself through its own expanding professional media of dedicated journals, conferences, courses, publishing houses and so on. Moreover, our deeper knowledge of ourselves is not unconnected with knowing our ancestry and our own tribal ways, a point that has been emphasized in the introductory chapter to the present volume (Keenan, Chapter 1). Academic life has a self-image and, to some extent, a public reputation, partly associated with what Talcott Parsons called the 'expressive revolution' (cf. Martin 1981) of the 1960s (but pre-dating it somewhat) as a zone of high tolerance of dress freedom. How accurate is this impression today? Are the corporate dress signs indicating that the trend towards 'formalization of informalization' (Wouters 1986) is becoming reversed with the 'businessing-up' (Readings 1996; Smith and Webster (eds) 1997) of the postmodern university? Are the 'new Puritans' in the ascendancy over dress codes, following counter-revolution against the permissive 'Cavalier' decades of 'doing your own thing'?

As inveterately multi-disciplinary, dress studies is energized by the synergy of cross-disciplinary intellectual cross-pollination. Consider a case in point, that of the politics of dress, particularly the question of dress freedom, arguably the most important fundamental issue concerning dress, body and society. How might the question of the rights to dress self-determination be approached drawing upon the insights and investigations of the many areas of scholarship that potentially have relevance to this basic question of culture and personal liberty? There are countless 'ways in' to a topic as many-sided as this. Let us consider following a trail set off by reflecting on Eileen Barker's luminous chapter in the present volume.

Of Hats, Hair and Ideology

An indication of the wider historical resonance of Barker's explorations (see Chapter 2) of an elective affinity between ideology or implicit religion and dress can be illustrated with reference to the (re-)presentations of sect-like political formations in literature and art (Akrigg 1963; Greenblatt 1984). As one example of this, consider the way in which the contemporary unknown artist has depicted the failed 5 November 1605 conspiracy to blow up Parliament in *The Gunpowder Plot* (Fig. 9.1). The anti-Puritan look[1] of the small band of extremists – clearly with something other than a 'fashion conspiracy' (Coleridge 1989) in mind – is vividly signalled in the flamboyant clothing and flowing hairstyles of the arch-conspirators (cf. Gent and Llewellyn (eds) 1990). The whole seam of the comparative politics and ideology of individual and collective self-presentation through body language and modifications and supplements to the human body, opened up here by Professor Barker in the context of implicit religion, offers rich pickings for prospective scholarship and research in dress studies.

Figure 9.1 Detail from *The Gunpowder Plot Conspirators, 1605* by unknown Artist c1605. National Portrait Gallery, London.

While the history of formal sumptuary rules and legislation is extensively covered in the literature (for example, Hooper 1915; Vincent 1935; Freudenberger 1963; Hurlock 1965; Hunt 1996a and b), the comment by Roach and Eicher (1979: 15) that 'adornment has long had a place in the house of power' invites much further investigation of the proliferation and pervasiveness of informal dress codes seeking to manage and control the body in everyday life. 'Quasi-uniforms' (Joseph 1986) are ubiquitous in the professional and occupational environments, shopping malls, sports, health and leisure clubs, restaurants and other contexts of contemporary society. If we are to advance the complex project of understanding self-identities, difference and representations – individual and corporate – it is essential that we 'get inside' the dressways and dress worlds that we ourselves inhabit or closely rub shoulders with or distantly look upon from the outside. Hall (1996: 4) makes a relevant point here:

> Precisely because identities are constructed within, not outside, discourse, we need to understand them as produced in specific historical and institutional sites within specific discursive formations and practices, by specific enunciative strategies. Moreover, they emerge within the play of specific modalities of power, and thus are more the product of the marking of difference and exclusion, than they are the sign of an identical, naturally-constituted unity – an 'identity' in its traditional meaning (that is, an all-inclusive sameness, seamless, without internal differentiation).

For students of freedom of expression and self-determination, individual liberty and human rights, the paradox of dress unfreedom in modern liberal polities arises here with considerable force. The site-specific 'marking of difference and exclusion' so often takes place 'within the play of specific modalities of power' in regard to which the individual subject is grossly disempowered. Such contexts of dress unfreedom cry out for close, systematic investigation and analysis, and, indeed, ethico-political concern. Arguably, the question is not just one of legal ownership, entitlements and control of the human body; and where the line is drawn between personal body-self possession, on the one side, and external – state or corporate – intervention, regulation and discipline (Foucault 1977; Crossley 1996; Entwistle 2000), on the other side. A tacit and voluntary integration or collusion is generally to be found among the various interests (individual, group, governmental, markets, traditional and cultural) involved in subjecting the body-self (Turner 1996; Featherstone 1991) to formal and informal dress rules. At times, any mutual and harmonious accommodation proves difficult to arrange. The line between the dress freedom of one party and another may be difficult to draw. In contexts of 'detraditionalization' (Heelas 1996), moreover, established justifications of dress code regimes cannot be presumed universally acceptable in advance (as recent cases worldwide of school uniform regimes and occupational dress codes coming under criticism and review make clear). This turbulence in formerly comparatively steady-state sartorial regimes can presage new opportunities for translating the rhetoric of human rights principle into the lived experience of the work-a-day world (Risse et al. (eds) 1999).

Whenever dress codes are imposed for whatever reason – health and safety, esprit de corps, corporate identity, a sense of equity, group discipline, collective order, human resource management and personnel control, the fancies of employers and owners, force majeure, loyalty to tradition, and so forth – those who would remain vigilant about the small, basic, perennially vulnerable freedoms that matter in everyday life, should be on guard with a healthy hermeneutic of suspicion. As David Martin so aptly puts it in the Foreword to this volume, we are called to 'be ware and be ready', especially when the case is far from clear and self-evident regarding the authority or rationale for restrictions, reductions and repressions of dress liberty.

On Dress and on Liberty

Dress freedom is never absolute. In both of its modalities – *positive* dress freedom to dress as we please and *negative* dress freedom to be free from the clothing regimes imposed by others, to adopt and adapt Isaiah Berlin's concepts (Berlin

1958) – we, typically, experience social, economic, cultural and personality constraints. The question of dress liberty is one of degree. The jaunty tilt of the subaltern's regimental dress cap; the schoolgirl's trendy necktie-knot; the vicar's jazzy shirt tucked discretely under the clerical black cassock and dog-collar; the 'Che Lives: Boss Class Sucks' badge adroitly pinned on the lapel-underside of the factory operative's 'issued' overalls, and other such sartorial strategies of independence, are often dogged expressions of valued dress freedom. Such forms of discretionary dress innovation and symbolic rebellion, emerging within and against the clothing regimes prevailing in a given form of life, typically denote unregenerate, irrepressible personal identities aiming to cock a snook at imposed uniformity and alienating dress controls. In contexts where scope for self-expression is highly circumscribed, these opportunities for sartorial self-assertion and 'deviance' can take on considerable political significance (Mazrui 1970).

In the final analysis, the entire issue here of dress freedoms and their implicature in the multi-layered political, economic, cultural, ethical, aesthetic and spiritual grounds of human embodied personhood (cf. Csordas (ed.) 1996; Kirk 1998; Coakley (ed.) 1997), may devolve on the principle of the sanctity or inviolability of the body-self itself. What space is sacrosanct for the body to dress as it pleases? The problematic here is inherently dualistic. Power manifests and plays itself out upon fleshly body-selves according to the different 'logics' of revelation and concealment, the double function or twin essence of dress.

Thus, in contexts of physical and psychological abuses of human rights, power impresses itself on the body-self by forcibly removing clothing, the better to enforce victim status. 'Revelation', hence, incarnates as violation. Forcibly divesting the body of its self-chosen dress symbols of personal identity and belonging assigns 'animal' identity to flesh and bones, exposed ready for recreation in the image and likeness of its new 'owners'. The Carlylean issue on this front becomes: What authority ever rightfully strips us of our garments? On what moral grounds are we ever justifiably rendered naked before the courts of man? Yet, in other circumstances, that may, indeed, closely follow on 'degradation rituals', power commands that the dress of subservience be worn. Here, 'concealment' equates with the coerced assumption of an alien identity, a loss of self-identity as the dress recognition symbols of other tribes and their gods, so to speak, are paraded on the backs of sartorial slaves.

The Carlylean concern here is with the hubris and arrogance of power. In the former instance, the body-self is rendered symbolically unprotected, denuded of common humanity. In the latter instance, the body-self is symbolically over-protected, infantilized and re-identified as belonging to new masters. In such contexts of usurpation of dress freedom, the 'agency' of the actor is invalidated (Bauman 1988). At both extremes, there is a curtailment of the basic human right of body-self-control, a denial of self-empowerment in relation to the 'foreign bodies' that impact most palpably, closely and intimately – clothing – on the body-self. That this process of dress divestment and reinvestment should take place on a voluntaristic basis within ritual contexts, such as ceremonies of taking the religious habit or other such investitures, is one thing; that it can proceed, often unchallenged, and sometimes in the name of democracy, welfare and good governance, in sites as diverse as prisons, geriatric homes, residential establishments for the infirm and mentally handicapped, and elsewhere, is another thing entirely. Whenever enforced dress codes are employed as a deliberate instrument of repression, torture and dehumanization, we are in an order of things where civilization itself is at risk. There is much to be done, in the context of the more general concern to expose persecution and discrimination world wide (Boyle & Sheen 1997), to advance and protect our basic dress freedoms while remaining sensitive to culture and tradition.

From the standpoint of an advocate of dress freedom, the temptation to react to the 'crisis of discipline' (Wagner 1994; Bauman 1995) of late modern society by the wholesale institutionalization of a matrix of dress code controls introduced for reasons of corporate image management, organizational efficiency, economy, and social discipline, is a decidedly uncomfortable prospect, to say the least. The last thing an open society needs is an all-encompassing shroud of uniform dress rules and regulations. Any and every step in that illiberal direction is to be feared and resisted. In this regard, dress studies is far from an effete, superficial pastime on the fringes of the big issues of the day and marginal to the profound questions of intellectual and political life. *Au contraire*, dress studies, conceived in this Carlylean framework, lives, moves and has its true being and larger purpose, precisely at the point of intersection – the point of impress – where the body-self of the human subject encounters society in some of its starkest forms.

One of the first, ostensibly innocuous – and massively revealing – acts of would-be tyrants and control freaks everywhere and down the ages, from Peter the Great's interdictions on facial hair to the Nazi imposition of the yellow star on the soon-to-be victims of the Holocaust, is to make their dictatorial presence felt through the inauguration of 'socially useful' symbolic means of impressing their political and ideological weight upon human flesh. For dress libertarians, such abuse of soft sartorial powers represents a particularly insensitive crime against humanity in that it brings the whole apparatus of the repressive state to bear on the sacred fragility of the body-self. Part of the necessary safeguards of dress freedom lies in understanding the 'paradoxical nature of freedom' (Hook 1962), that our liberties and rights, as Durkheim understood (cf. Lukes 1991; Turner 1993) are often a product of and best guaranteed by appropriate regulation.

Dress freedom is a social freedom; a freedom to 'deviate' from the normative sartorial expectations of our social group. That most of us are likely to 'deviate' in conventional or 'normal' dress terms should not blind us to the fact that now and again the boundaries of dress tolerance and freedom are likely to be stretched to breaking-point, an insight not lost to style rebels from Teds, Mods and Rockers to Hippies, Punks, Goths, Grebs, Grungies, and so on, in recent decades. That right has to be protected in law against those who might take offence under the banner of Decency, Good Taste, Standards, Respectability, Responsibility and other flags of 'moral majority' convenience.

At such times, and more of them may be coming into view under late modern social and cultural conditions as we become increasingly accustomed to 'the aestheticization of everyday life' (Featherstone 1992; Chaney 1996), dress 'deviance' may well assume heightened political and cultural salience as symbolic 'resistance' (Jenkins 1996; Hall & Jefferson (eds) 1976). Neither the individual nor the society can rely for the security of our dress freedom upon the so-called free market. When vast differences in the respective sartorial powers of corporations and persons are palpably omnipresent, the non-interventionist principle is a dress authoritarian's charter. In such circumstances of real sym-bolic inequalities, a constitutional and legal framework for the resolution of disputes and the safeguarding of dress rights and liberties is necessary. However, we must be sensitive to the potential in this area for the clash of interests, as claims for dress liberty rub up against competing claims for justice. My freedom to wear at the cinema an illuminated, candy-striped chimney-top hat festooned with glazed fruits and bells, must be balanced against your right to see the film – say, *Prêt-à-Porter* – in comparative peace; your freedom to express your racial, sexual and religious prejudices and predilections in graphic form has to be balanced against my right to personal safety and freedom from harassment and abuse.

Towards Sartorial Justice

When high street stores sell tops bearing the ambiguous, but lucrative, logo: 'FCUK' (sic); and t-shirts display activities and proclaim slogans that might make an anarcho-syndicalist blush, we have entered into an unprecedented phase of communication through dress, once deemed to be the subtlest and most indirect of the media. The span of corporate dress control expands at the same moment as society has become more litigious and rights-conscious. The private/public dichotomy, 'as crucial to ancient as it is to modern thought and society' (Slater, in Jenks 1998: 138), has never been so strongly articulated in sartorial terms as in the late modern 'society of the sign'. The contrasting pressures to 'individuate' or 'belong', to signal 'difference' or 'similarity', 'independence' or 'interdependence', 'rebellion' or 'conformity', are all woven into, and partially worked out through, the new explicit language of dress where there are few, if any, restrictions on profanity or nudity.

In this quasi-Saturnalian sartorial culture, displays of ideological alignment bordering on the illegal and anti-social, overlap with displays of body parts whose private nature it was once deemed a key function of clothing to conceal. Unrestricted dress freedom rapidly leads not to 'the naked public square', as the right-wing 'culture wars' arguments of Neuhaus (1984), Carter (1993) and others imply; but ushers in an implosion of sartorial signs and symbols that are as likely to engender reactions of revulsion, fear and anxiety, as they are to evince aesthetic pleasure and evoke a sense of wonder and enchantment. Part of the challenge of the postmodern turn in culture and society is learning to inhabit a public square that sends out, frequently via the portable, flexible, changeful medium of dress, mixed and multiple ideological messages; some we like, others we find reprehensible. An educated citizenry of a mature democracy, perhaps, has a better chance of finding peaceful and constructive ways of addressing the polarized sartorial expressions of love, hate and cold materialistic indifference than other forms of 'experiment in living' (to employ Mill's phrase).

This topsy-turvy carnivalized (Bakhtin 1968) clothing culture engenders a condition of dress license where little is left to the imagination, nothing is inherently sacred, and everything is profaned, including bodies – and dress modes themselves – once deemed holy and set apart (Keenan 1999a, b). Can authentic dress liberty survive a boundaryless postmodern condition in which personal clothing can assume the function of a commercial hoarding or an ideological weapon or a public invitation to sexual activity or an extension of corporate signage? How are real dress freedoms expressed in a globalized consumer culture where corporate liveries are designed by leading fashion designers to create the illusion that air stewards and chain store sales personnel are engaged in an exquisite catwalk parade far removed from the common-or-garden business of serving pre-packed foods and deodorants? Part of the dialectic of revelation and concealment in which dress is caught up, is the scope clothes provide for self-deception and public duplicity, on the one hand, and open exposure of private, interior life within public settings, on the other hand. This aspect of the capacity to employ and enjoy our dress freedom to manipulate and negotiate Truth, exploited to the full by politicians and media stars, but hardly monopolized by them, is worthy of further sociological consideration (cf. Simon 2000; Leonard 2000; Whitmore 2000).

An accessible, but not overweening or overly-intrusive legal-constitutional framework, currently in no more than an embryonic state of development around the world,[2] helps to provide some protection and recourse in law against the whimsy and arbitrary will of powerful, patrimonial, bureaucratic leaders bent upon 're-feudalization' through the imposition of corporate liveries. Moreover, it serves as a basis for affording rights of international legal redress against 'sartorial crime', to coin a phrase, where human rights violations occur through violence against the person in which dress and body modification practices are instrumentally involved. Examples here would include: abusive strip searches; intrusive dress control regimes designed to dehumanize; degrading dress codes imposed on employees under the guise of adult entertainment or dubious personalized customer services; fetishistic victimization; mutilation and body-damaging practices such as harmful foot-binding rationalized as 'beautification'; legally and medically unregulated body modifications such as infibulation, piercing, implants and stretching; and, inter alia, cases of invasive cosmetic surgery (Davis 1995) wherever health and personal safety are put at high risk. The definitions of dress and the body and the boundaries between them are increasingly imprecise and free-floating in the context of contemporary somatic re-sculpting and re-engineering practices (Featherstone and Burrows 1995). How far the frontiers of cyberbody culture (Featherstone 2000) can be pushed before the ancient question of the sanctity of the human body ceases to have any meaning or referents remains to be answered. Explorations of dress freedom may well shed light on the moral and cultural limits of tolerance in this expanding new area of human experience.

What matters most here, is that, compatible with the 'no harm' principle discussed above, the power to make appearance and body-modification decisions is transferred as much as possible from powerful 'abstract' forces external to the body-self – the market, tradition, culture, society, the corporation or organization, the community, the state, the gods, the faith, elders, ancestors and so on – to the persons immediately involved, whose bodies and identities are, as it were, directly in the firing line. The general rule should prevail that no one, in short, should be expected to look a certain way or be pressurized into a prescribed 'look', without having first had the opportunity to volunteer for the 'part'. There should be no expectation that electing to assume the approved, required or desired dress modes of others should necessarily commit one to wearing them in the future. Changes in one's conscience, tastes and preferences regarding one's own body-self-(re-)presentation should entitle one to freedom to change one's 'look'.

With regard to infants, minors, conscripts, convicts, public servants, the dependent disabled, and other categories where dress choice restriction is the order of the day, there should always be, from a Mill-Carlyle perspective, at any rate, the presumption in favour of the right of dress self-determination whenever this is reasonably possible. Where this principle is breached and conditions other than dress freedom prevail, it is incumbent upon those who would deny dress liberty to others, to make the case for dress unfreedom in particular cases, having due regard for the rights of persons to control their own body-self. In this sense, dress freedom enjoys a moral status beyond state and social boundaries and can be deemed a basic human right and entitlement (Stammers 1995) which may well be dependent upon local social and political conditions for its operationalization, but transcends these contingent conditions with regard to its ethical power.

How intriguing to have been an eavesdropper on the mystic Carlyle's conversations on such a topic with his ultra-cerebral friend, John Stuart Mill (Neff 1924), doughty champion of 'self-regarding action' (Hamburger 1965; Campbell 1993; Levin 1998)! One might conceivably just have heard the dress philosopher recall lines from *Sartor Resartus* (Carlyle 1869: 281) proclaiming: 'A day of justice, when the worth of Breeches would be revealed to man, and the Scissors become forever venerable.' The earnest Mill did not always see eye to eye with Carlyle's more fantastical phraseology (Mill-Carlyle correspondence, in Sanders 1992: 448–9), but they had a shared enthusiasm for fundamental freedoms expressed, embedded and embodied in the ordinary business of living.

Notes

1. The sober and sombre modes of Puritan 'plain dress' are well documented (Mann 1986: 463–72; Murdock 2000) as is the association between hair and hedonism (Leach 1957; Hiltebeital and Miller (eds) 1998).

2. Internationally, we are only now beginning to make some headway in this respect as cases of dress rights and freedoms come before the national and international courts. See, for instance, the European Union Citizen's Guide on Equal Rights and Opportunities where, in the 'Working Conditions' section, dress code gender parity is asserted in the context of employment rights (http://citizens.eu.int/en/en/gf/eq/pdf/l.pdf). From North America, there is the set of directives issued from Alberta from a Canada Government Policy site on Appearance/Dress Code and Employers' Rights (http://www.gov.ab.ca/mcd/citizen/hr/pubs/drescode.htm); and, from the United States site 'ERIC': Clearinghouse on Educational Management, there is a rapidly growing body of cases and case law references (http://eric.uoregon.edu/publications/digests/digest117.html). Finally, an American site that has good links to relevant Supreme Court deliberations, federal, district and local jurisdiction law cases and other related sites on the expanding universe of dress code formulation and contestation, see http://www.tentler.com/dress.htm.

References

Akrigg, G.P.V. (1963), *Jacobean Pageant or the Court of King James 1*, Cambridge, Mass: Harvard University Press.

Bakhtin, M. (1968), *Rabelais and His World*, Cambridge, MA: MIT Press.

Bauman, Z. (1988), *Freedom*, Milton Keynes: Open University Press.

—— (1995), *Life in Fragments: Essays in Postmodern Morality*, Oxford: Blackwell.

Baxter, R. (1707), *Practical Works*, London: Thomas Parkhurst.

Becher, T. (1989), *Academic Tribes and Territories*, Oxford: Oxford University Press.

Berlin, I. (1958), *Two Concepts of Liberty*, Oxford: Clarendon Press.

Boyle, K. & Sheen, J. (1997), *Freedom of Religion and Belief: A World Report*, London: Routledge.

Campbell, I. (1993), *Thomas Carlyle*, Edinburgh: The Saltire Society.

Carlyle, T. (1869), *Sartor Resartus: The Life and Opinions of Herr Teufelsdröckh*, London: Chapman and Hall.

Carter, S. (1993), *The Culture of Disbelief*, New York: Basic Books.

Chaney, D. (1996), *Lifestyles*, London & New York: Routledge.

Coakley, S. (ed.) (1997), *Religion and the Body*, Cambridge: Cambridge University Press.

Coleridge, N. (1989), *The Fashion Conspiracy: A Remarkable Journey Through the Empires of Fashion*, London: Heinemann/Mandarin.

Collini, S. (ed.) (1989), *On Liberty and Other Writings*, Cambridge University Press.

Crossley, N. (1996), 'Body/Subject, Body/Power: Agency, Inscription and Control in Foucault and Merleau-Ponty', *Body & Society* 2(2): 99–116.

Csordas, T.J. (ed.)(1996), *Embodiment and Experience: The Existential Ground of Culture and Self*, Cambridge: Cambridge University Press.

Dale, P.A. (1981), '*Sartor Resartus* and the Inverse Sublime: The Art of Humorous Deconstruction', in M.W. Bloomsbury (ed.), *Allegory, Myth and Symbol*, Cambridge, Mass.: Harvard University Press.

Davis, K. (1995), *Reshaping the Female Body: The Dilemmas of Cosmetic Surgery*, London: Routledge.

Entwistle, J. (2000), *The Fashioned Body: Theorizing Fashion and Dress in Modern Society*, Cambridge: Polity.

Featherstone, M. (1991), 'The Body in Consumer Culture', in M. Featherstone, M. Hepworth, and B. Turner (eds), *The Body: Social Process and Cultural Theory*, London: Sage.

—— (1992), 'Postmodernism and the Aestheticization of Everyday Life', in S. Lash & J. Friedman (eds), *Modernity and Identity*, pp. 265-90, Oxford, UK and Cambridge, USA: Blackwell.

—— (ed.) (2000), *Body Modification*, London: Sage.

—— & Burrows, R. (eds.) (1995), *Cyberspace/Cyberbodies/Cyberpunk: Cultures of Technological Embodiment*, London: Sage.

Foucault, M. (1977), *Discipline and Punish*, Harmondsworth, London: Penguin.

Freudenberger, H. (1963), 'Fashion, Sumptuary Laws and Business', in G. Wills and D. Midgley (eds) (1973), *Fashion Marketing*, London: Allen and Unwin.

Gent, L. and Llewellyn, N. (eds) (1990), *Renaissance Bodies: The Human Figure in English Culture c.1540–1660*, London: Reaktion Books.

Giddens, A. (1991), *Modernity and Self-Identity: Self and Society in the Late Modern Age*, Oxford: Polity Press, in association with Basil Blackwell.

Greenblatt, S. (1984), *Renaissance Self-Fashioning from More to Shakespeare*, Chicago: Chicago University Press.

Hall, S. (1996), 'Introduction: Who Needs Identity?', in S. Hall and P. du Gay (eds), *Questions of Cultural Identity*, pp.1–17, London, Thousand Oaks, New Delhi: Sage.

—— & Jefferson, T. (eds), (1976), *Resistance Through Rituals*, London: Hutchinson.

Hamburger, J. (1965), *Intellectuals in Politics: John Stuart Mill and the Philosophic Radicals*, New Haven and London: Yale University Press.

Haney, J.L. (1978), '"Shadow Hunting": Romantic Irony, *Sartor Resartus*, and Victorian Romanticism', *Studies in Romanticism* XVII: 319–32.

Harris, D. (1996), *A Society of Signs?*, London and New York: Routledge.

Heelas, P. (1996), 'Introduction: Detraditionalization and Its Rivals', in P. Heelas, S. Lash and P. Morris (eds), *Detraditionalization*, Oxford: Blackwell.

Hiltebeitel, A. and Miller, B.D. (eds) (1998), *Hair: Its Power and Meaning in Asian Cultures*. Foreword by G. Obeyesekere, Albany: State University of New York Press.

Hook, S. (1962), *The Paradoxes of Freedom*, Berkeley and Los Angeles: University of California Press.

Hooper, W. (1915), 'The Tudor Sumptuary Laws', *English Historical Review* 30: 422-49.

Hunt, A. (1996a), *Governance of the Consuming Passions: A History of Sumptuary Legislation*, London: Macmillan.

—— (1996b), 'The Governance of Consumption: Sumptuary Laws and Shifting Forms of Regulation', *Economy and Society* 25(3): 410–27.

Hurlock, E.B. (1965), 'Sumptuary Law', in M.E. Roach and J.B. Eicher (eds), *Dress, Adornment and the Social Order*, New York: John Wiley and Sons.

Jenkins, R. (1996), *Social Identity*, London & New York: Routledge.

Jenks, C. (ed.) (1998), *Core Sociological Dichotomies*, London: Sage.

Joseph, N. (1986), *Uniforms and Nonuniforms: Communication Through Clothing*, Westport, Conn: Greenwood Press.

Keenan, W.J.F. (1999a), 'Of Mammon Clothed Divinely: The Profanization of Sacred Dress', *Body & Society* 5 (1): 73–92.

—— (1999b), 'From Friars to Fornicators: The Eroticization of Sacred Dress', *Fashion Theory* 3 (4): 389–410.

Kellner, D. (1992), 'Popular Culture and the Construction of Postmodern Identities', in S. Lash and J. Friedman (eds), *Modernity and Identity*, pp. 141–77, Oxford, UK and Cambridge, USA: Blackwell.

Kirk, J.A. (1998), *The Meaning of Freedom: A Study of Secular, Muslim, and Christian Views*, Carlisle: Paternoster Press.

Langer, L. (1965), 'Clothes and Government', in M.E. Roach & J.B. Eicher (eds), *Dress, Adornment and the Social Order*, pp. 125-7, New York: John Wiley & Sons.

Lash, S. and Urry, J. (1994), *Economies of Signs and Space*, London: Sage.

Leach, E.R. (1957) 'Magical Hair', *Journal of the Royal Anthropological Institute* 88(2): 147–64.

Leonard, T. (2000), 'TV News Veteran Warns of Obsession With Style', *Daily Telegraph*, 28 August, p. 3.

Levin, M. (1998), *The Condition of England Question: Carlyle, Mill and Engels*, London: Macmillan.

Lukes, S. (1991), *Moral Conflict and Politics*, Oxford: Clarendon.

Mann, M. (1986), *The Social Sources of Power*, Volume 1, Cambridge: Cambridge University Press.

Martin, B. (1981), *A Sociology of Contemporary Cultural Change*, Oxford: Blackwell.

Mazrui, A.A. (1970), 'The Robes of Rebellion: Sex, Dress and Politics in Africa', *Encounter*, February issue: 19–30.

Mill, J.S. (1859), 'Of Individuality, as one of the elements of well-being', *On Liberty*, ch.3, in M. Cohen (ed.) (1961), *The Philosophy of John Stuart Mill*, New York: Modern Library.

Murdock, G. (2000), 'Dressed to Repress?: Protestant Clerical Dress and the Regulation of Morality in Early Modern Europe', *Fashion Theory* 4(2): 179–200.

Neff, E.E. (1924), *Carlyle and Mill: Mystic and Utilitarian*, New York: Columbia University Press.

Neuhaus, R. (1984), *The Naked Public Square*, Grand Rapids, MI: Wm. B. Eerdmans.

Readings, B. (1996), *The University in Ruins*, Cambridge, MA: Harvard University Press.

Risse, T., Ropp, S.C. & Sikkink, K. (eds), (1999), *The Power of Human Rights: International Norms and Domestic Change*, Cambridge: Cambridge University Press.

Roach, M.E. and Eicher, J.B. (1979), 'The Language of Personal Adornment', in J.M. Cordwell and R.A. Schwarz (eds), *The Fabrics of Culture*, pp. 7–21, The Hague: Mouton.

Sanders, C.R. (ed.), (1992), *The Collected Letters of Thomas and Jane Welsh Carlyle: October 1831 – September 1833*, Vol. 6, New York: Duke University Press.

Simon, S. (2000), 'The Empty Sound of Martin Bell', *The Daily Telegraph*, 28 August, p. 20.

Slater, D. (1998), 'Public/Private', in C. Jenks (ed.), *Core Sociological Dichotomies*, pp. 137–50, London: Sage.

Smith, A. and Webster, F. (eds) (1997), *The Postmodern University?*, Buckingham: Open University Press.

Stammers, N. (1995), 'A Critique of Social Approaches to Human Rights', *Human Rights Quarterly* 17: 488–508.

Stein, M. (1972), *The Eclipse of Community*, Princeton, NJ: Princeton University Press. First published in 1960.

Turner, B.S. (1993), 'Outline of a Theory of Human Rights', *Sociology* 27 (3): 489–512.

—— (1996), *The Body and Society: Explorations in Social Theory*, London: Sage.

Vincent, J. (1935), *Costume and Conduct in the Laws of Basel, Bern and Zurich, 1370–1800*, Baltimore, Md: John Hopkins University Press.

Wagner, P. (1994), *A Sociology of Modernity: Liberty and Discipline*, London and New York: Routledge.

Whitmore, R. (2000), 'Invasion of the Stylists', *Daily Telegraph*, 29 August, p. 17.

Wouters, C. (1986), 'The Formalization of Informalization: Changing Tension Balances in Civilizing Processes', *Theory, Culture & Society* 3(2): 1–18.

Name Index

Abler, T. 7
Akrigg, G.P.V. 184
Albrecht 79–80
Alexander, Jeffrey 32
Alexander, T.G. 130
Ali, Yusuf 120
Altschull, E. 115
Ariadne 41
Arnold, Matthew 16
Arthur, Linda B. 7, 15
Asad, Talal 133
Ash, Juliet 7, 92
Au, S. 77
Aziz, P. 111

Bailey, Edward 66
Bakhtin, Michael 190
Banim, M. 7
Barker, Eileen 51, 60, 65, 181, 183–4
Barnard, Malcolm 7, 18, 42
Barnes, Ruth 7, 35, 42
Barthes, Roland 16–17, 21, 174
Baudelaire, Charles 33, 150
Bauman, Zygmund 188
Baxter, Richard 179
Becher, T. 183
Beckford, James 65
Benjamin, Walter 33, 153–4
Bentham, Jeremy 24
Berg 36
Berger, Peter 15, 24
Berlin, Isaiah 186
Betterton, R. 159–60
Blumer, Herbert 7, 16
Bogatyrev, Petr 16, 38
Bourdieu, Pierre 15, 30–2, 87, 123, 123, 133–4, 138, 182
Bow, Clara 172
Boyle, K. 188

Braham, P. 101
Breward, Christopher 7
Brown, Malcolm 108–9, 181
Brownmiller, S. 159–60
Brutus 74
Brydon, A. 7
Buck-Morss, S. 153–4
Burchkhardt, Jacob 20
Burke, Edmund 24
Burman, B. 7
Burns, Robert 38
Burrows R. 191

Calefato, Patrizia 7
Callaway, Helen 7
Camargo, Marie 69, 72
Campbell, Ian 37, 40, 192
Carlyle, Jack 40
Carlyle, Jane Welsh 40
Carlyle, Thomas vii, xv, 1–42 passim, 181–2, 191–2
Carter, A. 166, 168, 172, 175
Carter, S. 190
Cavallaro, D. 42
Celarius 77
Chaney, David 189
Chaucer, Geoffrey 17
Cheikh, Soheib Ben 105, 111
Chesterfield, Lord 73
Clark, H. 7
Coakley, Sarah 187
Cole, S. 7
Coleridge, N. 184
Collini, S. 180
Comte, Auguste 24
Coq, Guy 113, 116
Corcoran, B. 137
Cordwell, Justine 7
Cox, C. 7

Craik, Jennifer 7, 35, 87, 89–90, 96, 100–1, 169–71, 173, 175
Crawley, Ernest 7, 16
Creed, B. 141
Cromwell, Oliver 20
Crossley, N. 186
Csordas, T.J. 187

Dale, P.A. 183
Darwin, Erasmus 1, 12, 16
Davis, C. 125
Davies, Douglas J. 125, 131, 181, 183
Davis, Fred 7, 32, 35
de la Haye, A. 42, 91
de Laurentis, T. 159
Defrance, Bernard 115
Delpierre, M. 72
Diana, Princess 7
Dickens, Charles 16
Dijkstra, Bram 141
Douglas, Mary 55, 57, 136–7, 182
Dreyfus, Alfred 106
du Gay, Paul 88
Durand-Prinborgne, C. 116
Durkheim, Emile 4, 16, 35, 188
Duvernay, Pauline 79

Edward III 163
Edwards, J. 16
Eicher, Joanne B. vii, xv, 7, 14, 16, 35, 42, 105, 185
Eissler, Fanny 78
Eissler, Theresa 78
El Guindi, Fadwa 7, 105
Elias, Norbert 17, 30, 69–70, 79–82, 165, 182
Emerson, Ralph Waldo 40
Entwistle, Joanne 7, 35, 146, 186
Erasmus, Desiderius 17
Esack, Farid 117
Evans, Caroline 7
Ewing, E. 167

Falk, P. 35
Farrell, J. 160, 162
Featherstone, Mike 24, 35, 92, 171, 186, 189, 191
Ferry, Jules 107
Festinger, Leon 60

Finch, C. 169
Finkelstein, J. 32, 70, 74
Flügel, J. C. 16, 74
Foster, H. B. 7
Foucault, Michel 186
Franklin, Caryn 95
Fraser, James 40
Frederick the Great 20
Freudenberger, H. 185
Friedman, Jonathan 32
Froude, J. A. 38–40

Gabor, M. 173
Gabriel, Norman R. 181
Gadamer, Hans-Georg 20
Garafola, L. 73
Garber, G. 7
Garber, M. 7
Garrick, David 164
Gaspard, F. 106, 115
Gay, A. 7
Gent, L. 184
Giddens, Anthony 32, 35–6, 175, 183
Gilman, S. 173
Giselle 79–81
Goethe, Johann W. 17
Goffman, Erving 21, 51, 182
Goodrum, Alison 181
Gordon, B. 7
Gould, S. 175
Gouldner, Alvin 29
Green, E. 7
Greenblatt, S. 184
Griffiths, I. 7
Guest, J. 72, 75
Guichard, Pauline 79

Hall, James 7
Hall, Stuart 185, 189
Hamburger, J. 192
Harberton, Lady 175
Harris, David 183
Harvey, A. 165, 174
Hawthorne, E. 16
Hawthorne, R. 160–1, 163, 167, 169, 172
Haynes, M. T. 7
Heelas, Paul 186
Heffer, S. 39
Helmling, S. 40

Hiltbeital, A. 192
Holland, H. 160
Hollander, Anne 7, 147–9
Hook, Sydney 188
Hooper, W. 185
Howes, D. 134
Hunt, A. 70, 185
Hurlock, Elizabeth B. 7, 185
Hyde, M. 169

Ilyas, Muhammad 110

Jackson, S. 159
Janin, Jules 76
Jefferson, T. 189
Jeffrey, Francis 38
Jenkins, Richard 189
Jenks, Chris 189
Johnson, Samuel 164
Joseph, Nathan 7, 42, 181, 185
Jospin, Lionel 105, 116
Juffer, J. 174

Kaiser, Susan 7
Keenan, William J.F. xv, 14 –15, 184, 190
Kellner, D. 180
Khosrokhavar, F. 105, 116
Kidwell, C. B. 7
King, J. 110
Kirk, J.A. 187
Ko, Dorothy 7
König, René 7, 16
Kroeber, Arthur 16
Kunzle, D. 160

Lacoste-Dujardin, Camille 111
Langer, Lawrence 179
Lash, Scott 32, 183
Laver, James 7, 35, 172
Leach, Edmund 138, 192
Lekain, Henri-Louis, 73
Leonard, T. 190
Levin, D.M. 134
Levin, M. 192
Lipovetsky, G. 7
Llewellyn, N. 184
Locke, John 17
Lottie, D. 172
Louis XIV 70

Luckmann, Thomas 24
Lukes, Steven 188
Lurie, Alison 7, 18
Lynch, A. 7
Lyotard, Jean-François 13

Macauley, Lord Thomas B. 20
Maffesoli, Michel 102
Mann, Michael 192
Marcus, S. 166
Martin, Bernice 6, 184
Martin, David vii, 186
Marx, Karl 20, 24
Mason, M. 171
Mauss, A.L. 123
Mauss, Marcel 8, 87,133
Mazrui, A.A. 187
McConkie, B.R. 124
McCracken, G.D. 7
McLintock, Anne 7
McRobbie, A. 7
McVeigh, B. 7
Medicine, Beatrice 7
Melchizedek 127
Mellor, Philip A. 35
Melville, Henry 16
Mernissi, Fatima 117
Merton, Robert K. 29
Mill, John Stuart 20, 24, 180, 190, 191–2
Miller, B.D. 192
Mitterand, Danielle 105, 116
Monnet, Jean-François 113
Monod, Jacques 63
Montesquieu 24
Morgan, Lewis Henry 16
Moscovici, Serge 137
Mukerji, C. 167
Mulvey, L. 170
Murdock, Graham 192

Neff, E.E. 192
Nerval, Gérard de 108
Neuhaus, Richard 190
Newman, John Henry 20, 24
Newton, Isaac 1
Nielsen, Jørge 107, 113
Niessen, S. 7
Nietzsche, Friedrich 16
Nisbet, Robert A. 15

O'Dea, Thomas 123
Obeyesekere, G. 138

Parsons, Talcott 184
Pater, Walter 16
Patterson, D.W. 133
Peacock, J.L. 133
Pearsall, R. 161
Pellegrin, N. 7
Perani, J. 7
Perrot, Philippe 7, 15, 74
Peter the Great 188
Polhemus, Ted 7, 14
Poll, Solomon 7
Pollock, Griselda 7
Popper, Karl R. 37
Porter, B.D. 128
Proclus 74
Pygmalion 72

Rameau, P. 71
Readings, B. 184
Ribeiro, Aileen 7, 72, 75, 81
Rice, Anne 149, 151
Richter Jean Paul 17
Ricoeur, Paul 20
Risse T. 186
Roach, Mary Ellen 7, 185
Roach-Higgins, Mary Ellen 16
Roche, Daniel 7, 15
Rouse, Elisabeth. 7
Rubinstein, Ruth P. 7, 35, 42
Rushdie, Salman 107
Ruskin, John 16

Sage 36
Said, Edward 108–9, 114
Saint-Simon, Louis R. Duc de 71
Salisbury, Countess of 163
Salle, Marie 72
Sanders, C. R. 40
Sapir, Edward 16
Sartre, Jean Paul 145
Schneider, Jane 7
Schwarz, Ronald 7
Sciama, L.D. 7
Scott, S. 159
Second, Alberic 77
Shakespeare, William xv

Sheen, J. 188
Shilling, Chris 35
Shipman, D. 172
Simmel, Georg 15, 21
Simon, S. 190
Slater, D. 189
Smith, A. 184
Smith, Adam 1
Smith, Joseph 129–30, 136
Solomon 36
Soper, K. 7
Spencer, Herbert 4, 16, 20, 24
Stammers, N. 192
Steele, Valerie 7, 14, 74, 78, 160, 165–6
Stein, Maurice 183
Stone, Gregory 7, 16
Swift, Jonathan 17

Taglioni, Filippo 76
Taglioni, Marie 76
Taylor, Lou 7
Teufelsdröck, Prof. Diogenes 12, 14,
    17–18, 24–5, 39–40
Todd, Emmanuel 112
Tseëlon, Efrat 7, 14, 19, 142–5
Tulloch, C. 7
Turner, Bryan S. 24, 35, 171, 175, 186, 188
Turner, Victor 130
Tylor, Edward B. 16
Tyson, R.W. 133

Underwood, Grant 125
Urry, John 183
Uzanne, Octave 168

Valette, Marquiss de la 79
Vasari 12
Veblen, Thorstein 7, 16, 21, 77
Vestris, Auguste 72
Villiers, John 72
Vincent, J. 185
Voltaire 74

Wagner, Peter 188
Warwick, A. 42
Weber, Max 14, 32, 167
Webster, Frank 184
Welters, L. 7
Wesley, John 16

Westermack, Edward A.16
White, N. 7
Whitmore, R. 190
Wieviorka, Michel 105, 115
Williams, Linda 141
Williamson, Milly 181
Willis, Paul 30
Wilson, D.A. 35, 40
Wilson, Elizabeth 7, 14, 35, 42, 88–9, 92,
   149–50, 172

Wilson, V. 7
Wilson-Kovacs, Dana 181
Wolff, N. 7
Workman, N. 174
Wouters, Cas 184
Wright, John 7

Young, Brigham 125

Zdatny, S. 7

Subject Index

Aaronic 127
Abbreviated 129
Absolutism 74
Abstract 191
Absurdity 39
Abuse 180, 187, 189
Academic 26, 29–31, 35, 39–41, 58, 108, 112
  enterprise 183
  feminist 183
  identity 23
  specialisms 183
  tribe 6, 183
Academics 29, 105
  Muslim 110
Accent 63–4
Accessories 92, 164
Accountancy firms 183
Acrobats 74
Actors 32
Actress 51
Actresses 164, 166
Adorn 92
Adornment(s) 24, 28 34, 36, 54, 74, 165, 185
Adornment hypothesis 5
Adult entertainment 191
Adultery 137
Advent of Christ 129
Advertising 162, 168–9, 174–5
  display 169
  laws 172
  techniques 169, 173, 175
Aesthetic 75, 77, 92, 187
  pleasures 190
Aestheticism 174
Aestheticization 87, 189
Aesthetics 15, 88

Affaire du foulard 106, 112, 116
Affect 133
Affiliate 181
Affirmation 118, 171
Affirmative 106
Africa 54
African 173
Age of empire 100
Agency 16, 187
Agent 100
Agnostic(s) 52–66 passim
Air stewards 190
Alberta 192
Alien identity 187
Allure 163
Alter egos 51
Alternative dress 146
Ambiguity 88
Ambiguous 88, 171, 189
  rebels 150
Ambivalence(s) 143, 153
America(n) 18, 40, 127, 160, 192
Amusements 80
Anacho-syndicalist 189
Analogical imagination 39
Analytical perspective 130
  traditions 138
Analytical-interpretative 25
Anamnestic communities 9
Anatomy 75, 171–4 passim
Ancestors 76, 127
Ancien Regime 80
Ancient society 28
Androcentric 86, 97
  ethos 95
Androgeny 153
Androgynous 154
Anglican 132

Church 137
Animal 58, 187
Ann Summers 174
Annointed 132
Annointing 129
Antagonism 80
Anthropological 22, 29, 133, 137, 182
   approach 136
Anthropologists 183
Anthropology 15, 34
   of sensation 134
Anti-bourgeois 149
Antifashion 147, 149
Anti-foundationalist 87
Antilaïque 113
Anti-Puritan look 184
Anti-republican 113
Anti-social 190
Anxiety 116, 190
Anything goes 66
Apparel 51, 54
Appearance(s) 37, 54, 63, 70–1, 110, 145,
   164, 175, 182, 191
Applicant 132
Apron 132
Aquascutum 88
Arab 120
   Muslim thought 110
Arabesques 72
Arabian nights 108
Arabic 113
Arcana 182
Archaic symbols 153
Archeology 15
Archetypal symbol 163
Archetype 173
Archimedean 35
Architecture 85, 129
Archives 182
Aristocracy 95
Aristocrat 150
Aristocratic 31, 34, 70, 74
Armour 39
Arms 72, 115
Arranged marriage 110
Arrogance of power 187
Art 27, 35, 77, 79, 165, 184
   and Design Studies 15

form 35, 91
Artefacts 160, 175
Article of faith 110
Artifice 143, 171
Artificial 133, 168
   silk 172
Artificiality 70
Artisan 27
Artist 62
Artistic 15, 32
Asafedita 40
Ascetic behaviour 138
Ascetic rationality 167
Asceticism 167
Aspirants 183
Aspirational 95
Assimilate 110
Atheist(s) 52–66 passim
Athletic 162
Attack 180
Attic 54
Attire 55, 74, 95, 170, 182
Attitudes 153, 160
Attractive 143
Audience 143
Aura 174
Austerity 75
Authentically feminine 145
Authenticity 136
Authoritarian 118
Authoritarian's charter 189
Authority 81, 90, 95, 102, 187
Autobiography 135
Autumn 55, 97
Availability 173
Aviator 97

Baby 59
Backstage 21, 77
Badges 128
Baggage 95
Ballerina 22, 69–82 passim
Ballet 69–82 passim
Ballet d'action 73
Ballet dancer 181
Ballroom 71
Ban 112, 118
Baptism 127

Barriers 39
Basques 167
Basquine skirt 75
Bathhouse 165
Bathing 164
  suits 172
Beautification 191
Beautiful 169
Beauty 96, 111, 143, 171
Bed 165
Bedeck the wicked 126
Bedlam 33
Behaviour(s) 26, 36, 66, 79, 115, 137
Behaviour-regulation 80
Belief(s) 37, 52, 59, 61, 107, 124, 133, 183
Belle Époque 166
Belletrist 29
Bell-shaped 76
Bells 189
Belong 190
Belonging 26, 33–4, 88
Besmocked 27
Beyond it 57
Bible(s) 52–3, 59
Bible-study 137
Biblical 17, 33, 56
Bifurcated undergarments 175
Big men 58
Bikini 117
Binary 90
Biographer 39
Biological 58
  freak 141
Biology 89
Biped 38
Birds of the air 34
Birmingham 18
Birth 150
Bisexuality 152
Bizarre 29
Black 55, 74, 115, 146–7, 150, 155, 173–4
  activist 183
  attire 148, 150
  garments 174
  lace 161
  Sobranie 55
  stockings 166
Black-clad villains 149

Blacks 58
Blakean 20
Blaspheme 62
Blokey 95
Blokeyness 94
Blood 80
Blouse(s) 57, 132
Blue mire 71
Blue-overalled 27
Blush 189
Board meeting 55
Bodice 72
Bodies 27, 37, 72, 78, 86, 146, 190–1
Bodily control 134
  functions 164
  movements 137
Bodily-felt knowledge 134
Body & Society 35
Body 34–6, 70, 72, 75–6, 91–2, 97, 124–41,
    159–60, 164, 181–86
  ideologies 170
  modifications 191
  parts 190
  politic 107, 179
  presentation 164
  studies 35–6
  symbols 14
  techniques 133
Body-damaging practices 191
Body-self 36, 186–92 passim
Body-self-control 188
Body-selves 181, 187
Body-technique 134
Bohemian 92, 150
Bond Street 54
Bones 187
Book of Genesis 179
Book of Mormon, The 126, 129
Boots 53
Bordello 78
Borderline figure 152
Born and bred 116
Bosoms 111, 151, 164
Bottom 171, 174
Boudoir 22
Bouffant skirt 77
Boundaries 28, 96, 164, 170, 191
  of gender 151

Boundary 88
  maintenance 62
Boundaryless 190
Bourgeois 63, 74–5, 78–9, 81, 149
Bows 71
Boys 71
Bra(s) 59, 162
Brand(s) 85, 88, 181
Branding strategies 88, 100
Brassiere(s) 162, 167, 169
Breasts 75
Breeches 38, 74, 192
Breeding 34
Brethern, the 128
Brides 126
Brigham Young University 126
British 53, 85–102 passim, 107, 133
  fashion 102
British Sociological Association vii
Britishness 85–6, 91–4
Brocade 161
Brooch 54
Brothers 111
Browns 55
Brutality 171
Brutalized 14
Bulletproof 130
Bum 165
Burberry 85–102 passim, 181
  ideology 98
  man 98
  woman 99
Bureaucratic leaders 191
Bureaucrats 113
Business 85, 94
Bust 72
Buttocks 78, 173
Buttons 95, 161
Buyer 164
Bygone eroticism 174

C and A 53
Cabaret 172
Cabrioles 69
Cairo 108
Calico knickers 77
Calvinist 39
Camisole(s) 166–7

Canada 192
Can-can dancer 161
Candy-striped 189
Canon of dress 69
Capes 146
Capital 77
  goods 32
Capitalism 56, 63, 81, 87, 150, 175
Carceral institutions 180
Cardigans 53
Caricature(s) 51–3
Caricatured 97
Carlylean vii, 1–42 passim, 187–8
  brio 29
  eye 181
  framework 23
  fun 183
  gaze 19
  legacy 25
  paradigm 12, 15, 31
  perspective 23
  pre-history 28
Carnival 78
Carnivalized 190
Carriage of the body 135
Cartesian legacy 90
Cassell's Magazine 166
Cassock 187
Cast-off 82
Castration 138
Categories 115
Catholic 114, 132
  Church 107
  priest 117
Catholicism 119
Catwalk 85, 182, 190
Causation(s) 62, 138
Cavalier 184
Celebration 171
Censorius 179
Censorship 95
Ceremonies 110–11, 188
Ceremony 80, 126
Chador 115
Chain store(s) 183, 190
Changing rooms 132
Chapel 128, 136
Character 64

Characterizations 76
Charlemagne-mantle 13
Charm 175
Charter 28, 30
Chartism 18
Chartism 20
Cheap 54
Cheapness 173
Check 85, 87
Cheese(s) 34, 77
Chelsea 29
Chemise 166
Child 136
Child dancers 82
Childbirth 130
Childlike 19
Children 107, 111, 132, 166, 180
Chimney-top hat 189
Choice 166
Choreographers 76
Christ 131
Christian 120, 125
  traditions 132
Christianity 130
Church 107, 119, 125, 129, 132, 137
  clothes 19
  leader 130
  meeting(s) 126–7
Cigarettes 55, 117
Cigar(s) 55
  butts 77
Cinema 144, 170, 172–3, 189
Circus riders 74
Cities 127
Citizens 107, 119
Citizenship 89, 107–8, 115
Civil liberties 106
  religion 66
  society 114, 164
Civilization(s) 25–6, 33, 80, 120, 188
Civilized 17, 81, 109, 120, 180
Civilizing process 21, 81
Civilizing Process 69
Clan 19
Class(es) 32, 80, 82, 88
  structure 34
Classic 14, 85–102 passim
  personna 181

Classical 76, 100, 131
Classier 180
Clean 55, 63
  -cut 127
Cleanliness 111, 126
Clergy 106
Clerical black 187
Clientele 95
Clingy nightgowns 172
Cloning technologies 34
Clotha Virumque cano 26
Cloth-animals 41
Clothed body 163
Clothes
  classes 35
  -Philosopher 36
  -philosophy 20, 26, 36
  -screens 36
  -shops 33
Clothing 69
  codes 74–5
  industry 102
  options 179
  organizations 94
  regimes 187
  stores 53
  system 87, 101
  theorems 23
  traditions 27
Club 58
Cockney 63
Code of behaviour 165
Coded 88
  sensory system 105
Codes 159–60
  of desire 173
Co-education 112
Cold weather 166
Collective 87, 93, 102
  fantasy 172
  identity 88
  order 186
  personality 96
  self-representation 184
Collectively 180
Colonial institutions 108
Colonized 14, 97
Colour 55, 167

Coloured labels 168
Combinations 166
Comfort 90, 175
Comfortable fit 170
Command of the Lord 125
Commanders 95
Commercial 78
  hoarding 190
  world 74
Commitment 123–5, 138
Commodification 36, 87, 175
Commodified 88
Commodities 160
Commodity 171
  culture 87
Common religion 66
Commoner 181
Communal 70, 165
Communally 135
Communities 37
  of memory 9
Community 26, 91, 115, 135, 137, 180
  bonding 136
  of believers 181
  self-surveys 183
Compass and dividers 130
Compassionate 27
Competitive 34
Compliance 179–180
Compulsions 70
Comtean 21
Concealment 41, 165, 187
Conceits 39
Conceptual-theoretical 182
Confession 120
Conflicts 60
Conformist majority 149
Conformity 16, 87, 190
Congregation 135–6
Congregational 127
Conjecture 182
Conjuration 81
Connections 182
Connoisseurship 34
Conscience(s) 79, 118, 180, 189, 191
Conscripts 191
Conseil d'Etat 116
Conservatism 55

Conservative 56, 59
  fantasies 152
  fantasy 153
Consistency/inconsistency 61, 66
Conspicuous consumption 34, 170
Constitution of society 35
Constitutional 189
Constraint(s) 57, 155, 171, 179, 187
Constricting garments 161
Constructed 87
Constructionist 24
Constructs of gender 152
Consumer(s) 81, 175
  culture 18, 20, 190
  desires 168
  groups 88
Consumerism 159, 164, 167, 171, 173
Consumerist 164
  culture 172, 175
  need(s) 160, 174
  psyche 172
Consumption 6, 87–8, 96
Contact lenses 149
Containment 165, 169
Contemporary 56
  society 185
Continent 166
Contingent conditions 192
Contours 171
Contradiction 144
Control 31, 123–5, 179, 186
  freaks 188
Controlled 53, 55–6
Convention (s) 74, 111, 136, 148, 165
Conventional 72, 189
  forms 153
Conventionalism 56
Convicts 191
Cool Britannia 85–6
Co-religionists 62
Corporate 185–6
  dress control 189
  dress signs 184
  identity 95, 101, 131, 186
  image 188
  liveries 190
  organization 183
  signage 190

Corporation(s) 96, 189, 191
Corporeal 38
Corpo-real 99
Correct 55
Correlations 138
Corset(s) 72, 76, 80, 162–71 passim
Corryphées 77
Cosmetics 87
Cosmopolitan 18, 181
Costume 70
    drama 94
Costuming of revolt 149
Cottage industry 163, 167
Counterculture 54
Counter-revolution 184
Country 92
    gent 22, 86, 101
    Gentleman 97
    squire 95
Country-look 89
Countryside 94
County 54
    set 87
Courage 96
Court(s) 69–71, 80, 192
Courtiers 71
Courtly 75
    profligacy 27
Covenants 136
Covert 165
Cradle 26
Craft shop 54
Craftsmen 57
Craze 55, 162
Creation 17, 19, 33, 35, 52
Creationist 60
Creative 85
Creativity 64
Credo 172
Creil 106
Crime(s) 33, 188
Crinoline 64
Crisis
    of discipline 188
    of representation 102
Critical distance 38
Critics 40
Crochet 16

Cross 54, 128
    -cultural 28, 42
    -disciplinary 184
Crucible, The 54
Crystal chandeliers 96
Cult(s) 29, 180
    dress 141
Cultivate 71
Cultural 99, 187
    capital 15, 32
    community 181
    construct 88
    construction 159
    construction 160
    development 123
    discourses 146
    displays 27
    expectations 145
    fantasy 143
    guises 41
    heritage 120
    homogeneity 90
    identities 87–8, 102, 181
    imagination 27
    intermediaries 91
    intermediary 92
    kudos 102
    limits 191
    pattern 37
    power 32–3
    practice(s) 123, 136, 138, 159, 175
    processes 174
    product 87
    representation 88–9
    salience 189
    stratification 31
    studies 22, 105
    styles 133
    symbol 105
    theory 28
    turn 30, 34
    values 89, 170
    visibility 32
Culture(s) 17, 81, 106, 181–2, 188, 191
    wars 183, 190
Cumulative tradition 136
Cunt 165
Currency 33

Current affairs 119
Curriculum 116
Curtsy 71
Curves 75
Custom(s) 28, 32, 37–9, 92
Customary religion 66
Customer services 191
Customers 169
Cut(s) 28, 74, 76, 153, 181
Cutting Edge Exhibition 91–3
Cyberbody culture 191
Cyborg revolution 34

Daily activities 132
  life 123
Daintily trimmed 161
Dance 69
  studio 22
Dancers 166
Dances 166
Dancing 180
  master 72
Dandiacal Body 19
Dandies 18, 35, 149
Dandy 150
Danger 70
Danseur noble 72
Dark
  blues 55
  colours 132
  glasses 53
  power 148
Darker coloured 126
Dead 123, 127, 131
Death 33, 126, 147
Decadence 109, 150
Decency 36, 189
Deceptive 145
Decision(s) 37, 179
Décor 96
Decorated 75, 77
Decorative 170
  boxes 168
Decorous 80
Decorum 17, 71, 73, 79, 180
Deeper layers 182
Deference 15, 32, 34
Defiant 151

Degradation rituals 187
Degrading 191
Dehumanization 188
Dehumanize 191
Delaicization 107
Demeanour 135
Demi-caractère 82
Demi-masculine 166
Demi-monde 77
Democracy 106, 150, 188
Democratic 81, 107, 113
  society 180
Demographic 54
Demos 85, 101
Demystified 38
Denial 171, 188
Denomination 129
Deodorants 190
Department stores 169, 170, 173–4
Dependency 15
Dependent disabled 191
Deportment 70, 133
Deprived 111
Derogatory status 173
Design 85, 100, 167
  changes 130
  Studies 15
Designers 92
Designing 88
Desire 97, 152, 154, 171–75 passim
  for alternative 155
Desirable 159, 169
  female body 169
Destiny 130
Detachment 38
Detraditionalization 186
Development 70
Deviance 173, 187
Devil 109, 126
Devil's dung 41
Devotee(s) 133, 181
Diable Boiteaux, Le 78
Dialect 64
Dialectic 110
  of revelation and concealment 190
Dialectical 63
Dialogue 118
Diaphonous 73

Dichotomy 96
Dickensian 33
Dictatorial 188
Didactic 27
Difference(s) 62, 89, 148, 185, 190
Different 155
Dignity 76, 111–2
Dining 180
Dirt 55–6, 173
Disaffected 150
Discipline(d) 169, 174
Disciplining 159
Discourse 87
Discretionary 187
Discrimination 188
Disdain 29
Disembodied sexuality 160
Disembodies 92
Disenchanted rebel 150
Disguise(d) 19, 34
Disorder 56
Displacement 173
Display 32, 34, 74, 92, 97, 105, 111, 145, 148, 159, 168, 171
Dissent 149
Distaff 58
Distinction(s) 23–4, 32, 94
Distinctive 71, 110
    dress 127, 132
Distorting 144
Diversities of Gifts 133
Diversity 57
Divine 28, 109
    imposition 179
    Principle 62
    revelation 128
    Spirit 136
Doctrine(s) 114, 129
Doctrine of Covenants, The (*D&C*) 125
Documentary films 27
Dog collars 54
Doing your own thing 184
Domestic 100, 169
    servant 148
Domination 31
Doorman 95
Door-to-door 128
Doughnuts 27

Drab 95
Dracula 148
Drama 76, 148
    school 64
Dramatic evenings 148
Dramaturgical 21, 24
Drape 36
Draperies 74
Drawers 165–68 passim
Dream 153–4
    world 108
Dress 188
    choice restriction 191
    class 34
    control regimes 191
    controls 179, 187
    culture 183
    deviance 189
    expression 180
    for success 17, 183
    freedom 179–92 passim
    innovation 187
    liberty 179–92 passim
    license 190
    modes 191
    of subservience 187
    philosopher 192
    recognition symbols 187
    rights 189, 192
    scholar 181
    studies 1–42 passim, 182–3 (see also New dress studies)
    symbols 187
    tolerance 189
    unfreedom 192
    worlds 185
Dress-body 36
Dress code(s) 34, 37, 179–83 passim, 186, 192
    enforcers 180
    formulation 192
    code regimes 186
Dressed race 17
Dressed self-expression 181
Dresses 71
Dressing 143
Dress-in-society 180
Dress-self-determination 184

Dressways 4–5, 15, 28, 30, 34, 181–2, 185
Drudgies 18, 35
Dualism 56
Duality 155
Dumfriesshire 12
Dusty 54
Dyspepsia 20

Ear implants 28
Earth 132
East End 54
Eastern 54
Eating 133
    habits 32
Ecclefechan vii, 12, 41
Ecclesiastical vesture 28
Economic 81, 124, 161, 170, 187
Economics 15, 35
Economistic 32
Economy 81, 188
    of signs 6
Ecstatic speech 135
Edinburgh 18
Educated citizenry 190
Education 105, 107, 111
    system 115
Educational 29, 32, 107, 113
    institution 126
Efficiency 188
Eighteenth-century 69–70, 72, 74, 80, 149, 164
Elaborate 132, 170
Elastic 161, 168
Elbow 54
Elder 127–8
Elective affinity 184
Elegance 72, 166
Elegant 96
Elements 66, 107
Elite 100
Elitism 96, 102
Elitist distinctions 150
Elizabethan fop 27
Embedded 192
Emblematic 5
Embodied 100, 192
Embodiment 123–4, 127, 129, 133
Embourgeoisement 33

Embroidered 57, 71
Embroidery 73, 168
Emotion(s) 97, 135
Emotional experience 134
Empathy 141
Empire 96
Empirical-historical 25, 182
Employees 191
Employers 186
Empowerment 100
Enchantment 190
Encouragement 135
Encyclopedic 28
Endogamy 112
Endowment(s) 129, 136
    ritual 132
Enemy territory 180
Enforced dress codes 188
English 30, 94
    magazines 168
Englishness 94
Englishwoman's Domestic Magazine, The 169
Entertainment 76, 183
Entrepreneurial 167
Entrepreneurs 167
Enunciative strategies 185
Environment 144
Epigrammatic 17
Epistemology 17
Epualetted 53
Equal rights 192
Equality 112–3
Equivocal status 153
Erlebnis 105
Erotic 22, 27, 159, 162, 166
    appeal 166
    frisson 161
    golden age 174
    iconography 161, 170
    iconography 170
    impact 172
    lingerie 175
    possibility 169
    potency 174
    qualities 169
    scenery 172
    status 163

stereotypes 174
value 164
Erotically 75
constructed 169
Eroticism 160, 170, 175
Eroticization 81
Eroticized 14
Esoteric comedy 40
Esprit 113
Esprit de corps 186
Esprit de Coutumes 24
Esprit des Lois 24
Essayist 26
Essence 34, 110, 145, 187
Essential 91
Essentialist 90, 96, 102
Establishment 30, 64, 95
Estampie 70
Eternal life 131
Eternity 124–5, 131–2
Ethical 36, 187
power 192
Ethico-political 186
Ethnic 27
Ethnicity 88
Ethnographic 29, 106–7
studies 133
Ethnography 28
Etiquette 17, 28, 73, 80, 164, 180
Eurocentric 100, 102, 106
Europe 107, 164, 167
European
dictator model 100
imagination 108
Union Citizen's Guide 192
Evanescence 92
Evangelical 17
Evangelists 124
Evening 148
Everlasting Yes! 16
Everyday
life 88, 185, 189
practices 160
rule 164
Everything goes 66
Evil(s) 56
sister 141
Evolution 164

Evolutionary 52
Exaltation 126
Excess 77, 92, 171
Exchange(s) 78, 88
Exclusion 96, 105, 114, 116, 185
Exclusionary 91
Exclusive 56, 79
Executive class 183
Exhibited 159
Existential 112
Exotic 28–9, 97, 108
Expenditure 70
Expensive 54
Experiment in living 190
Experimenting 59
Export 101
Exposed 82, 143, 164
Exposure 164
Express 189
Expressed 192
Expression 75, 135, 137
Expressive revolution 6
Expressivity 34
Extreme right 118
Extremism 113
Extremists 108, 184

Fabric(s) 71, 73, 76, 81, 85, 153, 167
Façade 86
Face 115
Facial expressions 73
Facial hair 188
Faddish(ness) 19, 42
Fads 90
Fair Isle sweaters 53
Fairy-like 76
Faith 117
Fame 26
Family 59, 125, 127, 135, 165, 180
members 130
resemblance 135
Famine 125
Fan 141, 181
Fanatical 115
Fanaticism 108
Fancy 166
Fandom 141
Fangs 148–9

Fantasies 81 175
Fantasist(s) 39, 181
Fantastic(al) 153, 192
Far East 54
Fascist 27, 63
Fashion Theory 35
Fashion(s) 26, 35–6, 42, 55, 57, 73, 85–6,
    89–90, 92, 125, 142, 149, 153, 163,
    166–7, 171, 174, 182
  conspiracy 184
  designers 190
  followers 39
  historian 168
  industry 87–8, 98, 100
  magazines 170
  market 179
  studies 15
  system 99
  theory 42
  trends 147
  world 101
  writer 163
Fashionable 28, 173
Fasten 161
Fatal man 148
Fathers 111
FCUK 189
Fear 116, 190
Feather(s) 28, 72
Feeling(s) 64, 79, 86, 133, 143, 145
Feet 53, 75
Fellow-feeling 27
Female
  body 98, 175
  dancers 70
  derrière 174
  loins 174
  sexuality 171, 173
Feminine 96–7
  norms 153
  realm 170
  sexuality 108
Femininity 96, 141, 150, 159, 173
Feminism 117
Feminist 42
  theory 159
Feminized 97–100
Fertility symbols 54

Festivals 111, 119
Fetishism 144
Fetishist(s) 39 169
Fetishistic
  enthusiasm 169
  victimization 191
Fetishized 14, 169
Fetishizes 141
Feudal 95
Feudalism 70
Fibre 168
Fiction 165
Field Lane 33
Fig-leaf 179
Figurante 78
Film industry 172
Financial Times 54
Fin-de-siècle 85, 97
Finery 74
Fine-twined 126
First World War 162, 167
Fisherman's smocks 54
Fit in 182
Fitting 60, 62
Fixtures and fittings 96
Flagship store 95
Flamboyant 184
Flâneurs 33
Flannel 166
Flared sleeves 146
Flesh 26, 35, 39, 97, 124, 187–8
Flesh-Garments 19
Fleshly 124, 187
Flexible production 88
Flounce(s) 75, 125
Flow 54
Flowers of the fields 34
Foe 70
Foibles 17
Folk religion 66
Folklore 28
Folk-tradition 130
Food 85
Foot-binding 191
Footwear 74
Fops 39
Force majeur 186
Foreign bodies 188

Form 167
Form of life 187
Formal 54, 70, 80–1, 186
  gatherings 126
  government 179
Formality 70, 183
Formalization 184
Formulaic 136
Foundation garment 129, 162
Founder 14–15, 28, 31, 41
Founding prophet 128, 134
Foyer de Danse 78
Fragility 96
Fragmentation 114, 148
Frailties 17
Frame 93
Frames 91
France 65, 71, 75, 105
Fraser's Magazine 10, 40
Freakishness 141
Free market 189
Freedom 70, 91, 118
  from harassment 189
  of conscience 118
  to deviate 189
Free-floating 191
Freemason 129
Freemasonry 130
French 70, 76, 78, 150, 168, 107, 133,
  161, 166
French Revolution 18
French Revolution vii, 20, 73, 75, 80
French-sewn 161
Freudian 108, 138
Friends 135
Frilly 145
  dresses 144
  underwear 174
Frocks
Frontiers 191
Frontstage 21
Function of clothing 190
Functional 87, 163, 170, 173
Functionality 169, 181
Fundamental freedoms 192
Fundamentalism 105
Fundamentalist(s) 52, 54, 108, 137
Funeral 127

  clothing 131
Future 56, 59, 92, 151, 153–4, 191

Galsworthian 15
Garb 100
Garden of Eden 130, 179
Garment(s) 26, 37, 113
Garter(s) 161, 164, 166
  belt 160, 174
Gauloise 55
Gayer 74
Gaze 99, 111
Gazette 175
Gegaw 125
Gemeinschaft 110
Gender 19, 89, 94, 151, 160
  barriers 152
  differentiation 164, 166
  distinctions 152
  ideology 96, 99
  meaning 145
  narratives 100
  parity 192
  power 89
  representation 153
  roles 111, 170
Gendered 7, 78, 86, 91, 100, 154
  discourse 100
  logic 97
  sexuality 151
  spaces 96
Genderized 14
Genealogical research 127
Genealogy 91
Generation 19
Generative principle 123, 136, 138
Genesis 52, 60
Genitalia 166, 171–4 passim
Genre noble 72
Gentleman 73
Gentleman/woman 181
Gentlemanly look 102
Gentlemen 77
Gents clothiers 22
Geographical
  discourse 97
  focus 109
  imagination 93, 102

Geography 15
Geriatric homes 188
Germanic 17
Germans 41
Gesture(s) 70, 133, 179
    of testimony 135
Gestus 123
Get inside 185
Ghettoization 114, 120
Ghost dance 130
Ghosts 33
Girl(s) 54, 113, 117, 162, 166
Girlfriends 58
Giselle 79, 81
Glad rags xv
Glamorous 162
    fashion 163
Glamour 69
Glasgow 18
Glasses 53
Glazed fruit 189
Global 86
    imagination 102
    perception 100
Globalization 101–2
Globalized 29
Globalizing 85
Glossolalia 129
Gloves 132, 146
Gnoses 56
God(s) 34–5, 52, 112, 112–5 passim, 130,
    134–6, 187
God-in-nature 17
Godlike 28
Going native 183
Gold 54, 126
Golden age 96
Good 56, 145
    and Evil 33
    Taste 189
Goods 88
Gothic 143
    novel 149
Goths 141, 189
Governance 179, 188
Governing bodies 180
Grace 70, 75–6
Gracefully 64

Gracefulness 72
Grand habit 70
Grandmother 54
Graphic form 189
Gratification 77
Grave 26
Great Britain 127
Great renunciation 74
Grebs 189
Greek 72, 120
Green and pleasant land 94
Greens 55
Greys 55
Grid/group 56–7, 136
Grooming 137–8
Group(s) 36–8, 53–66 passim, 76, 82, 96,
    119, 124–5, 179
    discipline 186
Grungies 189
Guardian, The 54
Guise 191
Gunpowder Plot, The 184–5
Gypsy-blanket 13

Habit 37, 39
Habit à français 70
Habitat 54
Habitus 21, 31–2, 37, 87, 128–38 passim
Hair 53, 56, 63, 115, 137–8, 184, 192
    dresser 144
Hampshire 95
Hand
    -coloured 168
    -knitted 53
    -me-downs 17
Harassment 180
Hard-wearing 100
Harem(s) 78, 108
Hat(s) 73, 82, 132, 184
Hate 190
Haymarket 95
Head 113
    dress 72, 181
    scarf 107, 112
Headscarf affair 106
Health 161, 175, 185, 191
    and safety 186
Healthcare 183

Heaven 38, 132
  in miniature 20
Heavenly Father 124
Hedonism 167, 192
Heeled 74
Hegemonic 86–7
Herbal 55
Heritage 69
Hermeneutic(al) 26, 33, 182
Hermeneutician(s) 21, 181
Hero 5
Heroes and Hero-Worship 18
Herringbone 86
Hetero
  sexist 152
  sexual 70
  sexuality 153
Hierarchical 71, 79
Hierarchies 31
Hierarchy 81
High
  fashion 91–2, 92
  minded 26
  modern 183
  society 40
  street 85, 172
  stores 189
Higher learning 63
Highlands 76
Hijab 105–20 passim
Hip(s) 77, 75
Hippies 189
Historians of fashion 160
Historic witness 135
Historical 81
  dress 151
Historiography 69
History 15, 36–7, 92
  syllabus 120
Hollywood 161, 172
Holocaust 188
Holy 190
  Spirit 131
Home 58
Homo religiosus 134
Homo-eroticism 151
Homosexuality 137
Honi soit qui mal y pense 163

Honour code 126
Hooped skirts 72
Hoops 71
Hope 153
Horizon of expectation 20
Horseback riding 166
Hosiery 168
Hottentot 173
Hoven clip 162
Hubris 187
Human
  association 27
  resource management 186
  rights 186–7
  violations 191
Humanistic ethic 52
Humanity 17, 27, 39, 188
Humdrum 182
Humean 18
Humility 135
Humour 39
Husbands 111
Hussar 78
Hybrid nation 101
Hygiene 161, 166
Hygienic 75
Hypotheses 61, 65

Iconic 27, 85–6, 88, 94, 128, 181
Iconography 160
Ideal
  femininity 146
  types 52
  typical 53, 134
Idealized 127
Ideals 80
Identifiable 127
Identifications 91
Identities 21, 86, 118, 191
Identity 32–4, 85, 105, 110, 125, 131, 135
  construction 153
  formation 133
  marker 130
  politics 87, 101–2
  statement 117
Ideological 19, 52, 57, 59, 64, 90, 161, 181
  alignment 190
  control 137

messages 190
 weapon 190
Ideologies 15, 55, 58, 160, 164, 171
Ideologized 14
Ideologues 111, 113
Ideology 37, 53, 61–3. 124, 129, 184
Idle 148
Illegal 190
Illiberal 188
Illusion 190
Illustrated posters 168
Image(s) 32, 86, 88, 141
 management 183, 188
Imagination(s) 16, 79, 141, 182, 190
Imbalances of power 152
Immigrants 116
Immorality 56
Imperfection 141
Imperial 97
 camp 100
 culture 96
Imperialistic 100
Implants 191
Implicit religion(s) 51–6 passim, 184
Impolite 33
Imposed 191
Imposition 115
Impress 181
Impressionistic 27
Impropriety 77
Impure 171
Inclusive 56, 183
Inclusivity 88
Incorporation 181
Indecency 74
Independence 82, 190
Independent on Sunday 85–6, 102
Indifference 190
Individual(s) 36, 80, 87, 93, 115, 118, 125,
 135, 137, 146, 180, 185–6
 liberty 180, 186
Individuality 23–4, 100
Individually 180
Individuate 190
Industrial 170
 processing 161
Industrial Revolution 81
Industries 85

Ineffable 52
Inequalities 115
Infantile 78
Infantilized 187
Infants 191
Inferior 82
Inferiorization 115, 119
Infibulation 191
Infirm 188
Informal 80–1, 186
 dress codes 185
Informality 70, 183
Informalization 184
Informalizing spurt 69–70, 75
Inner body 92
Innocence 19, 80
Innovation(s) 74, 164, 175, 183
Innovative 95
 styles 146
Inscribed 87
Insider(s) 37, 183
Insider-outsider 92
Insincere 145
Institutional 87
 affiliation 131
 sites 185
Institutionalization 89, 188
Institutions 39
Integration 112
Integration 112
Intégration 114
Intellectual 29, 64, 188
 elites 31
 field 6, 30
 foundations xv
 tradition 41
Interchanges 88
Interdependence 190
Interior 96
 life 190
Internal Orientalism 109
International courts 192
International Health Exhibition 175
Interpret 181
Interpretative 21, 33, 123
Interview dress 183
Intimacy 79
Intimate 170

universe 175
Intimately 188
Intolerance 33, 106, 114, 120
Intra-marital 137
Intrusive 191
Invented traditions 10
Investigations 183
Investitures 188
Inviolability 187
Invisible
    college 9, 183
    religion 66
Iranian 115
Ironic 18
Irrational 173
Islam 22, 109 (see also Muslim)
Islamic 105–20 passim
    headscarf 116 (see also *affaire du
    foulard*)
Islamists 113
Islamophobia 112
Issued 187

J C Penney 53
Jam making 16
Japan 102
Jeans 53, 63
Jerkin 71
Jesus 62
    Christ 134
    of Latter-day Saints 123–38 passim
Jeweller 57
Jewellery 54, 57, 75
Jewels 72
Jilbab 113
Job interviews 180
Jockey club 79
Joiner 181
Joke 38
Journal 40
Journalist 63
Joy 33
Judges 116
Justice 189

Kaftans 54
Kamiknickers 162

Kayser Bonder Teenage Advice Bureau 162
Khimar *113*
Kindness 135
King 181
Kinky 149
Kinship 124
Kirtland 129
Knee(s) 71, 163
    -breeches 73
Knickers 167
Knowledge(s) 37, 57, 87–8, 97, 110, 153
    -map 182
Knowledgeable
    look 97
    sexuality 163

Label(s) 52, 85
Labelled 85
    figures 128
Laboratory 60
    coat 183
Lace 26, 75, 161, 168
    gloves 146
Laced corset 160
Laces 150
Lad o'pairts 40
Ladies' department 96
Lady 165
Laïcité 106, 112
Laity 106
Landscape 94, 97–8
Language 33, 39, 42, 179, 181, 190
    -using 26
Lapel 54
Late modern(s) 18, 29–30, 188–9
    (see also postmodern)
Late modernity 26
Latin 133
Latter-day Saints 123–38 passim
    (see also LDS)
Laughing-species 26
Law(s) 106, 113, 119, 70
Lawmakers 107
Lax 56
LDS 124 (see also Latter-day Saints)
Leadership figures 128
Leather 54, 74
    patches 54

Left-wing 114
Legal
    framework 189
    ownership 1186
    -constitutional framework 190
Legislation 185
Legitimization 89
Legs 71, 75, 78, 129
Leisure 126, 180
    classes 95
    clubs 185
Leisured 73, 87
Leisurely discourse 169
Leniency 75
Lepenist 114
Less fortunate 34
Levi-Straussian 60
Liberalism 52
Liberals 52, 54
Liberated 174
Liberating 106
Liberation 117
Liberties 188
Libérty 113
Liberty 14, 115
Lifestyle(s) 87, 89, 95
    shopping 88
Lifestyling 88
Life-world 134
Lille 106, 113, 117
Limb exposure 181
Liminality 88
Lineage 127
Linen 126–7, 172
Lingerie 159, 163, 166, 168, 173
    fashion 175
Linkages 182
Literary 108
    studies 15
Literature 27, 77, 184
Litigious 189
Lived moment 153
Living
    Garments of God 16
    tradition 6
Loaded with significance 181
Local 144, 181
Localised rationales 101

Loges infernales 79
Logico-meaningful
    integration 60
    patterns 182
Loins 171
London 18, 95, 175
    pub 63
Long skirt 57
Look(s) 35, 85, 91, 181–2, 191
    the part 181
Lookalike 168
Loom 41
Lord, the 136
Love 76, 79–80, 17, 190
Lower classes 165
Lowland 18
Loyalties 180
Ludic 39
Luxurious 169
Luxury 75, 81
    lingerie 173
    underwear 168

Macho 31
Mail order catalogue 169
Mainstream society 150
Maize 161
Majestic 72
Make
    do 34
    oneself 135
    -over 85
Male
    dancers 70
    domain 96
    gaze 90, 144
    style 95
    see also Masculine
Manacles 26
Management 78
Manipulation 98, 115, 119
Mannequins 92
Mannerisms 51
Mannerly 80
Manners 17, 28, 57
Mantle 41
Manuals 71
Manufactures 91

Man-woman relationship 126
Marginalize 114
Market 166, 191
  Place 36, 76
Marketability 97
Marketable 88
Marketing 86, 160, 167
Marks and Spencer 53
Marriage 58, 79
Marxism 18
Marxist(s) 53–66 passim
Masculine
  gaze 97
  point of view 144
  values 96
  see also Male
Masculinised 89
Masculinity 73, 96, 159
Masked 19
Mass
  media 141
  production 164, 164
  scale 166
Masters 187
Masturbation 137
Material(s) 34, 36–7, 40, 77, 99, 118, 182
  accumulation 167
  culture 6, 160
  objects 153
Materialism 16, 52
Materialist 20
Materialistic 97, 190
Maternal 54
Mature 166
  democracy 190
Mausoleums 92
Mauve 161
Meanings 64
Measured 70
Meat 125
Media 116, 170–1, 183, 189
  representations 175
  stars 190
  see also Mass media
Medical 166
  practitioner 173
  science 165
Medium of dress 190

Meeting house 128
Melchizedek Priesthood 127
Memory 89
Mentalist 29
Mentality 29
Mentally handicapped 188
Metaphor(s) 23, 39, 97, 160, 171
Metaphysical 16, 41
Methodological 21, 51, 61
Methodologies 30
Middle
  Ages 70
  ground 57
Middle-class(es) 34, 94, 165, 170
  ideologies 173
  values 167
Migrated 109
Military 27–8
  uniforms 96
  -style 95
Mill-Carlyle perspective 191
Millenial 34
Millennium 29
Minimalist underwear 174
Minister for education 113
Minors 191
Minuet 70
Mirror(s) 92, 109, 141, 141
Mirza's Hill 33
Misfit 144, 149
Misogny 109, 141
Misperceptions 114
Mission 127
Missionaries 138
Missionary 28, 126, 128
Mistake 182
Mobility 77, 102
Modelling 173
Moderation 125
Modern 164, 180
  consciousness 153
  period 167
Modernists 52–66 passim
Modernity 56, 94, 97, 108–8, 165
Moderns 18
Modesty 71, 74, 111
Modifications 184
Modify the self 174

Modish 57
Mods 189
Molls 58
Monarch-of-all-I-survey 99
• Money 70
Monied 95
Monmouth Street 33
Monochromatic 55
Monopolized 190
Monstrosity 152
Monstrous 142
  feminine 141
Monty Pythonesque 39
Mood 133
Moonies 62
Moral(s) 17, 32
  grounds 187
  life 137
  majority 189
  spectrum 171
  standing 131
  tracts 28
Mores 17
Mormon 22, 123–38 passim, 181
  gestures 136
  history 123
  history 130
  ideology 126, 137
  teaching 134
Mormonism 123, 136
Mortal 76
Mosaic of dressways 182
Mosque 119
Motion 133
Mourning 71, 148
Movement(s) 70, 110, 180
Movie stars 172
Moviemakers 172
Mulberry 88
Multi-
  -cultural 86
  -dimensional 32
  -disciplinary 184
  disciplinary 22, 30
  -gendered 152
  vocal 129
Multiplicity 148
Muscles 77

Music 85
Musical 32
Muslim 22, 105–20 passim, 181
  (see also Islam)
  female 181
  identities 118
Mutilation 191
My Secret Life 165
Mysteries 27
  powers 90
Mystery 34, 37–8
Mystic 192
Mystical 20
Mythological 130
Mythologization 69
Mythologized 14

Naked 74, 164, 164, 181, 187
  body 163
  facts 24–5
Nakedness 26, 39, 164
Narratives 88
Nation 19, 86–102 passim
National 85
  Assembly 116
  culture 107, 113
  Health Society 161
  identity 87
  viginettes 100
Nationalism 88
Nationalist 120
Nationality 88
Nationhood 96
Nation-state 89
Native American 130
Natives 29
Natural 91
  history 38
  sciences 24
  Supernaturalism 16
Nature 97
Nazi 188
Necklace 77
Necktie-knot 187
Negative dress freedom 186 (see also
  Positive)
Neo-
  Cartesian 17

imperialism 97
  Platonist 18
Net 77
New
  dress studies 21, 28, 30
    (see also Dress studies)
  man 183
  Puritans 184
  religious movements 60
Newcomers 182
Nightclub 22
Nightwear 166
Nikah 110
Nineteenth-century 20, 28–9, 36, 69–70,
  78, 108, 161, 126, 1130, 148–9, 163–8
  passim, 173–4
Ninon corset 75
No harm principle 180, 191
Nobel Prize 31
Nobility 71
Nonconformity 150
Non-
  -believers 56
  -conformist 149
  -identities 155
  -fulfilment 155
  -interventionist principle 189
  -members 62
  -Mormons 124
  -official religion 66
  -practising 117
  -verbal communication 105
Norm(s) 91, 109, 115, 146, 172
  of femininity
Normal 189
Normative 189
North
  America(n) 18, 127, 160, 192
  Carolina 133
Nose-bones 28
Nostalgic
  feeling 174
  reveries 174
Not fitting in 143–4, 152
Notepads 53
Not-yet 153–4
Nouveaux riches 34
Novel 172

Novelty 167
Nudity 190
Nylon 77
  stocking 162
Nymphs 77

Obedience 124, 128
Objectification 99
Objectifies 144
Obligation 111, 114
Obscurantism 107
Obscurity 26
Observation 165
Obsolete 148
Occupational 185
  Dress 28, 186
Officer 78
Official(s) 127, 180
Off-the-peg 53
Old-Clothes market 33
Older Woman 54
Older women 163
Omnipresent narrator 17
On show 35, 143
Onlooker 35
Ontological 34
Open society 180
Openness 114, 120
Oppositional
  dress 155
  style 149–51
  symbolism 143
Oppressive 152
Opulence 72
Orbis Vestitus 22
Ordinand 39
Ordinary
  business of living 192
  clothes 126, 136
  social dress 129
Organization 96, 191
Organizational 188
Orient 109
Oriental studies 108
Orientalism 108
Orientalist(s) 108
  discourse 114
  stereotypes 109

Ornamentation 71, 159
Ornaments 39, 111
Orthodox 132
Ostentatious 116, 148
Otherness 97
Otherworld 132
Other-worldly 76
Outer garments 111
Outfits 145
Outlawed 56
Out-of-fashion 33, 148
Outsider(s) 96, 148
Outsiderdom 142, 148, 151, 181
Outward 70
Overalls 187
Overcoats 53
Overskirts 163
Owners 187
Ownership 95
Oxford Blue 96

Pack of cards 77
Packaged 159
Packaging 175
Pageant 33
Pain 39
Painful joys 79
Panentheistic 19
Panniers 72, 76
Pantaloons 78
Paradigm wars 10
Paradox 186, 188
   of dress unfreedom 186
   of femininity 145
   twofold 145
Paradoxical
   category 143
   experience 142
   nature of freedom 188
   parameters 154
Paradoxicality 21
Paradoxically 57, 86, 94
Paranoia 112
Paraphernalia 96
Parents 65
Paris 18, 77, 106
   Opera 72–3, 78

Parliament 184
Pars totalis 134
Participant observation 53, 64
Participant observer 33
Passer-by 129
Passionate 79
Passions 33
Past 57, 92, 100–1, 150–1, 154
   modes 154
Pastime 188
Patented 162
Pathos 149
   -steeped outsider 155
Patriarchal
   structures 141
   unconscious 144
Patriarchy 144
Patrimonial 191
Patronized 14
Patterns 182
Pauper 32
Peace 26, 189
Peasant 18, 76, 80
Pedagogic 113
Pendant 54
Penthouse Magazine 173
Perceived expectations 146
Performance 78
   -choreographer 69
Performing rites 137
Permissive 56
Perpetual change 150
Persecution 114, 188
Personal 130, 179
   appearance 143
   beliefs 180
   choice 179
   control 137
   emancipation 154
   faith 136
   habits 175
   identities 187
   identity 187
   liberty 184
   safety 189, 191
   significance 131
Personality 80, 187
Personalized 191

Personhood 187
Personnel control 186
Perverted 149
Pessimism 85
Petit rat 77
Petticoats 72, 162, 166–7
Petty 179
Phenomenological 34
Phenomenology 18
Philosophical 28, 35, 90
Philosophy 15
 of clothes 23
Photography 172
Physical 99
 control 126
Physicality 92
Piercing 191
Pink 144–5, 150
 femininity 146
Pin-striped accountant 27
Pioneer(s) 29, 135
Pipes 55
Plain dress 192
Plan of salvation 123–4
Plastic 35
 label 128
 sexuality 175
Playful 18
Playground 119
Plays to the gallery 149
Pleasure 39, 74, 174
Plural marriage 125
Pluralism 102
Pluralistic 18
Plurality 144
Pocket(s) 53, 77, 82
Poet 38
Polar Explorer 97
Polarization 118
Polemic(s) 113, 171
Police 63
 officer 182
Polite 73
 society 33
Political 36, 53, 85, 114, 124, 170, 179,
 181, 187, 189
 activist 22
 economy 12, 24

formations 184
sociology 118
motivated 75
naïve 180
Politicians 105, 190
Politico-ideological 116
Politics 85
 of dress 184
 of reaction 150
Polity 23–4
Polka 166
Polo-neck sweaters 54
Polycentral system 102
Polymorphous sexuality 152
Poor of the earth 34
Pop psychology 21
Pope 182
Popular 108
 consciousness 100
 image 124
 mythology 172
Pornographic 165
Portia combined stocking suspender 162
Poses 80
Positive dress freedom 186
 (see also Negative)
Positivistic 20–1
Post-
 -colonial 102
 -feminist 152
 -fordist 88
 -Freudian 152
Postgraduate 183
Postmodern 14, 18, 29, 38–9, 118
 (see also Late modern)
 condition 190
 intellectual 183
 turn 190
 university 184
Postmodernity 26
Post-structural 91
Postulates 60
Posture 56, 133
Posturing 152
Post-war period 94
Pot 55–6
Potwallopers 19
Poverty 26, 33

Power 13, 29, 32, 36, 70, 79, 82, 89,
    95, 99, 105, 109, 151–2, 180,
    185–7, 191
    hard/soft 18
    relations 160
Powerful 191
    images 164
    presence 102
Practical 181
Practicality 163
Practice(s) 32, 59, 62, 110
Praise the Lord!'s 53
Praxes 59
Prayer 110, 137
Preaching 111, 153
Precision 70
Preface 40
Prejudice(s) 29, 31, 38, 189
Pre-
    -marital sex 137
    -packed foods 190
    -Revolutionary 75
    -symbolic 152
Prerogatives 119
Prescribed 113
Presence 29, 72
Presentation 64
    codes 172
Presentational devices 17
Presented 87
Press 112–3
    advertisements 168
Pressures 190
Prestige 70, 80, 82
Prêt-à-Porter 189
Priesthood 52, 127
Prim 85
Prime Minister 116
Primeval 97
Primitive(s) 20, 29, 173
Primitivized 14
Prince 32
Principle(s) 28, 111–2, 187
    of control 136
    of liberty 180
Print technology 168
Prison(s) 26, 33, 188
Privacy 79, 132

Private 39, 78, 138
    nature 190
    self 181
    /public dichotomy 189
Private Eye 53
Privatised 34
Privilege(s) 80–1, 91, 95–6 135
Privileged 91, 95
Problemstellung 12
Production 6, 167
Products 87, 164
Profaned 190
Profanity 190
Profanized 15
Professional 81, 185
    career 182
    trends 181
Progressive 54, 112
    tradition 10
Promotional strategies 100
Prophet(s) 111, 135
Prophetic 36
    leaders 125
    -president 135
Proprietorial gaze 98
Propriety 74, 126
Props 21–2, 94
Proselytism 116
Prosperity 26
Prostitute(s) 173, 182
Prostitution 173
Protect 117
Protection 111, 119
Protective 95
Protectors 77
Protest 150
Protestant 125, 132–3
    ethic 86, 92
Proto-political act 150
Prototype 169
Proustian 18
Provençal 70
Provo, Utah 126
Provocation 55
Prudery 40
Psychanalytic 144
Psychoanalysis 144, 1152
Psychological 137–8, 187

danger zones 165
Psychologistic 32
Psychology 15
Pub 148
Public 78, 96, 107, 117, 138
  beach 117
  boundary marker 125
  domain 170
  exposure 39
  life 107
  sector 120
  servants 191
  settings 190
  sphere 170
  square 190
  world 127
Publicly visible 123
Puffed sleeves 75
Punks 189
Pupils 117
Purification 96
Puritan 125, 192
Puritanism 165
Purity rule 137

Quasi-Saturnalian 190
Quotidian dress 126
Qur'an 111–19
Qur'ranic 105

Race 89, 114
  relations 114
Racial 189
Racialized 14
Racism 115, 117
Racist 114, 119
Radical(s) 19, 63
Radicalism 16
Ragged-trousered 17
Rank(s) 70, 82
Rational
  choice theory 32
  Dress Society 175
Rationality 96, 165
Rationalized 15, 191
Rayon 168
Reactionary 150
Ready-to-wear 89, 94, 100, 102

Reason 90
Reasonable prices 168
Rebelled 69
Rebellion 155, 190
Rebellious colour 150
Recognition 108
Recourse in law 191
Red 71
Reductionist 52
Re-engineering 191
Reference group 181
Re-feudalization 191
Refined 170
Refinements 71
Reformers 28
Refutation 182
Regimental dress cap 187
Regimented 75
Régimes 87
Regionalist 120
Regulation(s) 79, 165, 171, 188
Regulatory 180
Re-identified 187
Reincarnated 57
Rejection 56
Rejector 64
Relative improvisations 133
Relaxation 75, 81
Religion 51, 62, 119, 132, 136,
Religious 227, 32, 36–7, 59–60, 64, 105,
  116, 181
  behaviour 123
  belief(s) 66, 110, 114, 119
  convictions 119
  creeds 39
  devotion 115, 118
  festivals 119
  garment 118
  habit 188
  institution 136
  liberty 106, 112–3
  life 134
  obligation 117
  services 126
  signs 116
  studies 15
  tradition 132
Renaissance 28

Renegotiation of identities 102
Repertoire 32
Representation(s) 21, 53, 87, 90, 92, 128, 152, 159, 165, 169, 171, 185
Representational 64
Representative(s) 127
Repression 188
Repressive fashion 112
Reproduction 87, 165
Republic 107, 115, 119
Republican 105, 113
  principles 113
  radical 150
Re-sculpting 191
Research 36, 65, 85, 106
  in dress studies 184
  programme 183
  workers 63
Reserve 74
Resistance 105, 144, 165–6
Resisted 188
Respect 111
  for the law 114
Respectability 79, 189
Respectable 55, 170
Responsibility 128, 189
Restaurants 185
Restoration 174
Restrained 135
Restraints 70
Restricted 71
Restrictions 80, 179, 190
Restrictive 69, 164
  clothing 174
Resurrected 131
Resurrection 125
  body 131
Retail
  goods 172
  prices 167
Revelation 41, 187
Reverence 17
Reverential 19
Revolt 149
Revolution 63, 106
Revolutionary 56, 64, 74, 112, 149, 153
Revulsion 190
Rhetorical 5

Rib cages 80
Ribbings 75
Ribbon(s) 26, 161
Rich 148
Right(s) 111, 180, 184, 188
  of dress self-determination 191
  -conscious 189
Rings 54
Risk 188
Risky 39
Rite de passage 62
Rite(s) 127, 129–30
  of endowment 130
  of sealing 129
Ritual(s) 124, 129, 133
  clothes 123
  contexts 188
  of endowment 131
  of remembrance 9
  prescriptions 181
Ritualizations 90
Ritualized 95
Robe(s) 72, 130, 132
  of splendour 17
Robotic humanoids 34
Rockers 189
Role 33, 70
Roman(s) 74, 120
Romance 170
Romantic 16–17, 19, 69, 71, 75–80 passim, 92, 147, 150–1, 154, 173
  rebel 155
Romantics 149
Routine(s) 36, 136
Royal 72
Rugged masculinity 96
Rules 119
  for dress 126
Rural 100
  idyll 94
Rurality 94

Sacrality 34
Sacralization 15
Sacred 17, 19, 181, 190
  domain 132
  fragility 188
  garb 180

text 112
Sacredness 131
Safari suit 57
Sage of Chelsea 31
Saint(s) 19, 125, 129–31, 134
Sales personnel 27, 190
Salvation 126 128, 130, 132
Salvation 130
Sameness 97
Same-sex congregation 126
Samplers 34
Sanctity 187
  of the human body 191
Sandal 74
Sanhedrin 33
Sardonic 40
Sartor Resartus vii, xv, 1–42 passim, 181,
  192
Sartorial 85
  archetypes 27
  behaviour 142, 147
  choices 142, 146
  context 88
  credo
  crime 191
  culture 190
  decorativenes 74
  embarrassment 54
  expectations 189
  expressions 190
  identities 141, 144–7, 155
  identity 146
  inspiration 142, 148, 150, 153
  portrait 91
  powers 188–90
  rebellion 154
  revolt 149, 151
  schemes 142, 146, 149
  signs 190
  slaves 187
  strategies 187
  tolerance 180
  vulgarity 150
Satanic 147
Satanic Verses, The 107
Satin(s) 76, 161, 146, 150
Satire 17
Satirical 40, 77

Scanties 172
Scarecrow 29
Scarf 180
Scarification 28
Scarlets 126
Sceptical 26
  gaze 181
Scepticism 39
Sceptre 13
Scholarly 35
Scholarship 27, 184
Scholastic 12
School 180
  girl(s) 22, 105, 113, 162, 187
  uniform 186
Science 29, 35, 52, 62
  of clothes 12
Scientific 15, 29, 31–2, 36
  disciplines 133
  discourses 175
  explanation 169
  world view 110
Scientist 52
Scissors 192
Scots 38
Scotsman 76
Scottish vii, 26
Second
  Empire 76
  naïvety 20
  World War 91
Secret 131
Sectarians 22
Sect-like 184
Sects 19, 29
Secular 105
Secular 22, 37, 52, 115
Secularization 107
Security 100
Seductive 109, 170
Segmented consumption 88
Segregation 116
Selective gaze 96
Self 55, 59, 62, 64, 87, 143–4, 151
  -affirmation 74
  -assertion 187
  -confident 180
  -consciousness 148

-constraint 71, 79
-control 74
-deceits 39
-deception 37, 190
-definition 144, 154
-determination 186
-discoveries 108
-effacing 146
-empowerment 188
-exclusion 114, 119
-exclusion 119
-fashioning 70
-identities 185
-identity 130, 187
-image 32
-perception 147
-presentation 36, 51–66 passim, 146–7
-promoting 69
-protection 180
-reflexive 183
-regarding action 192
-restraint 81
Selves 92
Seminal study 181
Semiotic(s) 118, 160, 170
Senegal 109
Sense(s) 165
   of self 145
   -making devices 174
Sensible shoes 53
Sensitive 165, 188
Sensitivity 37, 66
Sensual 108
   reference points 169
Sentiment 89
Sequins 72
Seraglio 78
Servant 165
Set apart 190
Seventeenth-century 174
Sewing machines 167
Sex 33, 74, 89, 111, 119
   differences 58, 126
   discrimination 115
   for sale 173
Sexes 54
Sexism 117
Sexual 55, 77, 189

activity 126, 190
attractiveness 160
behaviour 169
conduct 171
contact 171
desire 173
desireability 164
deviant 169
difference 152
enhancement 175
iconography 174–5
identity 89
impulses 171
license 78
life 137
meanings 160
organs 169
pleasure 165
possibilities 169
preference 19
recognition 164
revolution 172
sophistication 174
stereotypes 170
symbols 108
temptation 117
Sexuality 88–9, 127, 165
Sexualized 14, 27, 163
Sexually
   attractive 175
   stimulating 163
Shaitan 109
Shame 111
   frontier 164–7, 170
Shameful 151
Shaved heads 138
Shaven 63
Shawls 82
Shipboy 78
Shirt(s) 63, 126
Shoddiness 27
Shoes 74, 82, 127, 132
Shopping malls 185
Short(er)
   skirts 126, 162, 174
   -back-and-sides 63
   -sleeved 127
Shoulder(s) 72, 113

harness 162
Show 92
Showgirls 173
Showy 126
Shroud 188
Siberian winter 53
Sign(s) 28–9, 1225
Signage 26
Signature 85
Signifying 87
Silhouette 71
Silk(s) 126, 148, 164, 168
  stockings 75, 168
Silken hose 172
Silkiness 174
Silky dresses 146
Silver 71, 126
Similarity 190
Simplicity 126
Sincerity 135
Singapore 102
Singing 133
Sinister 147–8
Sisters 111
Situated practice 146
Sixteenth-century 164
Skill 70
Skin 163, 171
  -tight 78
Skinny 151
Skirt(s) 39, 69, 71, 76
Sky 161
Slacks 53
Slaves 111
Sleeping 164
Sleeves 129
Slippers 74
Slips 172
Slogans 172, 189
Slouch 56
Smoke 55–6
Smoking 117
Snake charmers 108
Snapshot 94
Sneakers 53
Snobbery 29
Soap 77
  operas 27

Sobriety 149
Social
  animal 26
  anthropology 123
  bond 23, 25
  codes 71
  commentary 33
  conduct 87
  construction 32
  control 133, 136, 138
  conventions 70
  critic 26
  dances 71
  developments 69–70
  exclusion 33
  fabric 181
  facts 25
  freedom 188–9
  gaze 35
  group 189
  hierarchy 70
  history 27–8
  identity 32
  interactionist 24
  intercourse 27
  legitimacy 74
  life 36
  markers 88
  niche 31
  norms 175
  order 77
  pageant 27
  pageantry 9
  philosophy 24
  placement 26
  position 70
  presentability 175
  pressure 82
  processes 69
  proprieties 80
  psychology 21, 59
  roles 26, 28, 31
  scientific 37
    analysis 123
  scientific study of religion 134
  script 25
  semiotics 27
  stratification 32

systems 35
theorists 160
theory 16, 18, 28
workout 63
world 146
Socialization 62, 66, 127
Socialize 86
Society 35, 181, 191
  in dress 30, 180
  of the sign 5, 183, 189
Socio-cultural production 87
Sociological 22, 27, 32–3, 39, 118, 160,
    190
  description 138
  gaze 9
  imagination 18, 26
  perspective 138
  research 35
  theory 59
Sociologist(s) 64–6, 183
Sociology xv, 15, 21, 24, 30, 35, 51, 60,
    105, 118
  of religion 133
Soft 174
Soldiers 133
Solemn 72
Solemnity 71
Solidarity 88
Somatic 29, 191
Sombreness 74
Sons 111
Sophistication 166
Soul 10, 19, 38, 79
Southern 40
Space 19
Spanish shape 77
Speaking in tongues 135
Speaks volumes 181
Specialist 95
Speciality shops 174
Spectacle 86
Spectatorship 144
Speech 53, 55, 133
Spinner 39
Spinster 85
Spirit 16, 76, 131
  -body 124–5
  -child 124

-influenced 135
of enquiry 36
of the Founder 10
of tolerance 120
Spiritual 16–17, 19, 39, 41, 52, 187
  unrest 148
Spirituality 20, 125
Splendours 70
Spontaneity 80
Spoof 12, 38
Sport, Le 166
Sporting 32, 87
Sports 183
  team 27
  man 97
  men 95
Spy 63
Sri Lankan 138
Stake House 128
Stand out 146
Standardization 101
Standards 189
  of dress 146
Standing 71
Stanislavski method 64
Stare 99
Stark 171
Stars 69
State 63, 89, 107, 186
  education 114
  schools 105
Station in life 181
Statue 72
Status 32, 70, 125
  differentiation 36
  symbol 77
  -driven lifestyles 34
Steel 35
Steps 71
Stereotype(s) 27, 108, 115
Stereotyped 76
Stereotyping 141
Stigma 12
Stitch 38
Stockings 73, 161, 167, 174
Stomachs 80
Straightened means 148
Strata 89

Street style 86
Strength 168
Stretching 191
Strips 187
Strollers 33
Strong 147
Structural Functionalism 18
Structure 16
Struggle 70
Struggle 80
Stuffy 85
Style(s) 28, 53–4, 71, 75–7, 86, 90, 94, 125,
    148
  arena 101
  circuit 102
Styling 88
Stylised 71
Stylization 91
Stylized 17
Subaltern 187
Sub-
  culture 22
  fields 42
Subjugation 79, 113
Submission 160
Subversive 152
  identities 152
Subverted 149
Suit(s) 33, 53, 63, 124, 126–7
Summarizing symbol 181
Sumptuary 80
  laws 70, 179
  legislation 28
  rules 185
Sumptuously 74
Superior 80
Supplements 184
Suppress(ed) 118
Suppressed 29, 172, 118
Suppression 175
Supreme Court 192
Surface(s) 17, 31, 87
Surgical appliance 171
Surgicalized 14
Surprises 182
Surveillance 95
Surveys 28
Suspender-belt 159–75 passim

Suspenders 161
Swaying 135
Sweden 102
Sweetheart 76
Swiftian 5
Swimming 133
Sylphide(s) 77, 79
Sylphide, La 76
Sylvia's Home Journal 168
Symbol(s) 16, 18, 23, 29, 74, 79, 85, 91,
    96, 114, 118, 128
  of outsiderdom 142
Symbolic 24, 36–7, 40, 87, 118, 129
  articulation 141
  bearer 100
  capital 32
  code 26
  difference 132
  dress 132
  exchange
  goods 32
  inequalities 189
  -metaphorical 36
  order 153
  power 32
  rebellion 187
  understanding 127
Symbolical 36
Symbolically 89
  over-protected 187
  unprotected 187
Symbolism 21, 138, 147, 173–5
  of seduction 173
Symbolized 100
Sympathy 27
System of values 109

Table manners 32
Tablighi Jama'at 110
Taboo 34
Tailoring 92
Take the stand 135
Taste(s) 17, 31, 33, 35, 37, 39, 70, 75,
    172, 191
  classes 31
  culture 26
  norms 33
Tattered 31

Tavern-waiter 33
Tea party 55
Teachers 63
Team shirt 180
Technical innovation 167
Technological 164
    advance(s) 169
Technologies of gender 159
Technology 170
Teenagers 180
Telenomic filter 63
Teleology 56
Television 172
    comedies 27
Temple(s) 129
    ceremonies 123
    clothing 127, 132
    garment 129, 134, 136
    rites 132
    ritual 126
    undergarment 130
    -Mormon 130
Temptation 117
Tensions 60
Terrorism 113
Testimony 123, 128, 134–6, 138
Text 25–6, 111, 126
Texture(s) 75, 166
Theatre 53, 57
Them and Us 55, 62, 91
Theological 16, 131
Theology 15–6, 34, 55
Theoretical 36, 59, 137, 182
    analysis 131
Theoreticians 73
Theories 37
Theorization 35
Theorize 182
Theory 59, 80
Thigh 77
Thirst for the past 153
Thongs 54
Tie(s) 126–7
Tights 162, 166, 172
Time 19, 25, 131–2
Timeless 143
Times, The 86
Titillation 172

Togs 94
Tolerance 37, 106
    of diversity 180
Tonlets 72
Tool-using animal 24
Tops 189
Topsy-turvy 190
Torso 75
Torture 188
Tourists 85, 96
Towns 127
Trade 86, 167
Traders 110
Tradition(s) 15, 32, 37, 97, 116, 147, 174,
    181, 183, 188, 191
Traditional 29, 52, 86
Traditionalism 56
Traditionally 96
Trained eye 37
Trains 72
Trans-Atlantic 54
Transcend 155
Transformation 132
Transforming 182
Transgenetic experimentation 34
Transitional society 80
Travel 151
Travellers 28
Travesty 78
Trends 145
Trendy 144, 187
Tribal 28
Tribes 102
Trickle-down 101
Trimmed 168
Trimmings 71
Troubadour 78
Trousers 78, 126, 132
Truth(s) 37, 56, 130, 136, 190
T-shirts 53, 189
Tulle skirts 75
Tunics 73
Tutu 76
Tuxedo-style 126
Tweed(s) 55, 86, 100
Twentieth-century 87, 94, 108, 125,
    130
Tyrants 188

Umbrella 54
Unapproachable 147
Unashamed 151
Uncluttered 55
Uncontrolled 56
Unconverted 110
Underclothes 164, 169, 174
  industry 160, 164
Undergarment(s) 123, 132, 136
Undergraduate 183
Underground meanings 174
Underpants 166, 169
Underskirts 163
Underwear 168
  industry 167–8
Undress 132
Undressing scenes 172
Unfashionability 27
Unfeminine 175
Unfreedom 170
Ungendered space 152
Unification
  Church 62, 65
  theology 62
Uniform(s) 26, 28, 95
Uniformed services 180
Uniformity 16, 81, 137, 179
United Kingdom 114
Unity 114
Universal values 106
Universe 23
University of Edinburgh vii
Unregulated 191
Unrestricted 190
Unseen 123
Uplift 54
Upper classes 34, 70, 74, 165
Upper-middle class 54
Upstairs 63
USA 102 (sell also America)
Uterus 171
Utilitarian 19, 100
Utopian 153

Values 10, 15, 17, 37, 65, 106, 133,
    152, 164
  neutrality 38
Vampire Chronicles 149, 151

Vampire(s) 22, 141–55 passim
  mother 152
Vampiric
  attire 155
  imagery 143
  images 147
Vampirism 141
Vanity 17, 33, 181
Veil 105
Velvet Grip Hose Supporter 162
Velvets 146, 148, 150
Verbal performance 135
Versailles 72
Versatility 168
Verses 11
Vested 134
Vicarage 55
Vice 33
Victim 109
  status 187
Victoria's Secret 174
Victorian(s) xv,1, 2, 5, 14, 18, 21, 25–6,
    33–4, 40, 54, 170
  obsession 173
  sensibility 15
Victorian and Albert Museum, London 91
Vie Parisienne, La 170
Viewer's gaze 174
Vigilance 180
Vignettes 94
Violation 187
Violence 180
Virtual reality 34
Virtues 33
Virtuosic performances 69
Virtuosity 72
Virtuoso 76
Visible 36
Visions 129
Visitors 165
Visual 165
  clues 174
  displays 173
  power 97
Vitalist 18
Vocabulary xv
Voile islamiste *113*
Voluntaristic 188

Volunteer 191
Voyeur 165
Voyeurism 144, 169
Vulcanized rubber 161

Waist 72, 161
Walking 71, 133
Waltz 78, 166
Wantonness 173
War 26, 190
Wardrobe(s) 32, 147
Warfare 70
Warmth 36, 163
Washed 132
Wasp-like figure 75
Wealth 32
Wealthy 87, 95
Wearer 164
Weberian 52
Weddings 126
Wedlock 137
Weight 175
Weightlessness 76
Welfare 183, 188
Well-kept 137
Well-turned-out 181
West 106–8, 110, 114, 143
Western 109, 160
  culture 110
  discourse 108
  Europe 109
  ideas 146
  identities 118
  society 179
Whale-boned 72
Whim 39
Whipping 169
White 75–6, 132, 161, 164, 171
  shirted 127
Whore 165
Wicked villain 148
Wife 40 (see also Wives)
Wild 100
Willingness 174

Wines 34
Winfield 53
Winter 53, 97, 125
Wisdom 13
Wish image 153
With it 57
Withdrawal 110
Wives 58, 132
Woe 33
Woman 162
Womanhood 170
Womb 173
Women('s) 58, 65
  performers 69
  magazines 16
  periodicals 170
  subject 16
Wonder 190
Word of Wisdom 125, 127
Wordplay 25
Words 70
Work 180
  of genius 40
  wear 126
Workers 63
Working-class 77–8
Workshop of the world 92
World Federation of Scientific Workers
  53
World-faith 181
World-rejecting 110
Worship 33

Xenophobia 113, 115–6
Xenophobic 105

Yarn 168
Yellow star 188
Young 54
  people 180
  person 136
Youth 172

Zen Buddhists 54